Health Information for Youth

The Public Library and School Library Media Center Role

W. Bernard Lukenbill and Barbara Froling Immroth

LIBRARIES
UNLIMITED
A Member of the Greenwood Publishing Group

Westport, Connecticut • London

Library of Congress Cataloging-in-Publication Data

Lukenbill, W. Bernard.
  Health information for youth : the public library and school library media center role / W.
  Bernard Lukenbill and Barbara Froling Immroth.
    p. cm.
  Includes bibliographical references and index.
  ISBN 978-1-59158-508-4 (alk. paper)
  1. Libraries—Special collections—Medicine. 2. Libraries—Special collections—Health. 3.
  Youth—Health and hygiene—Information services. 4. Children—Health and hygiene—
  Information services. 5. Health education. 6. Communication in medicine. I. Immroth,
  Barbara Froling. II. Title.
  Z688.M4L86 2007
  025.2'761—dc22   2007017731

British Library Cataloguing in Publication Data is available.

Library of Congress Catalog Card Number: 2007017731
ISBN: 978-1-59158-508-4

First published in 2007

Libraries Unlimited, 88 Post Road West, Westport, CT 06881
A Member of the Greenwood Publishing Group, Inc.
www.lu.com

Printed in the United States of America

The paper used in this book complies with the
Permanent Paper Standard issued by the National
Information Standards Organization (Z39.48–1984).

10 9 8 7 6 5 4 3 2 1

Contents

Illustrations

Acknowledgments

We would like to thank all of the people and institutions that have helped us in the preparation of this book. The technical support offered by the School of Information made this book much more feasible. The General Libraries of the University of Texas at Austin provided excellent reference and online database services that again facilitated the development of this book. Our illustrator, Richard Hendler, was most helpful with his design suggestions. We thank Anne-Frances Lightfield for her help in identifying and analyzing many of the health-related resources that appear in Chapter 11 and for her contributions to the action research scenario in Chapter 13. Lucy Hansen, Lead Librarian of the Biblioteca Las Américas, and her staff have built an award-winning library featuring health information, and they were most generous and gracious in sharing their experiences and insights with us. Finally, we thank our families for offering understanding and support as we worked on this worthwhile project.

W. Bernard Lukenbill, Professor
Barbara Immroth, Professor
School of Information
University of Texas at Austin

Introduction

Health is an important issue for everyone in today's complex world. Having appropriate information about health is especially important for youth and their parents and caregivers in all parts of the world. No country or society can exist successfully without good health care and health information for all its citizenship, including children and adolescents.

Purpose of the Book

The major purpose of this book is to consider how librarians working with youth in public and school libraries can provide better and more accessible health information and services to their various user groups. We feel that this responsibility goes far beyond acquiring and organizing health information. This information offers youth librarians opportunities and responsibilities that require a considerable amount of knowledge about materials and management. We also feel that the responsibility for providing health information requires a deep and ever-expanding knowledge of health policies, issues, and problems in society and how various agencies in society respond to those needs and issues. Perhaps the best way that librarians can address issues of providing health care information is to approach it from a broad, conceptual framework, drawing on the works of many individuals and fields of professional practice. On the basis of this assumption, this book addresses the following concerns and issues:

- Historical development: What does the historical development of health care in society mean to us today?

- Policy formation and impact on youth: Who makes health policies, and how are they implemented?

- Modern health issues and their impact on youth: What are the major issues today, and what is their impact on youth?

- Community models for health delivery to youth: What kinds of models have developed over time that support youth health and health information?

- Consumer information for youth and caregivers: What is consumer information, and how can it be better disseminated?

- Parents and other caregivers as health information providers: What are their responsibilities and how can youth librarians help?

- Information for youth with critical health needs and their caregivers: What are these needs, and how can youth librarians respond to those needs and behaviors?

- Youth health information needs and products designed and produced to meet those needs: What are some of the expressed needs of youth for health information? What are some design and production problems, and how can youth librarians respond?

- Strategies for planning health and fitness programs and services: What are some of the major principles of planning that can benefit youth librarians in providing health care information?

- The role of youth librarians in health information: Do youth librarians have a specific role to play in health care information? Can they develop one that is accepted by society?

- Health care and health care information within a world context: How can youth librarians respond to a growing health crisis throughout the world?

- Globalization and health information: What are the major trends in health care information around the world? How might these trends affect youth and their need for health information and health care? How does globalization affect youth librarians?

- Research and development needs: What are the pressing research needs concerning health care information in public and school environments? How can youth librarians become active researchers and developers of health information services?

- Protecting the rights of youth to health information. What are the social, political, legal, and cultural problems that prevent youth of all ages from having access to good, reliable health information? What are the legal and professional responsibilities of youth librarians to protect the rights of youth to health information?

This book is largely based on literature published in a variety of fields, personal observations, reviews of government services and policies, reviews of Web sites, and interviews with selected persons. We also consider various social and psychological theories that appear to us to offer guidance toward a better understanding of how people seek information and how they relate to various persons and institutions in their environments. This interaction certainly includes youth librarians. We have attempted to place these theoretical concepts into the work-a-day world of librarians in both public and school libraries.

Realizing that more research is needed in this area, we also propose research that we believe invites investigation, especially in terms of how users perceive the need for health information, how they search information, and how libraries of all types can meet their needs. The "Selected Bibliography" provides basic information useful for librarians, but it also includes materials that encourage further discussions of issues raised in this book.

The book closes with an overview of the importance of health information throughout the world. In this regard, we celebrate the International Federation of Library Associations (IFLA) and its various sections dealing with the interest of youth in recognizing the importance of health information and the role that librarians and school library media center specialists can play in providing health information to youth. By selecting a health-information theme for their part in IFLA's 2007 conference titled "Libraries for the Future: Progress, Development, and Partnerships" held in Durban, South Africa, school librarians have said to the world that we, too, play important roles in bringing better health care and health care information to children and youth everywhere.

A Brief Statement Concerning Terminology

To lessen confusion, throughout this book we generally use the term "youth librarian(s)" when we are referring to both school and public librarians. We use "school librarians" when we refer to librarians that work in school settings. Although the American Association of School Librarians (AASL) prefers the term "school library media specialist," we generally do not use this term here.

Chapter 1

Health Information for Youth:
Policies and Directions

Introduction

Health care is one of the primary driving forces in human history. For healing, the ancients turned to shamans and gods. Over the years, health care has developed into a wealthy industry as well as a powerful political and social force in most societies. Nevertheless, in the popular mind it still retains a great deal of romanticism, as illustrated in Figure 1.1, showing a concerned physician caring for an ill child. The stamp was issued by the U.S. Post Office (now the United States Postal Service) in 1947 commemorating the 100th anniversary of the American Medical Association.

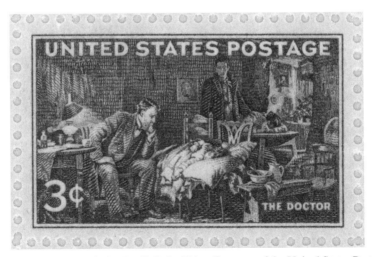

Figure 1.1. *The Doctor.* A painting by Sir Luke Fides. Courtesy of the United States Postal Service.

Health care is in crisis in most countries of the world. It is expensive, the availability and the distribution of services and facilities are not equal, and the demands placed on it are tremendous. These problems are exacerbated in developing countries where social and political issues often overwhelm the ability to respond to ever-increasing health demands.

Over the years, libraries and other public agencies have attempted to help provide various levels of health information to the public in efforts to address some of these issues. Libraries have been involved in these efforts in several ways. Large public libraries have established consumer health departments to help provide nontechnical information to the general public. Many public libraries have also been active in providing community information that includes health information. Schools have often been centers for neighborhood health services in areas where health care is limited. Often the school libraries within these institutions have played roles in the development of special collections that can meet the needs of students, teachers, and parents and other caregivers. These resources are discussed in more detail in later chapters.

Policy, Problems, and Issues

Public policy of any country outlines how it will meet health needs and respond to health issues facing it. Policy can be looked at as a narrative statement designed to direct action as well as to inform the general public about health issues and how the government proposes to respond to various health-related situations. Public health policy must represent the culture, society, and the general expectations inherent to it. Public health policy is necessary for public order and stability, especially in times of crisis. Public policy is further necessary to direct institutions in performing the delivery of health care, including information dissemination. Most important, public health policy must be based both on individual health needs and information and the broader needs of society. Like all public policies, public health policies often carry the weight of law and accountability.[1]

Public policies must be well understood before any type of public information system can be developed within a library or school community. Most health care policies are informed by both social and political considerations. In the United States today, these considerations play out in terms of controlling health costs, reimbursements to providers, insurance for children of low-income families, and managing various health care crises as they arise. Good public health policy must always consider both the failures and successes of the policy as it unfolds in society.[2,3]

Howard Waitzkin, sociology professor at the University of New Mexico, outlines several ways that health policies are made. These include advocacy for health care policy, science-based/evidence-based policy construction, consensus building toward policy, advisory councils and their influences on policy, coalition building in support of policy, public input for policy, and political considerations and impact on policy.[4] The library community often plays roles in several, if not all, of these options.

Most developed Western European countries, as well as Canada in North America, have health care systems that are centralized and operated under government authority and centralized policy. In Canada, this type of delivery has come under fire in recent decades because of its perceived failures to deliver adequate care to their populations due to increasing costs and demands placed on their services.[5] In most countries, health information and how information is delivered to the public or should be delivered has become an integral part of discussion, debate, and policy development.

Some of the pressing health issues that affect large numbers of children and influence policy are common in most countries. These include emotional and behavioral issues, obesity, diabetes, mental health, allergy and allergy control, autism, childhood depression, suicide, and sexually transmitted diseases. Other important issues include health care to minority children, children of addicts, infant mortality, especially those from lower socioeconomic backgrounds, child abuse and neglect, immunization problems and delivery, childhood injury and poisoning, childhood cancer, and awareness of dangers from exposure to sun. In developing countries, these problems are also encountered, but in these countries, we can add prevention of childhood diseases, malnutrition, epidemics, birth defects that need specialized attention, and HIV-AIDS.[6]

Government Health Information Policy

Health information policy defines and states what kinds of information will be formulated, promoted, and disseminated to the public. Policies exist at all levels ranging from international to local governments. Most information policies regarding health are stated in general terms in the organization's objectives and mission statements. For example, the World Health Organization (WHO), part of the United Nations, states that

> WHO's objective, as set out in its Constitution, is the attainment by all peoples of the highest possible level of health. Health is defined in WHO's Constitution as a state of complete physical, mental and social well-being and not merely the absence of disease or infirmity. (World Health Organization—"About WHO." Available at: http://www.who.int/about/en/, accessed May 16, 2006.)

National, state, provincial, and local governments have similar policies.

At the operational level, health information policy deals with content, creation of formats, distribution, and interpretation. At some levels, policy also deals with enforcement of policy through rules, regulations, and laws. Content simply refers to the topics being addressed. This may range from simple procedures for boiling water to how to prevent serious bacterial infections in hospitals. Content relies on authorities who understand the issues—both technical and scientific, as well as cultural and social. Creation involves complex issues of how to relate content to appropriate formats such as print, television, or instructional settings. Issues of readability and illiteracy must be taken into consideration, as must cultural and religious values, attitudes, and behaviors. Marketing assumes an important role in health information policy. Simply stated, marketing considers issues of how and to whom the health information will be targeted. Health policy is likewise concerned with the impact of the information being disseminated. Does it have the desired effect? Will the information produce the desired changes in attitudes and behaviors, and will such changes be long lasting?

Health information policies are always in a state of flux. New health issues arise frequently and must be integrated with existing policies, or new policies must be created to address new issues. These include newly discovered diseases, new infection agents, and social and cultural changes, such as the impact of globalization.

The Role of Libraries in Health Information Policy

Libraries play an important role in the dissemination of health information. Activities supporting this role include the following:

- Collection development and services (book, periodical, and film collections, consumer health, interlibrary loan)

- Promotion of health information produced by other agencies and organizations (government announcements and publications)

- Cooperation with others in developing and presenting programs and services (local, state and regional health authorities)

- Establishment and networking with government agencies and individuals

- Production of health information products such as bibliographies, finding guides, and Web sites

These activities and opportunities are discussed in more detail in other parts of this book.

Health and Public Outreach Programs

The progressive era of the 1880s and 1890s in the United States and other Western countries introduced public health care services that went out into the communities to provide health care to the poor. These services were largely centered in large, urban areas where large populations of poor people lived. Many of these people were foreign-born and had little access to costly health services.

In the United States, public health nurses often visited settlement houses, providing basic health care and health information to the residents. During this period, public librarians also developed outreach programs to children who lived near settlement houses, often reflective of public health models in contact and delivery. Public library services were focused largely on literacy and on bringing books to poor children; they were not directed toward health care information. The important element here is that public libraries, along with other social agencies, established a tradition of outreach to their communities.

Figure 1.2. Early drawing illustrating efforts to control diseases through government action. Courtesy of the United States Department of Health and Human Services.

Policy and Current Health Delivery Issues

Like all programs that school and public libraries offer, health delivery systems must be based on the overall mission and objectives of the parent institution. Aside from that, most health delivery issues reflect the tone of national policy about how best to serve the information needs of children and their parents and caregivers.

Librarians often react to government initiatives and take action to address unmet needs. For example, "Teen Health Information Network (THINK)" was a government-supported research project conducted in the United States in the Aurora, Illinois, area to determine how public libraries in that service region might better meet the health information needs of adolescents. Surveys and interview data showed that adolescents received their health information largely from parents, television and radio, magazines, books, health care providers such as doctors, and classroom instruction. In terms of their interests in health information, youth in this survey were interested in violence, personal safety and self-protection from attack, AIDS and HIV, bodybuilding, physical fitness, rape and rape prevention, child abuse, drugs and teenage use of drugs (including marijuana, alcohol, and teen drinking), diseases and disease prevention, and teen suicide.[7]

This survey also showed that adolescents prefer their health information in the form of videos (now DVDs) that can be checked out, speakers and demonstrations, magazines and newspapers, computers and print facilities, books, and pamphlets. The survey did not ask about gay and lesbian issues, guns and gun control and availability, and premarital sex and relationships.

As a result of this survey, the libraries in the area created a teen advisory board to help develop policies and programs. They also decided to collect better information in the form of paperback books and to acquire books on disease and social issues connected with health. In addition, more attention was paid to buying materials on puberty and sexual development. General references on health topics were also identified as an area to develop, as were fiction titles dealing with health.

Multiple copies of popular titles in the areas of HIV-AIDS, abortion, drugs, and gangs were added to collections, along with materials directed at professionals, parents, and caregivers. Outreach and health-related programs were also developed and/or increased. A special speakers' program was initiated. Topics in this series included teen sexuality, parenting programs at hospitals, positive parenting of teens, and training sessions for professionals in various fields. An information and marketing program was developed including open houses at high schools, development of community contacts, and the development of materials for display at various community locations. A more detailed profile of this program is found in Chapter 7.

Policy Formation

The following discussion considers some of the important elements in developing a health information system within a school and public library.

As stated, good health information policies are based on and grow out of the general missions and goals of institutions and governments. At the highest levels of government, health policy is the official plan that explains and embraces the general goals of how a government will bring health services to citizens. This policy embraces the government's general goals, and it presents acceptable procedures as to how the government will execute that policy in relation to health issues. Good health policies reflect social and institutional expectations and mandates.

In a democratic society, health policy reflects the prevailing ideals of democracy and the principles of providing adequate health care information for everyone. The official policy reflects the philosophy of government and traditions and expectations of citizens. Good policy also reflects acceptable means of delivery of services and programs within the boundaries of the society and culture of the country. In some countries such as the United States, the overall direction of health care has been left in the hands of individuals, businesses, and the health benefits that businesses provide to their employees. In many other Western countries, the philosophy has taken on a more centralized approach in which the government has assumed a major role in health care delivery. Although the U.S. government has taken on a less direct role in the providing of services (with certain exceptions, such as some care for the elderly, the poor, disabled, those who serve and have served in the military, and concern about the uninsured), it has been active in providing health care information in accordance with it prevailing policies.

At the building level, such as in schools and libraries, policy helps direct actions in how to provide services, programs, and materials. Good policy at all levels is based on consideration of many factors and alternatives to operations and, from there, selecting the best actions based on good, sound evidence. School library policy regarding health information will, of course, reflect the needs of the curriculum and the information needs of students, staff, and parents. Public library health information policy will likewise reflect the information needs of the community and will consider the sociocultural aspects of how health information is perceived within various community groups. Programs and services will be based on the well-considered policy statements. All events and services offering health information can and must be assessed against the established policy. Questions such as the following should be asked: Are such programs and services in agreement with policy? Are such programs and services in agreement will the overall missions and goals of the institution? Good health information policies can help in the everyday activities of planning, scheduling, designing, performing, evaluating, and, when necessary, redesigning and restructuring of health information services and programs.

Policy developments are very much influenced not only by government but also by professional groups and their perceived mission in society. In fact, government often turns to professional groups to ask for direction and guidance while considering policy associated with certain governmental directives. Professional groups represent expert opinion based on observations, consensus regarding good programs and services, and research. Often suggestions for national, state, provincial, and local health information policy are stated through the standards and guidelines that these professional groups issue in their role of meeting the needs of and improving conditions in society.

Policy is also influenced by law and legal considerations. Sometimes policies are formulated by legislative mandates or court rulings. Many policies are developed as a result of public pressure for services that are not being provided, applied by client or special interest groups or when such groups ask or even demand a reformulation of policies that do not work properly when placed in operation.

In recent years, we have seen governments at many levels respond to social needs regarding health. These include programs that encourage pregnant teenagers to stay in school to learn skills that will benefit both themselves and their children. The issue of teenage fathers and their roles and responsibilities is also a health and social issue that some levels of government are now addressing.

Often such programs and services for youth are specifically designed to prevent teenage pregnancy through better awareness of the biology of sexual reproduction, as well as responsibility involved with sexual activity and the possible resulting pregnancies. For example, official U.S. policy is to support sex education but within the framework of abstinence only. This abstinence-only policy is controversial because many of its critics claim that it is not effective in preventing inappropriate sexual behavior of youth or teenage pregnancies. Nonetheless, the U.S. Food and Drug Administration (FDA) does provide information on birth control methods on its Web site for teens (http://www. fda.gov/oc/opacom/kids/html/7teens.htm).

In a 2007 special issue of *U.S. News & World Report,* the Swedish sex education program, which begins at an early age in Swedish schools and is comprehensive in its approach, was highlighted as an exemplary model for the United States.[8] Canada, unlike the United States, follows a more comprehensive sex education policy that offers several alternative means of pregency prevention, including the use of contraceptives.

Parenting programs centering on family health care issues and the development of services to help parents access the health needs of their children have been a part of government policy for many decades in the United States. The U.S. federal government has supported library-based parenting programs for many years. These programs concentrate on parenting skills and reading readiness, but their structure certainly permits the integration of health information into information literacy.

Public Policy Issues and Concerns

Information Provision

Information is fundamental to good public health policy. The U.S. government, as governments in other countries, has developed through its various departments and laws, systems of delivery of information designed to influence the attitudes, behaviors, and actions of its citizens. These include information about smoking and drug use, child care and child-rearing issues, literacy, environmental care, and other areas considered vital to a healthy country. Some of these have been effective in changing attitudes and behaviors. For example, in the United States, smoking and tobacco use has decreased significantly since the government initiated its antismoking campaign in the 1950s. In fact, this information campaign was so successful that the warnings of the Surgeon General of the United States on tobacco use are not only coded in law but have become a part of popular culture.[9]

School and public libraries' information policies can and often do adapt and reflect the government information campaigns and designs in their own programs and services. This adaptation can ensure consistency and uniformity in providing better services and programs to the public.

Models of Delivery and Models of Services

Public health policy is often influenced by what has already proved successful in the community. Programs and services may develop from research supported through government funding. Such research often encourages the creation of new models for health programs that then find their way into public health policy as suggestions or even mandates for action. This book considers some of these models in later chapters.

Collection Development and Materials Selection

The development of good health information collections for both public and school libraries must be based on sound collection development policies. Professors Robert Stueart and Barbara Moran advise that a good collection policy must articulate answers to these fundamental questions.

- Why and for what purpose is the collection developed?
- Who will be involved in developing the collection?
- When and how will the plan be implemented?
- Where will the plan be executed?
- How will the plan be executed?[10]

For example, collection policies for health information for youth will need to consider community expectations, including boundaries that a culture might impose on the collection. Curriculum and age and concepts of appropriateness of materials and information must also be considered, as must readability and graphic design of materials.

Community Information

Community information or information that is produced for the nonspecialist community plays an important role in health information delivery. In terms of health information, this includes information on health delivery and support services, educational services regarding health issues, and information regarding personal aid available to individuals and families in times of need.

Library and Interagency Coordination

Almost all public health initiatives require the cooperation of agencies that can support each other through resources, personnel, policy experiences, and services and programs. Public libraries and schools have a long record of such cooperation, and this history should serve them well in the development of health information services and programs.

Networking in the Community

Closely related to interagency coordination is community networking. Networking can take on many meanings. It can mean how persons relate to and interact on personal and professional levels, as well as how agencies such as librarians in public and school libraries establish and maintain contacts with persons and agencies in their communities. Relationships, information from networks, and ideas that arise from networking certainly affect health information policies. In most communities, networking involves the news media, government agencies, businesses, persons, religious bodies, clubs, and service groups.

Marketing of Services

In modern society, the public is bombarded with information of all kinds. Some information is useful, and some is not. Individuals as well as groups must negotiate through this maze of information. In recent years, the idea of social marketing has come to the forefront in helping nonprofit agencies place their agendas, services, and programs more forcefully before the public. Essentially social marketing relies on the techniques of commercial marketing, and the overall message is the selling of a socially beneficial program or service, to improve society in some definable way, or both. A social marketing message and campaign is designed to change attitudes and behaviors and to reinforce already-existing positive attitudes and behaviors. Health information has already benefited from social marketing as exemplified by the U.S. government's campaign to decrease smoking and tobacco use among the public. Recent legislation against smoking in public places and businesses in some European countries such as Ireland perhaps reflects the success of social marketing. Another useful social marketing campaign is that waged against breast cancer and other cancers that can often be detected early for successful cure.[11]

Evaluation of Programs and Services

In all policy statements, a clear explanation of how services will be evaluated is necessary. This includes guidelines for personnel evaluation and for program and service assessments. It also states how evaluation will be conducted and perhaps even lists some appropriate methods such as client surveys, interviews, staff observations, and anecdotal evidence. Policy statements should also include how and to whom results of the evaluation will be distributed. For example, most evaluation reports are sent to management and to funding sources. Evaluations might also be adapted for distribution to the news media and other agencies that have an interest in youth health information.

Impact Assessment

Impact assessments of programs and services are an ever-increasing expectation of evaluation. Funding bodies and governments are interested in having documentary evidence that programs and services have an impact on behaviors and attitudes of persons who receive those services. If a program is designed to increase better health attitudes through information delivery, the program must be able to provide clear and convincing evidence that the program and its services are having the desired outcomes in terms of behavior and attitude changes. United Way of America, in its *Measuring Program Outcomes: A Practical Approach* (1996), provides guidance as to how to assess impact on groups and individuals.[12] Joan Durrance and colleagues' *How Libraries and Librarians Help: A Guide to Identifying User-Centered Outcomes* places many of these principles into a library context with examples of how impact evidence can be acquired.[13] This approach and its application to public and school libraries, based on health information programs, will be discussed later in this book.

Policy and Building a Healthy Community

In recent years, the idea of a "healthy community" has developed. This certainly means health support provided in local communities, but it goes further by saying that certain characteristics must exist in a community for it to be healthy. A statement for the President's Council on Sustainable Development defined a healthy community in this way during President Bill Clinton's administration (1993–1999):

> Sustainable communities are those communities which support the dignity of families and individuals and in which the quality of life is renewed and enhanced

within the context of responsible environmental practice through collective decision-making and action. Sustainable communities depend upon the existence of a social infrastructure which provides for the basic needs of shelter, jobs/income, health, education and social support.[14]

Good health information policies for both public and school libraries can be guided by the principles outlined in this and other documents and analyses coming from this council. Figure 1.3 illustrates these major concepts in relationship to school and public library services.

Figure 1.3. The healthy community and the library.

Conclusion

Health, police and fire protection, and education are at the top of the lists when governments are asked to name and defend their top considerations. Libraries must quickly align themselves with these movements, including health information provision, and demonstrate how their programs and services are central to governmental priorities. The history and successes of both the public and school library movements have given us direction, theory, and conceptual definitions to articulate clearly how this can be accomplished. The remaining chapters in this book attempt to lay out some basic guidelines for action.

Notes

1. Kant Patel and Mark E. Rushefsky, *Politics of Public Health in the United States* (Armonk, NY: M. E. Sharpe, 2005).

2. Patel and Rushefsky.

3. Thomas S. Bodenheiner and Kevin Grumbak, *Understanding Health Policy: A Clinical Approach* (Norwalk, CT: Appleton & Lange, 1995). [Note: This is a continuing series.]

4. Howard Waitzkin, "Syllabus, 'Public Health Systems & Globalization, Sociology 595,' " University of New Mexico, Spring Semester, 2006. Available at: http://www.unm.edu/~socdept/Course%20Descriptions/Spring%202006%20Syllabi/398595.025.spr06.doc, accessed January 17, 2007.

5. David Gratzer, *Better Medicine: Reforming Canadian Health Care* (Toronto: ECW Press, 2002).

6. Australian Institute of Family Studies, "Welcome to the Information Floor in Children's House." Available at: http://www.aifs.gov.au/ch/infoindex.html, accessed May 19, 2006.

7. Judith Kuzel and Sue Erickson, "The Teen Health Information Network (THINK)," *Illinois Libraries* 77 (Fall 1995): pp. 157–182.

8. Thomas K. Grose, "Sweden—Straight Facts about the Birds and Bees," *U. S. News & World Report*, March 28–April 2, 2007, 56.

9. U.S. Code, Title 15, Chapter 36, §1333 includes these required statements for tobacco products: SURGEON GENERAL'S WARNING: Smoking Causes Lung Cancer, Heart Disease, Emphysema, and May Complicate Pregnancy. SURGEON GENERAL'S WARNING: Cigarette Smoke Contains Carbon Monoxide.

10. Robert D. Stueart and Barbara B. Moran, *Library and Information Center Management*, 5th ed. (Littleton, CO: Libraries Unlimited, 1998), pp. 31–86.

11. Philip Kotler et al., *Social Marketing: Improving the Quality of Life*, 2nd ed. (Thousand Oaks, CA: Sage, 2002).

12. United Way of America, *Measuring Program Outcomes: A Practical Approach* (Alexandria, VA: United Way of America, 1996).

13. Joan C. Durrance et al., *How Libraries and Librarians Help: A Guide to Identifying User-Centered Outcomes* (Chicago: American Library Association, 2005).

14. Explanation of the working group of the President's Council on Sustainable Development. Available at: http://www.rand.org/publications/MR/MR855/mr855.ch2.html, accessed October 11, 2005.

Chapter 2

Health Issues and Libraries in the Modern World: An Overview

Introduction

This chapter provides a brief overview of the major developments in health in society and how it affects health care information policy development and operations. Brief introductions are given to contemporary health issues: globalization and health, the role of technology and libraries in health information, public health policies and educational initiatives, consumer health information, and consumer health advocacy. Most of these topics are considered in more depth in later chapters of this book.

Health in Society

As mentioned in Chapter 1, health and disease have been with society from the beginning of human existence. History gives evidence of how various ancient societies attributed disease to many sources including demonic creatures and witchcraft, the influence of astral forces, and the will of the gods. For protection against the ravages of disease, the ancients often turned to faith healing and religion, as well as to the influence of powerful tribal authorities and shamans.[1]

Although the ancient Israelites were religious, in their early social structure and unlike other ancient societies, they turned the care of the sick over to physicians rather than to their priests. Biblical evidence suggests that physicians in Israel were held in high esteem. We read from Ben Sira:

> Honor a physician with the honor due unto him for the uses which ye may have of him, for the Lord hath created him. . . . The Lord has created medicines out of the earth; and he that is wise will not abhor them. . . . And He has given men skill that He might be honored in His marvelous works. . . . My son, in thy sickness be not negligent; . . . give place to the physician; . . . let him not go from thee, for thou hast need of him.[2]

In later periods the role of the Israeli physician became even more institutionalized through civic ordinances. For example, physicians were called on to provide expert testimony in criminal cases, to provide opinions about the nature of assaults, to supervise corporal punishment, and to be licensed by local judicial councils. Every city was required to have at least one physician.[3]

Anthropological and historical evidence suggests that a vague understanding of scientific medicine existed in ancient societies. The previous passage mentions that "the Lord created the medicine out of the earth." Cave drawings from Lascaux in France suggest that herbs were used as early as 13,000 to 25,000 B.C.E. Surgery was practiced as early as 7300–6200 B.C.E. in the Kiev region of the Ukraine. The ancient Egyptians also used surgical techniques as early as 2700 B.C.E.[4]

The Islamic world advanced scientific medicine well into the beginning of modern history through such thinkers as Ibn Sina (Avicenna), Ibn Nafis, and Rhazes (also known as Razi). Ibn Sina produced *The Canon of Medicine*, a book that became the standard textbook on medicine used in Europe until the Enlightenment. Another Islamic scientist, Ibn Nafis, described blood circulation in the 1200s, well before William Harvey did so in 1628. The Academy of Gundishapur produced the great Persian physicians including Rhazes, who not only wrote about medicine but was the first medical doctor to use alcohol in his treatments and medical practice. Rahzes compiled the *Comprehensive Book of Medicine*. In this book, he wrote about clinical cases based on his own experiences, describing various diseases. In another work, he presented useful information about measles and smallpox. The world's first teaching hospital was also established at Gundishapur.[5] The Crusaders established health facilities to care for both pilgrims and soldiers.

Figure 2.1. *Ruins of a Medieval Hospital: The Hospital of St John in Jerusalem, founded by the Knights of St. John to Aid the Sick.* Line drawings by Richard H. Hendler based on photographs by James McDonald, published in 1865.

Historical Overview of Public Health Services and Government

Elements of public health date back into antiquity with governments and religious communities assuming or requiring that the sick and dying be cared for in various ways. Modern public health movements as we know them today in Western countries did not begin until later in the nineteenth century when germ theory as advocated by Robert Koch was accepted by medicine along with the recognition that vaccination could prevent the spread of certain infectious diseases. The early mission of public health was one of preventing infectious diseases from spreading. Helping individuals understand that behaviors often caused infection and illness and that the spread of disease could be prevented by changes in behaviors and attitudes were important attributes in this newly emerging public health movement.

Following the lessening of infectious diseases in Western countries during the late nineteenth and early to mid-twentieth centuries, the public health movement began to address chronic diseases such as cancer, heart diseases, obesity, and tobacco-related illness. Today the emphasis is on population health in which the concern is on understanding and addressing situations that cause health problems among population groups, exacerbated by inequality, poverty, and the lack of education. New concerns include conditions of disability, the effects of aging, HIV/AIDS, tuberculosis and its growing resistance to antibiotics, smoking, and obesity in children and youth. In recent years, public health directives have addressed the special health needs of minority populations.[6] Nevertheless, considerable effort continues to be directed at reducing disease throughout the world through vaccination programs.

Health Issues Facing Contemporary Society

Governmental Responses and Concerns

Governments and health organizations and services throughout the world have recognized pressing health problems facing all populations. Observing how governments recognize and organize their resources and respond to health needs and issues gives us an overview of major health issues facing society today. The World Health Organization (WHO) has identified hundreds of health issues ranging from accidents caused by radiation to zoonoses and veterinary public health. WHO also tracks health crises such as outbreaks of contagious diseases as they emerge throughout the world.[7] The information provided by WHO can serve well as a guide to resource development for youth librarians.

National governments are also important sources for understanding the role of health in society. For example, the U.S. Department of Health and Human Services currently highlights these concerns:

- Diseases and Conditions
    - Heart Disease
    - Cancer
    - HIV/AIDS
    - Diabetes
    - Mental Health

- Genetics
- Addictions, Substance Abuse

- Safety and Wellness

  - Eating Right
  - Exercise, Fitness
  - Safety Tips and Programs
  - Smoking, Drinking
  - Traveler's Health

- Drug and Food Information

  - Drugs, Dietary Supplements
  - Food Safety
  - Recalls and Safety Alerts
  - Medical Devices

- Disasters and Emergencies

  - Bioterrorism
  - Homeland Security
  - Natural Disasters
  - Hurricanes (e.g., Katrina Recovery)

- Families and Children

  - Medicaid, Other Health Insurance
  - Child Support, Child Care, Adoption
  - Domestic Violence, Child Abuse
  - Vaccines

- Aging

  - Medicare (e.g., national health care for the elderly)
  - Health Issues
  - Coping and Caring

- Specific Populations

  - Women, Men, Children, Seniors
  - Disabilities
  - Racial and Ethnic Minorities
  - Homeless

- Resource Locators

  - Hospitals and Nursing Homes
  - Other Health Care Facilities
  - Physicians, Other Health Care Providers

- Policies and Regulations

    - Policies, Guidelines
    - Laws, Regulations
    - Testimony

Included here are issues and concerns which reflect current U.S. government views about the role of government in pubic life. The Center for Faith-Based & Community Initiatives located in the U. S. Department of Health and Human Services encourages research and services in a variety of health issues including community services, HIV/Reproduction health, services to minority populations, social and economic issues, and substance abuse and mental health issues.[8]

Figure 2.2. Campaign by U.S. government to combat the 1918 flu epidemic. Courtesy of the U.S. Department of Health and Human Services.

On the basis of government policies, the British Department of Health articulates its concerns about health similarly, identifying these major areas of concern:

- National service frameworks (NSFs)

- National standards for a defined service or care group

- Social care

- Conditions and diseases

- Health improvement and promotion

- Environmental health

- Ethics, research, and genetics

- Health care standards[9]

Canada is similar in that its Ministry of Health notes targeted concerns as follows[10]:

- Addictions
    - Alcohol, Drugs, Tobacco ...
- Conditions and Diseases
    - AIDS, Cancer, Cardiovascular ...
- Clinics and Services
    - Regional, Health Counseling ...
- Dental Health
    - Treatments ...
- Emergency
    - First Aid, Preparedness
- Environmental Health
    - Air, Water, Global Change
- Health Care
    - Benefits, Home Care, Organ Donation
- Health Legislation
    - Regulations, Acts
- Healthy Lifestyles
    - Fitness, Nutrition
- International Development (Nutrition and Nutrition Information)
- Medications and Treatments
    - Alternative, Drugs, Palliative ...
- Mental Health
    - Anxiety, Depression, Stress ...
- Occupational Health
    - Civil Aviation, Ergonomics, Safety ...
- Organizations
    - World Health Organization ...
- Public Health and Safety
    - Food, Pests, Immunizations ...

- Reproductive and Sexual Health

  – Birth Control, Pregnancy, Sexually Transmitted Infections

- Travel

  – Advisories, Clinics, Immunizations ...

Countries that have federated systems, such as the United States, Canada, Australia, and New Zealand, as well as other countries that operate with a more centralized organization have provincial, regional, or area health departments that offer services and information reflective of specific government policies and directives. Cities and counties also maintain health departments. Many governments maintain Web sites containing various types of information, including policies, directives, and services.

A search of the Internet often reveals an abundance of information concerning both governmental and private organizations interested in promoting good health and safety. These lists provide youth librarians with an abundance of ideas relating to needs, services, programs, and resources developed to address pressing health and social needs.

Globalization and Health

Globalization is often considered in economic and technological terms, but with the advent of HIV/AIDS, the world has become painfully aware that the old patterns of social communication are breaking apart because of widespread travel and the relative ease of crossing geographic boundaries. Travel is now available to many people in society for recreation, business, and government.

Globalization produces both positive and negative effects. As populations become more prosperous due to improved economies, child health improves, and this in turn places more demands on social organizations such as schools and health care institutions for expanded services and programs. For some, globalization may bring social and economic dislocation, which then leads to declines in health and social support systems.

Health is perhaps one of the more visible effects of globalization. Health conditions serve as indicators of social infrastructures and social care networks and as such can serve as one barometer of the overall successes or failures of globalization.[11] Again, this is an important topic that must be considered in building a viable health information collection for youth. See Chapter 10 for a further discussion on globalization.

Technology, Health, and Libraries

No discussion of health information would be complete without considering the impact that recent computer and information technology has had on the availability of health information to both the professional as well as the lay public. An abundance of health-related information is available on the Internet, enhanced by ready access to computers. Because of the abundance of information coming from various sources, the ability to apply critical judgment and to use such information based on principles of sound information literacy are crucial. The National Library of Medicine advises that these criteria be applied to online resources[12]:

- Authority—author(s), editor(s), advisors, board of directors

- Contact Information

- Content Accuracy

- Currency

- Purpose

- Audience

- Readability

- Organization

- Site Maintenance

To this list we must also add the importance of site usability and the appropriate application and understanding of learning and design theories and techniques in the design of online resources that enhance access to information.

Networking is another important part of health information. Enhanced by the development of the computer, networks facilitate cooperation and sharing of resources and information. Electronic networking, influenced by conventional concepts of person-to person and organization-to-organization networks, now allows for all sorts of partners to become involved in health information, including hospitals, governmental agencies, libraries, health organizations, as well as private health care, and public and nonprofit health information providers.

Technology has also introduced the concept of telemedicine. Generally telemedicine is defined as "health care delivery where physicians examine distant patients through the use of telecommunications technologies."[13] As defined by the European Commission, telemedicine is the "rapid access to shared and remote medical expertise by means of telecommunications and information technologies, no matter where the patient or relevant information is located."[14] Although telemedicine may not be of immediate application for youth librarians, this concept illustrates how well developed and sophisticated information technology is in its application and use.

Public Health Services, Education, and Libraries

In Western countries such as England, France, and Germany, public health services were underway in various ways by the1880s.[15] Public health movements in the United States and England were influenced by progressive social reform movements of the era. Urban Western society was in crisis. In the United States, slums existed in almost all major cities, especially along the East Coast. Labor unrest was rising, labor strikes were numerous, and labor unions were gaining in political and economic power. Huge differences existed between the middle and upper classes, and the very poor lived in squalor and disease in tenements. Public health officials, public health practitioners such as nurses, as well as volunteers from the middle classes went into the slums determined to improve the health of those they often regarded as victims of a society that had lost touch with its equalitarian concepts.[16]

The rise of the American public library was contemporaneous with the rise of the public health movement. Libraries and public health were influenced by progressive ideology of the period.

Like public health workers, American librarians were involved in programs and services that reached into the tenements and slums of the nation's cities. According to

Rosemary DuMont, librarians saw as their primary mission the improvement of literacy and the offering of books to those who needed education. Librarians also attempted to help in the Americanization of immigrants. What might differ from the public health movement in terms of motivation is what DuMont maintains is social control. She contends that the public library movement as it extended its reach into the slums was intended to lessen the effects of labor unions and the growth of socialism and, in so doing, to stabilize the growing working-class population.[17]

With the advent of compulsory education and limitations on child labor in Great Britain and North America as well as other Western countries, schools became important to facilitate contact with children. By the 1880s, librarians in the United States had begun to make school visits bringing books and programs to schools with the idea of fostering literacy and promoting education and Americanization. Public school and health officials in Great Britain and North America also saw the value of the emerging school system as important to their work. As more and more children were placed together in school settings, public health policy for children began to emphasize the importance of hygienic education, especially among the working classes, and the sharing of information designed to promote better health behaviors. The role of health information included parenting information and emphasized the important role of mothers in protecting the health of their children.[18]

Although health information was recognized within the school context, the prevailing approach within the public health movement was disease-oriented, and schools were seen as an efficient way to control and monitor diseases. In effect, they became laboratories for observing and containing the spread of disease within the population.

Even as late as 1915, the United States paid little attention to public health education, with disease-orientation being the dominate model. However, another competing model at this time emphasized the role of public health within a broader social context and saw the community in a much more complex way. This model advocated education of individuals in personal hygiene, supported organized nursing services directed at the control of disease, and encouraged the development of social structures that would ensure standards for adequate health maintenance and prevention.[19]

Figure 2.3. American Public Health Examination Board, ca. 1912. Courtesy of the U.S. Centers for Disease Control.

The Social Security Act of 1935 in the United States encouraged a shift toward the educative and information role of public health. The act supported public health programs through grants to state and local governments; by 1935, the American government was providing funds to states to develop public health education programs. The war years of the 1940s likewise saw further expansion of public health educational campaigns.

The change in disease patterns experienced by the American population played an important part in furthering the role of public education and information. For example, leading causes of death in 1900 were tuberculosis, pneumonia, diarrhea diseases, and enteritis; by 1946, that had changed to heart disease, cancer, and accidents. These diseases could not be addressed by the old prevailing model of treating infectious disease, and by the 1950s, the concept of social medicine emerged as one means of combating these chronic diseases.

Although the medical community had no clear answers to curing or preventing these ailments, education and information were considered important in the total framework of social medicine. Legislation of the 1960s, with its emphasis on social reform and the reduction of poverty, played an important role in supporting the further expansion of social medicine and community-based services and information provision within that concept.

Social medicine, as well as community and neighborhood-based health and mental health services that developed during the 1960s, was largely based on federal legislation of the period. This legislation largely favored a centralized, federal approach to medical programs rather than state and local government control.[20]

Nineteenth-Century Libraries and Health Information

As stated earlier, health issues and programs were introduced into schools as early as the 1880s. At the same time, debates concerning the role of the library in the schools were underway. For example, Charles Adams wrote *The Public Library and the Common Schools* in 1879, followed by Melvil Dewey's *Libraries as Related to the Educational Work of the State* in 1888. Few library-focused discussions addressed the role of health information directly, with the role of the school library viewed as a means of improving literacy and providing information to faculty, staff, and students being paramount.

Perhaps librarians and public health officials had different goals in mind in these early service agendas. Nevertheless, they seemingly joined together in progressive social ideologies that focused on improving the population, including the poor, and helping to ensure that all might enjoy the benefits that Western democracies and prosperity had always promised.

Community Health and Libraries

As stated earlier, the social movements and activism of the 1960s profoundly influenced health information. Although existing in various formats before the 1960s, an organized and more forceful concept of community health information and services emerged from the dialogues of that era concerning roles and responsibilities of society and government in the lives of individuals and groups.

Although there are many components to community health, this discussion focuses on its educative role and how it relates to public and school libraries. Community health education is based on theoretical and practical concepts that promote health and the prevention of diseases. Schools have an important role within this concept in that school health programs involve

> the development, delivery and evaluation of planned, sequential and developmentally appropriate instruction, learning experiences, and other activities designed to protect, promote, and enhance the health literacy, attitudes, skills, and well-being of students, pre-kindergarten through grade 12.[21]

Within this context, a coordinated approach to health education in schools includes

- Comprehensive health education

- School health services

- Healthy school environments

- School counseling

- Psychological and social services

- Physical education

- School nutrition services

- Family and community involvement in school health

- School-site health promotion of school staff[22]

These ideas of health education are based on the National Health Education Standards and directives and guidelines available in many states. The connections between all these components (students, staff, faculty, parents, community) and youth librarians are apparent and are discussed further in later chapters in this book.

As in other areas of education and public service, outcome measures are an important aspect of community health education; they are defined as follows:

> Measurable changes in or reinforcement of health knowledge, attitudes or beliefs, personal behaviors, and/or skill of individuals or populations; changes in social norms and actions; and organizational practices and public policies that are attributable to health education and health promotion interventions.[23]

Outcome measures are designed to gauge the impact of educational strategies on target audiences.

Consumer Information, Advocacy, and Libraries

Consumer health and advocacy for better health among the population have become major issues in society within the last few decades. Patrick and Koss (1996) define consumer health information as:

> Information that enables individuals to understand their health and make health-related decisions for themselves and their families.[24]

Libraries of all types play significant roles in that they often serve as gateways to consumer health information and can help develop appropriate skills of evaluation and application in users. The Library of Medicine has identified the following as important skills for librarians to know when involved in consumer health information at any level:

- Trends and issues affecting consumer health information

- Consumer health information resources

- Providers of consumer health information

- Management of consumer health information services and programs

- Collection development

- Evaluation of consumer health information

- The consumer health information interview

- Consumer health information sources available from the National Library of Medicine

These issues, problems, and skills are discussed in more detail in later chapters.

Figure 2.4. The United States National Library of Medicine Building. Courtesy of the National Library of Medicine.

Conclusion

Disease and illness have been linked with human development from the beginning of our evolution. Disease has influenced religion, government, and social and cultural order and has caused the rise and fall of powerful governments and institutions throughout history. Similarly, government and religion have played powerful roles in how diseases are viewed and contained. Both ancient and modern governments have defined fundamental ways in which disease and its effects are integrated into social contexts.

Progressive movements of the nineteenth and twentieth centuries have influenced our view of the role of government and other social agencies in the containment of disease and illnesses. Within these movements, librarianship and information workers have found a place and have asserted themselves into important roles. Modern society and medicine together have encouraged the involvement of all aspects of society in information concerning the many aspects of health, wellness, disease, and illness. It is within this social context of how to organize, access, and use information in well-informed ways that youth librarians can and will play important roles as the twenty-first century unfolds.

Notes

1. "History of Medicine." In *Wikipedia, The Free Encyclopedia*. Available at: http://en.wikipedia.org/w/index.php?title=History_of_medicine&oldid=52808 542, accessed May 13, 2006.

2. Solomon Schechter et al., "Medicine" (Ecclus. [Sirach] xxxviii. 1–12). In *Jewish Encyclopedia*. Available at: http://www.jewishencyclopedia.com/view_friendly. jsp?artid=325&letter=M, accessed May 13, 2006.

3. Schechter et al.

4. "Surgery." In *Wikipedia, The Free Encyclopedia*. Available at: http://en.wikipedia. org/w/index.php?title=Surgery&oldid=53003531, accessed May 13, 2006.

5. "History of Medicine—Islamic Medicine." In *Wikipedia, The Free Encyclopedia*. Available at: http://en.wikipedia.org/wiki/History_of_medicine#Islamic_medicine, accessed May 17, 2006.

6. "Public Health." In *Wikipedia, The Free Encyclopedia*. Available at: http://en. wikipedia.org/w/index.php?title=Public_health&oldid=52834626,   accessed May 13, 2006.

7. World Health Organization. Available at: http://www.who.int/en/, accessed May 19, 2006.

8. U.S. Department of Health and Human Services, the Center for Faith-Based and Community Initiatives. Available at: http://www.hhs.gov/fbci/funding.html, accessed May 19, 2006.

9. Department of Health, Great Britain. "Health and Social Care Topics." Available at: http://www.dh.gov.uk/PolicyAndGuidance/HealthAndSocialCareTopics/fs/en, accessed May 19, 2006.

10. "Canada Health Portal. Targeting Health." Available at: http://chp-pcs. gc.ca/CHP/index_e.jsp, accessed May 19, 2006.

11. "Globalization and Health." Answers.Com from *Wikipedia.* Available at http:// www.answers.com/topic/globalization-and-health, accessed August 10, 2007.

12. U.S. National Medical Library, "Consumer Health Information (6 hour course): A Workshop for Librarians Providing Health Information to the Public." Available at: http://nnlm.gov/train/chi/lws.html, accessed May 23, 2006.

13. ADV Communications, "Telemedicine." Available at: http://www.advcomms. co.uk/telemedicine/definition.htm, accessed May 24, 2006.

14. ADV Communications.

15. Dorothy Porter, ed., *The History of Public Health and the Modern State* (Amsterdam: Editions Rodopi B.V., 1994), 1 ff.

16. Elizabeth Fee, "Public Health and the State: The United States." In *The History of Public Health and the Modern State*, Dorothy Porter, ed. (Amsterdam: Editions Rodopi B.V., 1994), pp. 233–235.

17. Rosemary DuMont, *Reform and Reaction: The Big City Public Library in American Life* (Westport, CT: Greenwood Press, 1977).

18. Graham Mooney, "History of Public Health." The John Hopkins Bloomberg School of Public Health JHSPH Open Courseware. Lecture 5. "Education and Mothering." Available at: http://ocw.jhsph.edu/courses/HistoryPublicHealth, accessed May 19, 2006.

19. Fee, p. 238.

20. Fee, pp. 242–259.

21. Mary Ellen Wurzbach, ed., *Community Health Education and Promotion: A Guide to Program Design and Evaluation,* 2nd ed. (Gaithersburg, MD: Aspen, 2002), p. 5.

22. Wurzbach.

23. Wurzbach, p. 6.

24. National Library of Medicine, "MedlinePlus: Your Gateway to Consumer Health Information on the Web," quoting Patrick and Koss. Available at http://www.nlm.nih.gov/nno/MEDLINEplus.ppt#298,3,3, accessed August 10, 2004. This definition is discussed fully in Kevin Patrick and Shannah Koss, *Consumer Health Information White Paper* (Washington, DC: U.S. Department of Health and Human Services, 1996).

Chapter 3

Community Models for Health Information Delivery

Introduction

In this chapter, we discuss various models for the delivery of health information within the context of various environments: public libraries, school libraries, and hospitals, and other places where children and youth come for health care and attention. The final part of the chapter offers suggestions from the field as to how youth librarians in various environments can better serve their users.

Consumer Health Information and Consumer Support Models

As mentioned in Chapter 2, consumer health information is health information that is not technical and can be readily understood and applied by the layperson and young adults as well. Nevertheless, to use consumer health information adequately, one must know how to acquire and evaluate it. One must become health-information literate.

One of the overriding concepts of health information delivery today is the responsibility that the consumer of health information has assumed in recent decades. No doubt this is the result of the growing power of consumers to make decisions in the marketplace about what they will or will not purchase or use. The consumer advocacy and protection movements championed by such forceful personalities such as Ralph Nader give this movement some of its political and social power.

Consumer behavior is informed by a number of factors including psychology of consumer behaviors, social considerations, and individual characteristics. Personnel in institutions such as libraries and schools, built on a legacy of community support and involvement, understand these influences and have developed and continue to develop numerous models for health care and delivery of health information to the consumer public.

Because the general public now has social and political power and permission to be involved in their health management, many people have become assertive in the management of their own health and view themselves as partners with their professional health care providers. Generally this has been supported by the professional health community, but there are problems. Some physicians complain that the overuse of antibiotics has been influenced by patients' insistence on being given a quick cure to sickness so that they can resume their busy lives without the inconvenience of illness.

With the relaxing of the rules by the American Medical Association regarding promotion of services, some physicians have undertaken advertising and public relations campaigns directed at consumers. Notable among these are plastic surgeons and, with the wider use of computers, surgeons who treat the hands (e.g., for carpal tunnel syndrome). Sports physicians also make use of advertisements. All of these advertisements to consumers are limited to what is considered ethical and in good taste as determined by the medical profession. Physicians now better understand the value of public relationship in terms of promoting their services, while encouraging good health attitudes.

Youth Librarians as Facilitators of Health Information

Youth librarians often help facilitate the dissemination of health information to several components of society that consume health information. They need to connect and cooperate with physicians and other health care workers in the community. All health care workers, including physicians, have a need for good public relations within the context of their professional and societal mission. Some suggested approaches that all librarians working with youth can take include encouraging physicians and other health care workers to[1]

- appear at school events and discuss with parents, staff, and students relevant health issues such as test anxiety, adolescent depression, childhood obesity.

- write educational columns for the school's Web site, newsletters, and newspapers.

- make suggestions about topics and formats to be included in collections, including internet sites.

- suggest local health resources and events for advertising through the public library and school library.

- suggest class field visits when appropriate.

- visit classes to give presentations.

Because these activities are time-consuming, youth librarians can offer assistance in writing and editing articles and newspaper columns and, if situated in a secondary school situation, link these activities to the business or journalism departments or programs.

Connecting with the Health Care Community

The medical profession is divided into many areas, ranging from the physician and nursing staff to laboratory technicians and pharmacists. All of these professions function in cooperation with each other to provide health care and health information to their clients, but they all operate as separate professional groups and under separate educational and credentialing requirements. Nevertheless, all have a public image that they want the public to see. The suggestions given above are broad enough to apply to various professional groups: nurses, physical therapists, medical technologists, managers, and administrators. A review of these medical and health care groups offers all librarians working with youth opportunities for a vast array of contacts and networking possibilities. With the exception of some physicians, a sampling of these professional health care workers and their assisting staffs is provided here[2]:

- MEDICAL/LABORATORY
  - Clinical Laboratory Technologists and Technicians
- NURSING
  - RNs
  - LPNs and LVNs
  - Nurse Practitioners
  - Psychiatric and Home Health Aides
- PHARMACISTS
  - Pharmacy Aides
  - Pharmacy Technicians
- RADIOLOGY
  - Cardiovascular Technologists and Technicians
  - Diagnostic Medical Sonographers
  - Nuclear Medicine Technologists
  - Radiation Therapists
  - Radiology Technologists and Technicians
- SOCIAL SERVICES
  - Counselors
  - Dietitians and Nutritionists
  - Dietetic Technicians
  - Personal and Home Care Aides
  - Social Workers
  - Social and Human Service Assistants
- THERAPY SERVICES
  - Audiologists
  - Chiropractors
  - Occupational Therapists
  - Occupational Therapist Assistants and Aides
  - Physical Therapists
  - Physical Therapist Assistants and Aides
  - Psychiatric Technicians
  - Recreational Therapists

- Respiratory Therapists
- Speech-Language Pathologists

- OTHER MEDICAL

  - Emergency Medical Technicians and Paramedics
  - Health Educators
  - Medical Assistants
  - Medical Equipment Preparers
  - Physician Assistants
  - Surgical Technologists

- ADMINISTRATIVE/MANAGEMENT

  - Medical and Health Services Managers
  - Medical Records and Health Information Technicians
  - Medical Transcriptionists

- DENTISTRY

  - Dental Assistants
  - Dental Hygienists
  - Dental Laboratory Technicians

- VETERINARY SCIENCES

  - Veterinarian
  - Veterinary Assistants and Laboratory Animal Caretakers
  - Veterinary Technologists and Technicians

To this list can be added alternative and holistic health, massage therapy, wellness education, physical training, and bibliotherapy.

Hospitals and Health Care Information for Youth

Importance of Children's Hospitals in Service and Research

Hospitals devoted especially to the care of children began to appear in the middle of the nineteenth century. Children's Hospital of Philadelphia, founded in 1855, was the first hospital in the United States established especially for the care of children; today it is considered the best hospital of its kind in the country, if not the world. The University College of London's children's hospital dates from 1852, and Australia's first children's hospital was founded in 1870. Today children's hospitals exist in most countries and make fundamental contributions to pediatric medicine.

Children's hospitals differ from other types of hospitals in that they "benefit all children through clinical care, research, pediatric medical education and advocacy." They likewise serve as a "safety net for children [by providing] expert care for the most severe and complex medical problems."[3] Children's hospitals through their associations advocate for well-funded health care for children that is of high quality and comprehensive.

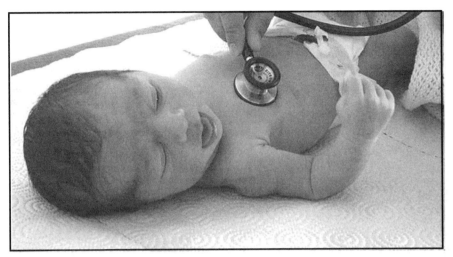

Figure 3.1. Newborn examination, 1967. Published by permission of Nevit Dilmen.

Two of the leading associations of children's hospitals in the world are the National Association of Children's Hospitals and Related Institutions (NACHRI) and its public policy affiliate, the National Association of Children's Hospitals (NAVH). NACHRI includes in its membership hospitals in Australia, Canada, Italy, Mexico, Puerto Rico, and the United States. Specifically:

> NACHRI promotes the health and well-being of all children and their families through support of children's hospitals and health systems that are committed to excellence in providing health care to children. NACHRI works to ensure all children's access to health care and children's hospitals' continuing ability to provide services needed by children. Children's hospitals work to ensure the health of all children through clinical care, research, training and advocacy.[4]

Many states in the United States have children's hospital associations and all of these have similar objectives. The goals of the Ohio Children's Hospitals Association are typical. They state their agenda as follows[5]:

- Goal 1: Strengthen Children's Health Care Coverage and Access

- Goal 2: Strengthen Investment in Patient Care, Teaching and Research

- Goal 3: Protect Children's Health and Wellness by supporting:

    – the development and use of quality measures and standards for pediatric care;

    – [prevention of] smoking among children and reduce exposure to second-hand smoke;

    – legislation requiring all children to be safely restrained in motor vehicles;

    – [promotion of] bicycle safety through legislation requiring children to wear helmets when bicycling; efforts to ensure adequate supplies of all childhood vaccines;

    – legislation requiring equitable coverage for treatment of mental illness and diabetes;

– continued eligibility and benefits for children covered by the Bureau for Children with Medical Handicaps;

– public health initiatives that advance child health, including preventive health services, more restrictive teen driving laws, child abuse treatment and prevention, trauma care, palliative care, and bioterrorism planning.

Although all three of these goals are relevant to health information needs in libraries, the specific needs as expressed in Goal 3 are particularly powerful in terms of collection development, community information, and providing information to parents, students, staff, and faculty. These topics also lend themselves well to Web site links within school and public library environments. Youth librarians can also offer outreach programs to local hospitals that support much of this agenda.

As mentioned earlier, the NACHRI has an international membership. It offers access to children's health care facilities in Australia, Canada, China, Italy, Mexico, and the United States. Its online search directory allows one to identify specialists, care delivery programs, community outreach services, camping facilities for children with special needs, and current research activities. This directory offers a convenient way to go directly to the Web pages of hospital and other care facilities (http://www.childrenshospitals.net/Template. cfm?Section=Hospital_Profile_Search).

Great Britain, Canada, Australia, and New Zealand have similar agendas and operate under social and governmental directives and/or policies. The University College of London operates an extensive children's hospital through its Institute of Child Health program. Its Great Ormond Street Hospital offers useful information to youth and their families called Children First for Health (CFIH). This information portal that is described as

> [A] child-centred health and hospital resource, supporting teenagers, children and their families. It provides comprehensive and age-appropriate health information from the UK's leading medical experts and paediatricians. This includes; health news, features, fact sheets, advice on health matters and hospital life plus young people's own views and stories. [CFIH's] website works across the NHS to support the Government's public health agenda in the dissemination of engaging health information to children and young people. The service is provided to NHS Trusts, health professionals and schools without charge.[6]

Canada, like other countries, has children's hospitals throughout the country. One of these is the Hospital for Sick Children. Operated by and affiliated with the University of Toronto, it is a research-intensive hospital and one of the largest centers in Canada "dedicated to improving children's health in the country." It is family-oriented, offering what it considers to be "compassionate care." One of its important missions is to advance and lead in scientific and clinical advancement. As a teaching and research institution, it has a mission of educating future researchers, practitioners, and leaders in children's health. Among its services is a library designed to meet the needs of researchers and hospital staff, and it offers help to parents and families with information that can be met through its services and collections. Its Web site offers useful information for youth librarians concerning children's health issues and resources.[7]

The Sydney Children's Hospital in Randwick is the teaching hospital for the University of New South Wales. It started in 1870 as the Catherine Hayes Hospital at Randwick for the care of poor children. Like similar teaching hospitals, it is devoted to research, the care of ill children, and the provision of health information to families. Its directory of services offers an extensive overview of complex medical and social needs facing families, children, and those who care for them. Their research and service agenda includes a vast and encompassing array of children's and adolescent health needs including cancer, trauma, HIV/AIDS, congenital abnormalities, disabilities, heart disease, and respiratory disorders. The hospital also offers community outreach services at its Randwick campus. This center provides services for children with developmental disabilities, mental health disorders, and other behavioral issues.[8] Health information for families is also available through its Web site (http://www.sch.edu.au/health). The inclusive information offered by the Sydney Children's Hospital is most useful in helping youth librarians understand the complexity and interrelationship of youth and children's health requirements and how they might assist in facilitating information access.[9]

Similar children's hospitals are located in other English-speaking countries such as New Zealand and South Africa. The Starship Children's Health and Starship Foundation is operated by the Auckland District Health Board (http://www.starship.org.nz). In South Africa, the Red Cross War Memorial Children's Hospital in Cape Town is the only children's hospital dedicated to children's health needs in sub-Saharan Africa (http://www.travellersworldwide.com/08a-south-africa/08-southafrica-medical.htm).

Informed by Practice

Information from the Health Care Field

Profiles of services provided in the community offer examples of ongoing community health care facilities and operations that can inform and offer librarians working with youth insight into both models of operations, as well as information needs that they might offer to meet within the contexts of these various environments. The following locally based situations are excellent sources of information and insight into the health needs of most communities.

- Local children's hospital or hospitals (a hospital in the service areas)
- Community health and outreach centers
- Physicians (pediatricians and/or family medicine)
- Health care workers (nurses, counselors, health care therapists)

Youth Librarians as Information Providers

Interacting with Health Care Providers

As we have just seen, health care is complex, and it is information rich. Because of these characteristics, youth librarians can play an important role in helping people access the information that they need. Providing health information in various ways to youth and those that care for and are responsible for them is challenging, but not impossible. The following are suggestions that should work in most situations when applied appropriately.

Personalize and Network in the Community

In a school environment, it is often necessary to take the initiative in establishing a personal relationship with parents, counselors, and the school nurse (if one is available), letting them know that as the school's primary information worker, you are willing to help provide health information as needed and an appropriate resource to meet the objectives and mission of the school and individuals associated with it. As the school librarian, one will also want to establish a relationship with health care providers in the local area of the school, letting them know that you are willing to help with their own health-information agendas. Public librarians serving youth will need to do much of the same type of networking and establishing of personal relationships within the health care communities so that they can provide health information to clientele who come into the public library.

Understand and Know the Major Issues Involving Health Care

To be creditable when talking to both laypersons as well as health professionals, one must know the major issues involved in health care. You do not need to be an expert, but when offering your services, you must be able to "talk the talk" and ask suitable questions that will better inform you about issues. Understanding major issues is an absolute necessity when offering your services to your various publics.

Learn What Is Needed

As we have seen from the field reports, librarians can play an important role in providing information to both laypeople and medical care workers. This information need not be technical and professional, but it can be user-friendly and selected or even designed to meet needs as expressed by your public. Parents may need certain types of information that can be easily made available through the public or school library. Health care providers may be most eager to accept services that they themselves may not be able to provide. For example, a regularly scheduled story hour in the children section of a hospital may be well received and appreciated. The Internet and its Web sites offer an abundance of health information, but this information is sometimes hard to access. Youth librarians can offer guidelines for better use of this information.

Market Yourself and Your Services and Programs

In line with your own library's and library media center's mission and objectives, market your services to your potential constituencies. Establish good public relations, and use standard marketing techniques to advertise the services that you can offer. Not-for-profit organizations, including libraries, have found that social marketing is useful when attempting to bring their services and programs to the attention of their identified market group. Social marketing uses the techniques of commercial marketing; however, the primary mission is not marketing for profit but marketing to offer services that will benefit society. In doing this, librarians design their programs and services in ways that will change behaviors and attitudes for the better or improve existing positive behaviors. Well-known examples of social marketing used in the medical field over the years have involved promoting better health behaviors and attitudes involving eating habits and weight control, use of tobacco, and periodic medical examinations. In recent years, the medical professions have been emphasizing and marketing information for parents and child-care providers.

Make Concrete Suggestions

Although many health care workers will welcome your help and will cooperate with you, they often will not know exactly what to expect from you in the way of services and programs. Come with a small list of suggestions that you feel will enhance their own programs and services. Be sure that these suggestions are logical in terms of time available and that they can be justified in terms of your own mission and objectives.

Know What Others Are Doing

If you are a public or a school librarian, make sure that you know what is happening in schools and in the community concerning health information programs and services. For ideas, read in the professional literature, visit programs, and talk to others. Concrete examples will help prove your interest and credibility in the marketing process.

Provide Models and Examples

Interesting models and examples coming from your reading and from visiting and observing library programs will prove useful in marketing your ideas to potential users. If possible, provide printed documents, photographs, and news reports about successful operations and programs.

Provide Useful Resources

It is always good to provide background items when you are marketing your ideas. A carefully selected package of readings, together with a listing of film media and Web sites, will aid your marketing strategies.

Advocate and Propose Services and Programs

Busy professionals like to have something concrete when they give you their time for discussion. Assuming that your discussions are fruitful, offer to develop a draft proposal of services and programs based on agreed-to ideas. Have it available for review and further discussion within a reasonable time. This will help you keep the dialogue open, positive, and continuing.

Conclusion

Health care in our communities is one of the pressing social, cultural, political, and economic factors in modern life. It is complex at the personal level and at local, state and provincial, national, and international levels. Youth librarians have a long history of providing information and outreach services. Providing health information and services is not a foreign concept. Librarians have been involved in health information for years.

Other chapters describe these programs in more detail. What is needed now is the will to forge new ground as community expectations and demands about health and health care information expand.

Notes

1. John McCormack, "Public Relations Services for Physicians." Available at: http://www.bymccormack.com/pr-physicians.htm, accessed May 24, 2006.

2. Health Care Monster, "Healthcare Job Profiles." Available at: http://healthcare. monster.com/articles/jobprofiles, accessed May 23, 2006.

3. Children's Hospital of Texas, "Home Page." Available at: http://www.childhealthtx. org, accessed May 26, 2006.

4. National Association of Children's Hospitals and Related Institutions and National Association of Children's Hospitals, Home Page. Available at: http://www.childrenshospitals.net, accessed May 26, 2006.

5. Ohio Children's Hospital Association, "Child Health Advocacy." Available at: http://ohiochildrenshospitals.org/advocacy.html, accessed May 25, 2006.

6. University College of London Institute of Children Health, "Children First for Health." Available at: http://www.childrenfirst.nhs.uk/about/index.html, accessed May 26, 2006.

7. Hospital for Sick Children (Canada), "SickKids." Available at: http://www.sickkids.ca/default.asp, accessed May 27, 2006.

8. Sydney Children's Hospital, Randwick (Australia),"Welcome to the Sydney Children's Hospital." Available at: http://www.sch.edu.au, accessed May 27, 2006.

9. "Services." Available at: http://www.sch.edu.au/services/services.html, accessed May 27, 2006.

Chapter 4

Consumer Health Information for Youth and Their Caregivers

Introduction

In preceding chapters, we have discussed policy development, issues and problems, and major models for health delivery. This chapter considers consumer information and how it relates to children, adolescents, and their caregivers in both school and public library environments. Some basic definitions are needed before we can begin our discussion.

A Brief Glossary

Consumer Health Information

Consumer health information is information about various aspects of health care that are written, produced, or given in some form to nonmedical persons who need information about health. The basic premise of consumer information is that individuals can make decisions about their own health needs provided they have well-written and accurate information.

Consumer health information involves theoretical principles that promote health and the prevention of diseases within populations. This theoretical base draws on sociology, psychology, political science, instructional and education theories,[1] nursing, public health, health promotion, health education, library science, and communication science.[2]

Community Information and Referrals

Community information is information that is available in the community, and it comes in many forms,[3] including people, organizations, government agencies, businesses. Often this information is nonbibliographic. That is, no bibliographic record has been made of it. Libraries do not necessarily acquire and store community information (although they certainly can) as they do for books or other produced items. Rather, they obtain knowledge about the whereabouts of information and create directories or other guides so that referrals can be made to appropriate sources. The referral aspect of community information is the act of directing someone to sources in the community where information or services can be obtained based on the nature of the information request. In libraries, referral is not advice giving; rather it is directional information given to patrons based on their needs after consultation with them. Consumer information is found in the large array of materials offered by community information providers that offer health care and information.

Health Information Literacy

Health information literacy is a part of information literacy. Basic information literacy involves the ability to solve problems through the identification of sources, evolution of sources in relation to needs, and the ability to place needs, demands, and sources into a priority context. Similarly, health information literacy allows an individual "to obtain, interpret, and understand basic health information and services." Health information literacy provides individuals with "competencies to use such information and services in ways" that will enhance their health and the health of those in their families and communities.[4] Chapter 7 also discusses health information literacy.

Community-Based Organizations (CBOs)

CBOs are organizations developed within the confines of a given community to meet specific needs within the geographic confines of that community. Many CBOs are health related. AIDS-HIV organizations serving local communities are examples of CBOs. More specifically, a CBO is "organized as a non-profit ... either public or private under the U.S. Tax Laws. These organizations are designed to facilitate community needs with public and private funds."[5]

Making Consumer Health Information Accessible: Designs and Concepts

One of the most important aspects of consumer health information is making it accessible to the public. Accessibility includes facility designs, social needs consideration, and publications that are accurate, appealing, age-appropriate, and readable.

Figures 4.1 through 4.4 illustrate how consumer health information can be made accessible in libraries and other health information centers through careful consideration of comfortable surroundings and accessibility to information.

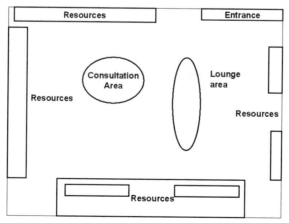

Figure 4.1. Diagram of major function areas of a consumer health information service and consulting center.

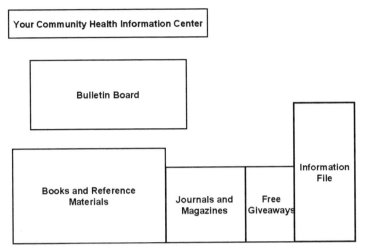

Figure 4.2. Consumer health information center: major resource components.

Figure 4.3. Consumer health information center: Interior design sketch. Design reflects storage for resources, comfort, and privacy. Windows and glass in door allow for openness and contact with outside surroundings. Drawing by Richard H. Hendler.

Figure 4.4. The Consumer Health Center, Frankfield County Public Library, Lancaster, Ohio.
Courtesy of the Frankfield County Library.

Figure 4.5 is an example of one of the many publications designed to provide easy-to-understand consumer health information to the general public. It is an example of how governments continue to be involved in health care management and information.

Figure 4.5. Consumer health pamphlet issued by the U.S. Environmental Protection Agency.
Courtesy of the U.S. Environmental Protection Agency.

Consumer Health Information, the Health Curriculum, and Schools

As we stated in Chapter 3, the connection between schools and health began with public health initiatives to control the spread of infectious disease in the 1880s in most of the industrial countries of England and North America. New school attendance laws and child labor laws resulted in more children and youth remaining in school for longer periods of time. Unlike earlier periods, large groups of children were now collected together and could be monitored, checked, and tracked for diseases as they arose in the communities. Schools began to serve as field laboratories for monitoring disease. Another benefit was that better health behaviors could be taught to children and their parents in a formalized setting.

Public health movements occurred alongside of, but somewhat separate from, the development of school libraries. In 1909, a collection of essays edited by Claude G. Leland and his colleagues appeared, explaining the important role of the school library in education. As mentioned in Chapter 2, the similarities between public health outreach into communities and the development of library outreach are similar. An essay by Homer Seerley describes how the Library Commission of Illinois managed traveling libraries, a book loan program for the blind, distribution of standard magazines through exchange programs, and development and loan of a traveling picture collection of great works of art.[6] Whereas public health stressed disease control, these library essays argued that although libraries provide information and enjoyment, good, well-selected books in libraries promote culture and appreciation of literature, development of good taste, and refinement in behaviors. This same collection carried a series called The Harper Juveniles: A Selected List of Harper's Books for Young People Alphabetically Arranged. Most of the selections listed dealt with literature, history, biography, with some attention given to science. Only a few titles specifically addressed health. One title, *How to Get Strong and How to Stay So* by William Blaikie, discussed muscle development and daily exercise. Curiously, this title was listed in "Harper's Girls' Handy-Books" series.[7]

Health education and physical education as terms are often used together, but they have different roles to play in the school curriculum. Most states and provinces in North America as well as the United Kingdom have mandated health curricula that address such issues as[8]:

- Emotional health and positive self-image

- Respect for and care of the human body

- Physical fitness

- Health issues related to addiction and abuse (e.g., drugs, alcohol, and tobacco)

- Health misinformation and misconception and quackery

- Exercise and its effects on the body

- Nutrition and weight control

- Sexual relationships

- Community and ecological health

- Diseases (communicable and degenerative)

- Disaster preparedness

- Safety and driver education

- Selection of health care providers

- Choices in health care professions

Similarly, physical education has an underlying goal of promoting good health. In fulfilling this goal, it emphasizes large-muscle activity through play and movement. Such activities are designed to develop motor skills, develop knowledge of games and understanding of game rules, promote teamwork, develop play skills, and encourage competitive activities. Activities generally followed in U.S. schools include aquatics, conditioning activities, gymnastics, sports (team and individual), and rhythm and dance. Activities favored in the United Kingdom include netball, cricket, and rugby. Softball, cricket, football (Australian rules), and rugby are played in New Zealand and Australia.[9] Soccer (football) and basketball are almost universally played in school environments around the world.

School-Based Health Clinics and Outreach Programs

Modern school-based health clinics located in schools began in the United States in the 1960s as part of the "War on Poverty" policy of the Johnson administration. Although not a complete success, there are more than 1,500 schools in the country that have health clinics attached to them. Similar to earlier disease control measures initiated by public health agencies from the1880s, schools are still convenient places for reaching and serving children and youth. In some health circumstances involving psychological needs, emotional and sexual abuse, or mental health issues, older youth feel more comfortable having problems addressed in a familiar school environment. A school setting also offers a more direct means for close observation and intervention by staff and teachers of students' health situations. School-based clinics also present avenues for formalized health instruction designed to promote positive health behaviors and attitudes.[10]

The National Assembly of School-Based Health Care, with headquarters in Washington, D.C., promotes school-based health clinics. Its basic activities include advocacy and public policy development, offering avenues for training and technical assistance, and evaluation and quality control of programs. It has chapters in twenty-one states. The association's national conferences offer information on such topics as clinical skills, cultural understanding, policy development, financial support, and management, parental involvement, adolescent risk-taking behaviors, bioterrorism, rural health needs, and child and adolescent obesity.[11] Another useful organization is the Center for Health and Health Care in Schools, operated from the George Washington University School of Public Health and Health Service. The center

> builds on a 20-year history of testing strategies to strengthen health care delivery systems for children and adolescents. For the past decade, with support from The Robert Wood Johnson Foundation, Center staff and consultants have worked with institutional leaders, state officials and clinical providers to maximize outcomes for children through more effective health programming in schools.[12]

The first clinics began in Dallas, Denver, and St. Louis. Successful school-based clinics also operated in Bridgeport, Connecticut, and San Fernando and San Jose California. The Orange County, California, Health Care Agency currently operates a public health clinic at Las Lomas Elementary School (http://www.ochealthinfo.com/Public/clinics.htm). Illinois operates forty-four clinics, with twenty-four of them in Chicago schools. Forty-three clinics exist in New Mexico, with thirty-five funded by the state. Syracuse, New York, has operated clinics in three schools for the last 10 years.[13]

School-based clinics are not without their critics. Some groups and individuals have protested that it is inappropriate and even harmful for clinics in schools to offer safer sex and family planning information. Other problems faced by school-based clinics include staffing, management, financing, community involvement, and support.[14]

The school health clinics of Santa Clara County, California, and Texarkana Independent School District in Texas are particularly useful to this discussion. The Santa Clara County Clinics states that its group mission is

> to keep kids healthy and in school by providing high quality, easily accessible primary medical care and preventative health services to low-income children and adolescents. We operate seven school health clinics that provide primary medical care for children, from birth through 18. Clinics are strategically located at three elementary schools and four high school sites. Enrollment specialists help families enroll in Medi-Cal, Healthy Families and Healthy Kids programs.[15]

The clinics in the system are staffed by licensed nurse practitioners, physician's assistants, and physicians. Bilingual Spanish-speaking staff members as well as translation services are available in any language. The specific goals of the services are as follows[16]:

- Ensure that children stay healthy and in school
- Deliver comprehensive care
- Advance health promotion activities
- Provide leadership in adolescent and child health care
- Involve students and their families in their health care
- Support the schools and the community

The Tiger Health Clinic in the Texarkana Independent School District (TISD) is similar. It is designed to meet the needs of TISD students and their siblings. Through a grant from the Texas Department of Health in 2001, TISD has been able to operate a health clinic on the Texas Middle School campus to serve the needs of all district students. The goal of this health clinic is to improve the overall physical and emotional health of children and adolescents within the school and community and to reduce some of the present barriers to learning.

School Libraries and School-Based Clinics

Little has been written about the direct involvement of the librarian in school-based clinics. Several years ago, one of the authors had a conversation with a school librarian who worked in an Austin, Texas, elementary school that had a neighborhood clinic based in the school. She stated that her main involvement with clinical operations was working with the teachers and the clinic staff to select materials for the collection. Because the clinic served the immediate neighborhood, the collection was open to the public therein. She explained that because funds for this collection were separate from her regular budget, she did not select materials alone but was guided by a committee. She did note that the committee was especially aware of materials that might cause controversy such as anatomy books. Because the library was open to the neighborhood, she worked closely with parents, many of whom had limited English language abilities.

A neighborhood-based clinic serving a well-defined population, as just discussed, is a model that has some support, although this support may be weakening. The idea is that the neighborhood school plays a central role in social support and networking for people. This seems especially true for low-income areas. Together with health facilities, the school can meet other needs such as public library services; it can also offer recreation and entertainment venues and provide for nutrition support and food services. Included in all of these activities are services and support for parents.

Role of the School Librarians in Supplying Health Information

School librarians can play a significant role in how schools meet various health information needs. Among these are the following:

- Understand major health issues facing society today

- Have knowledge of local community and health needs

- Cultivate contacts with health professionals and providers in the community

- Select appropriate materials for the collection

- Understand the structure, theory, and expectations of national, state or province, and local curriculum mandates and make sure that the center's, services, programs, and collections match and are integrated with those mandates

- Provide for parental support through collection development, information provisions, and information referral

- Develop health-related programs such as health fairs and speaker events

- Disseminate health information through appropriate means in the school environment such as the school Web site and through staff, faculty, and administration

- Maintain relationships with the health care providers on the school's staff

- Utilize and make referrals to community information services

- Ensure that information literacy skills are incorporated into consumer health instruction

Consumer Health Information: Public Libraries

Public Library Programs

The American public library has always provided health information to its users through traditional services such as references, reader advisement, and acquisition of health materials for collections. In the 1980s and 1990s, the concept of consumer health information came into larger focus when some public libraries began to conceptualize and then offer specialized health information tailored to meet the needs of the nonspecialized user. Professional writings about consumer health information management with reference to the role of public libraries appeared as early as the 1980s.[17] Field testing of the concept also started in the early 1980s. For example, a 1984 report of consumer health information funded through the New York State Library and other New York state agencies detailed experiences in pilot projects at the Nioga Library System and the Onondaga County Public Library in that state.[18]

In 1987, a community-wide survey of residents in Montgomery County, Maryland, showed that many of the county's residents wanted a place to obtain health care information without having to rely on physicians or other health care workers. In 1989, the county library system opened the Wheaton Regional Library's Health Information Center (http://www.montgomerycountymd.gov/libtmpl.asp?url=/content/libraries/HealthInfo/hic.asp). Services offered in 2006 included the following:

- Books, medical texts, videos, journals, and free pamphlets

- Access to articles on health-related topics

- Information on local and national health organizations, support groups, and health hotlines

- Senior Health Info Line—around-the-clock message service for senior citizens (240-777-0674) [for Maryland]

- Monthly blood pressure screening clinics

- Senior health insurance counseling

- Internet access

- Special health-related programs

- Enhanced reference assistance available from trained staff[19]

The center also provided a variety of services including Internet links (with descriptions) to health resources. Those related more specifically to the health of youth included the following:

- Children with Diabetes

  Kids, parents, and adults with Type 1 diabetes can learn about diet, diabetes camps, join chat rooms, and more at this searchable Web site.

- Dr. Greene's Housecalls

  Intended for parents, this Web site features a searchable list of answers to common questions about children's health.

- American Academy of Child & Adolescent Psychiatry

  This site is a resource for parents looking for mental health information concerning their children or teens. Excellent search engine. Brochures in English, French, and Spanish.

- Kids Home at National Cancer Institute

  Designed primarily for children, this site has stories for and by kids. Parent information regarding talking about cancer with children is also available.

- KidsDoctor

  Parents can search for information on topics concerning children's physical, nutritional, and emotional well-being.

- KidsHealth.org

  Maintained by the duPont Hospital for Children, children's health information is presented to three separate audiences: kids, teens, and parents. Searchable.

Health information services in public libraries vary as we might expect. For example, the New Hanover County Public Library located in Wilmington, North Carolina, maintains a Consumer Health Information Service that provides access to major databanks such as Hale Health and Wellness Database, MedlinePlus, and NC Live.Org (a password-based library network of North Carolina public libraries). The library says this about its services:

> The Consumer Health Library provides information, not advice, and does not imply medical recommendation or endorsement. This includes links to online journals, organizations, or any other type of website. Please consult your health care provider for specific health concerns.[20]

The services (mostly links to medical information) are divided into these major parts[21]:

Getting Started: Basic information and how to make judgments about health information

Disease and Conditions: Information about specific diseases, such as HIV/AIDS

Services and Providers: Contact information in the local area (physicians, hospitals, etc.)

Family Health and Fitness: Parent information and information for children and adolescents, labeled "For Parents," "Kids Site," and Teens Site." These sites are prepared by the Nemours Foundation.

Other Resources: Links to materials and resources in Spanish and easy-to-read items

The New York Public Library is one of the largest and most extensive public library systems in the world, offering many unique services. Its consumer health service is titled "Choices in Health Information." Its announcement of basic services states that "CHOICES is here to help you! We're the community health information service of the New York Public Library. Our job is to help you get the information you need to take care of your health and your family."[22]

CHOICES offers health-related programs related to current health interests and needs conducted by health and other experts and held in various branch locations around the city; health features drawn from the Internet, health information links prepared by reliable sources available on the Internet; and books on health information available in the collection, together with their location and other bibliographic information. The Toronto Public Library offers similar services through its Consumer Health Information Service (http://www.torontopubliclibrary.ca/uni_chi_index.jsp).

Continued U.S. National Efforts

Encouraged by the interest shown by the U.S. government, the American Association for the Advancement of Science (AAAS), recognized the need for health information and the role that public libraries could play in providing consumer health information to the public. With the aid of a grant from the National Institutes of Health Education Awards Program and working within the U.S. federal government's Healthy People 2010 project,[23] AAAS created Library Initiative, a five-year program designed to provide consumer health information through public libraries to minorities and other groups. A research component initially surveyed the present situation involving consumer health information in public libraries and then made some general recommendations as to how public libraries could better meet the goals in the Healthy People 2010 project. Published as *The Challenge of Providing Consumer Health Information Services in Public Libraries,* the study's recommendations included the following:

- Providing outreach programs and services

- Production of readable and visually appropriate health information

- Promoting the availability of reliable health information sources such as MEDLINEplus

- Providing for communication with non- or limited English speakers

- Collection and resource development

- Training of librarians in consumer health information[24]

Initially, the research report gave only general guidance as to programs and services to offer, but The Library Initiative has issued subsequent reports addressing some of these issues in more depth. The report also makes references to several outstanding public libraries that can provide guidance about dealing with many of these and other issues.

Programs and issues that seem to need special attention continue to be levels and types of programs and services to provide; types of materials to acquire; parenting information to make accessible and information created especially to meet the needs of children and adolescents; and methods appropriate for consultation and referrals. Many of these issues (e.g., parenting information, consultation and referrals, selection of materials) are discussed in more detail in other chapters.

Outreach Programs and Services

On the basis of information from focus groups of public librarians, AAAS through its Library Initiative, issued several suggestions for various types of outreach programs and services that librarians find essential in helping libraries reach further into their communities with consumer health information. Many of these are standard services and practices that librarians offer as a part of regular services, but others, within the context of consumer health information, can be used to advantage by libraries. These ideas include the following[25]:

- Partner with local groups such as:

  - Community health centers
  - Local hospitals or hospital libraries
  - Community outreach programs already in place
  - Groups and agencies serving the minority groups

- Engage in cooperative programming and outreach with others

- Identify minority health advocacy groups serving African Americans, Latinos, and religious groups

- Contact and use materials and ideas developed by the Office of Minority Health in the U.S. Department of Health and Human Services and the National Center for Minority Health and Health Disparities at the National Library of Medicine

- Seek the help of volunteers in the health professions, such as nurses and pharmacists, asking them to advocate for the library as a source of consumer information; invite health care professionals to give programs under the sponsorship of the library

- Contact and stay connected with the major CBOs in the community and publicize the consumer health information available in the library for their clients

- Disseminate information about consumer health information services available in the library, placing flyers and other information where they can be easily found by potential users. Distribute information at

  - Health fairs where health screenings are performed
  - Churches
  - Ethnic festivals
  - Day-care centers
  - Public schools
  - English as a second language programs
  - Workforce development programs

Although not mentioned by the focus groups just cited, use of the local news media is essential. A standard approach is to develop press releases and send them to news outlets. Such contact with news organizations requires a certain level of relationship development and cultivation. In larger communities, news staff members tend to specialize in certain areas such as education and community services. Identify these people, and explain how your program and the information you have will benefit the community and be of interest to readers or to viewers and listeners (or both). Using the same personal approach, contact producers and hosts of local radio and television outlets and suggest willingness to be interviewed or to present programs. Do not overlook community access television. With the help of staff members and of other community groups, produce and present programs that feature the consumer health information available in the library.

Naturally, consider how you can work with groups, organizations, and agencies that have special youth service missions (e.g., Boy Scouts, Girl Scouts, interest groups such as 4-H Clubs of America, church youth groups, youth detention programs, neighborhood youth facilities, parenting organizations, etc.). Make sure in all of these contacts that the needs and interests of children and adolescents are made clear as are the programs, services, and resources available to address these groups' special needs.

Consumer Health Information: Hospitals and Medical Institutions

Chapter 3 discussed in some detail the role that government agencies and children's hospitals play in children's health care. Many of these have consumer and family information services that are open to their clients as well as the general public.

One useful example is PlaneTree Library of Good Samaritan Hospital located in Los Gatos, California. The library's motto is "Walk in with questions. Walk out with confidence." It states that it is a

> comprehensive consumer health and medical library, free and open to the public. Our library's most fundamental service is providing you with access to information so you can make informed decisions about your health and healthy choices about your life.

> ... Resources range from easy-to-understand materials to the technical, professional literature. Our computer services feature Internet access, including health sites not publicly available, and help with online searching. PlaneTree covers both conventional and complementary (alternative) therapies. Some books, articles, and videos are available in Spanish and in Vietnamese.[26]

Consumer health information services are provided by academic medical centers, medical society libraries, and some special libraries. The Consumer Health Library Directory maintained by the Consumer and Patient Health Information Section of the Medical Library Association lists libraries and collections that offer information for patients as well as information about consumer health.[27] Included are NYU Medical Center, Women and Children's Hospital of Buffalo, Children's Hospital of Eastern Ontario, Ottawa Hospital and the Children's National Hospital in Washington, D.C., National Jewish Medical and Research Center, University of Iowa Hospitals and Clinics, and the Baptist Health System, Jacksonville, Florida. The directory provides information on the nature of collections and services offered.

Consumer Health Information: Rural and Small Towns

Rural America still is a very important part of the nation's social life, and the characteristics of rural and small-town life vary. The U.S. Department of Agriculture reports that the 2005 economy was favorable to rural life; employment growth was strong, and recreation and tourism was important. Nevertheless, some areas still experienced loss of population and dislocation of sources of employment as natural resources and farming declined. Overall population rates were low. Immigration into rural areas increased, creating more diversity of cultural groups in some areas. Poverty still remains a problem in most areas of the United States, with 14.2 percent living below the official poverty level. Southern states had the highest level of poverty at 17.7 percent, and the Midwest the least at 9.7 percent. Statistics for 2003 showed that 11.6 percent of all rural households with children were "food insure." "Food insure" is a term meaning that food is not readily available in a household.

In terms of health services, many rural Americans lack proper health care. These include the working poor and migrant workers, both legal and illegal. In most U.S. rural areas, there is a critical need for better hospitals and access to them. Medical personnel are in short supply, especially those who are highly trained and specialized. Many citizens lack health insurance and often have difficulty applying for government support. Recent solutions to some of these problems are the increased use of medical information technology and understanding on the part of government, policy makers, and funding agencies that health care involves an interdisciplinary and community-based approach.

Centralized governments such as the United Kingdom, Canada, and many European countries have government health policies that address the needs of rural areas. These countries rely less on volunteers, philanthropy, and community-based organizations to meet rural needs than does the United States.

The following excerpt from an essay on Canadian sociology may help us better understand the difference between the approach to health care in Canada (and in many European countries) and the United States:

> Canadians are often viewed as less individualistic than are people in the United States, with a greater emphasis on collective approaches in Canada. An associated development is the social welfare state as a means of organization, as opposed to greater reliance on individual initiative and private charity, as in the United States…. The strong central state or provincial government exercises control in many areas such as health care, education, unemployment insurance.[28]

Collaboration as a Model

Collaboration involving schools, public libraries, and health agencies is a model that can be adopted in both urban and sparsely populated rural areas. This model offers youth librarians opportunities to become involved in providing health information, programs, and services to their communities. They can collect and promote materials in their collections, provide parents and caregivers with services and information, and identify and promote available community health services through library Web sites and other types of communication avenues typically used by libraries and school library media centers. All youth librarians certainly need to develop skills and confidence in listening, consulting, and making appropriate referrals to health services and health information available in their area.

Conclusion

As society becomes more complex, individuals are expected to assume more responsibility for their own needs. This is undoubtedly the case with health care. This in turn implies that resources must be available to help people make good choices, but before this can happen, society must provide for the resources that are needed. Consumer health information services arose in the 1970s as an attempt to meet the needs of laypersons who need appropriate information to make good health choices. The rise of the Internet has both promoted and complicated the availability of consumer health information. So much health information is now available through the Internet that the adequate use of this information requires a great deal of health information literacy.

Medical facilities as well as libraries now offer a great deal of consumer information. But the question remains: Is this information accessible to all that need it on an equal footing? The answer is probably not. Public libraries and school library media centers have opportunities to act as "consumer health information providers." The prevailing practice in consumer health care delivery is based on the concept of a "community-based approach." Youth librarians have a role to play in this community endeavor. Not only is this involvement good public relations for existing youth library programs, it also offers a humane and personal connection with many aspects of our diversified communities.

Notes

1. Mary Ellen Wurzbach, ed., *Community Health Education and Promotion* (Gaithersbury, MD: Aspen, 2002), p. 4.

2. Gunther Eysenback, "Clinical Reviews: Recent Advances. Consumer Information Informatics," *BMJ* (*British Medical Journal*) 320 (June 24, 2000): 1713–1716. Available at: http://www.bmj.com/cgi/content/full/320/7251/1713, accessed January 18, 2007.

3. Children's Hospital and Regional Medical Center (Seattle, WA), Home Page. Available at: http://www.seattlechildrens.org/child_health_safety/health_advice, accessed June 15, 2006.

4. Wurzbach, 7.

5. Delaware County Business Resource Center, "Glossary." Available at: http://www.delawarecountybrc.com/glossaryterms.htm#1, accessed June 9, 2006.

6. Claude G. Leland et al., eds., *The School Library and the School* (New York: Harper & Brothers, 1910), 62.

7. *The Harper Juveniles: A Selected List of Harper's Books for Young People Alphabetically Arranged*, p. 98. In Leland et al., eds.

8. "Health Education." In *Wikipedia, The Free Encyclopedia*. Available at: http://en.wikipedia.org/wiki/Health_education, accessed June 8, 2006.

9. "Physical Education." In *Wikipedia, The Free Encyclopedia*. Available at: http://en.wikipedia.org/wiki/Physical_education, accessed June 8, 2006.

10. Carol Chemelynki, "More Districts See Benefits of School-Based Health Clinics." *School Board News* (Nov. 2004). Available on the National School Boards Association Web site at: http://www.nsba.org/site/view.asp? TRACKID=& VID=58&CID=1578&DID=34823, accessed June 9, 2006.

11. NASBHC Home Page. Available at: http://www.nasbhc.org, accessed June 9, 2003.

12. The Center for Health and Health Care in Schools Home Page. Available at: http://www.healthinschools.org/about.asp, accessed June 9, 2006.

13. Chemelynki.

14. Paul Brodeurk, "School-Based Health Clinics." Available at: http://www.rwjf. org/files/publications/books/2000/chapter_01.html, accessed June 8, 2006.

15. School Health Clinics of Santa Clara County, "Welcome to School Health Clinics of Santa Clara County." Available at: http://www.schoolhealthclinics. org, accessed June 8, 2006.

16. School Health Clinics of Santa Clara County.

17. Alan M. Rees, ed., *Developing Consumer Health Information* (New York: Bowker, 1982).

18. Christine A. Bain, *Health Information from the Public Library: A Report on Two Pilot Projects* (Albany, NY: New York State Education Department, New York State Library, Culture Education Center, 1984).

19. Montgomery County (Maryland) Public Libraries, "Health Information Center." Available at: http://www.montgomerycountymd.gov/libtmpl.asp?url=/content/libraries/HealthInfo/hic.asp, accessed June 5, 2006.

20. New Hanover County Library, "Consumer Health Library." Available at: http://www.nhcgov.com/lib/CH/CHmain.asp, accessed June 6, 2006.

21. New Hanover County Library. Available at http://www.nypl.org/branch/choices, accessed 6 June 2006.

22. New York Public Library, "Choices in Health Information." Available at: http://www.nypl.org/branch/choices, accessed June 6, 2006.

23. U.S. Office of Disease Prevention and Health Promotion, "Healthy People 2010." Available at: http://www.healthypeople.gov, accessed June 4, 2005.

24. American Association for the Advancement of Science, *The Challenge of Providing Consumer Health Information Services in Public Libraries* (Washington, DC: AAAS, n.d.).

25. "Healthy People Library Project: Health Outreach—Tips for Librarians: Outreach Models." Available at: http://www.healthlit.org/health_outreach/outreach_models.htm, accessed June 7, 2006.

26. "PlaneTree Health Library." Available at: http://www.planetreesanjose.org, accessed June 9, 2006.

27. "Consumer and Patient Health Information Directory." Available at: http://caphis.mlanet.org/directory/find_a_library.html, accessed June 9, 2006.

28. "Canadian Sociological Approaches Dec. 7, 1999." Available at: http://uregina.ca/~gingrich/d7f99.htm, accessed June 9, 2006.

Chapter 5

Families, Parents, Caregivers, and Health Information

Introduction

Families, parents, and other caregivers play fundamental roles in how health information is made available and used by children and adolescents. Earlier chapters in this book discussed the role of society and some of the provisions made by institutions and persons in society to meet a wide array of health information needs. This chapter looks more specifically at the role of families, institutions, and parenting in modern society.

Family, Society, and Health Information in Libraries

Family life in most countries is complex, and in Western countries, it is in flux. Some claim that the family is in decline because of challenges in society: divorce, economic and political instability, poverty, and homosexuality and the recognition of gay and lesbian marriage. All of these concerns affect how persons in libraries and schools respond in terms of providing programs and services. It is essential that youth librarians have a fundamental understanding of family life and how families are now defined.

The United Nations' Declaration of Human Rights in Article 16(3) states this about families: "The family is the natural and fundamental group unit of society and is entitled to protection by society and the State."

Earlier chapters have outlined how governments and other care providers have developed avenues for health care. In some cases, these developments have been in direct response to the UN statement, encouraged and helped by the World Health Organization (WHO). In others, they are results of available resources and social policy created to meet human needs within the specific understanding of social, cultural, and governmental responsibilities.

The idea of family varies from society to society and culture to culture; those of us who plan library and school library media services must understand how the concept of family is understood by our various user groups. In society, the term "family" has several definitions.

At a basic level, a family is a group of people who form a social group or a group of social groups. These groups are generally united by marriage, birth, or other types of relationships recognized by governments. These relationships include domestic partnerships, adoption, and foster families or foster care providers. Foster care families form a special relationship that is often a legal contract or agreement made between an adult or adults to care for a child as a surrogate for the state. In this role, the foster care parent(s) assume many of the responsibilities of a parent for the care of the child or children.

Power of Family and Clan Identity

The family has often been defined as a blood or genetic relationship in both modern and traditional societies. This may be too simple an explanation of family. Some social scientists suggest that the genetic "family" can be used only metaphorically and that family must be understood in much larger social and cultural contexts. For example, "clan" is a term related to family that takes on important cultural and social meanings in various cultures. In some cultures, clans and loyalty to one's clan have huge social, political, and cultural impact. A case in point is the role that clans have played historically in the political and social stability of such areas Scotland, Appalachia, Iraq, Afghanistan, and Pakistan. The deadly feud between the Hatfields and McCoys in the Appalachian Mountains of nineteenth-century America is well known.[1] Clan systems exist in most human society including Asian, Pacific, and Moslem cultures; African societies; and various caste systems. Clans are important for social and individual identities in Native American and Native Canadian tribes.

In one sense, clans are a group of families that claim descent from a common ancestor. In Western societies (with the exception of Celtic/Scottish and Native peoples in various countries), it has lost much of its importance.

In planning programs and services today, it is helpful to understand the metaphorical power of family clans and family alliances and how family and clans are viewed today by many who will use libraries and schools. This is especially useful when planning programs that serve native cultures.

Clans and Family in Western Society

The power of the clan in Western society is illustrated by how clans have survived in native North American cultures. Clans also have lingering power in Western European cultures as well. In the seventeenth century, the British government viewed Scottish clans as lawless and disloyal to the Crown (encouraged by its prevailing patriarchic system). The Crown engaged in continual attempts to destroy the influence of Scottish clans through much of the 1700s.[2] Following several defeats, including the Battle of Culloden, the clans were disarmed in 1746, and wearing clan tartans was a rigorously enforced penal offense. In 1822, George IV helped make the tartan acceptable by indicating that they could be worn in a public celebration. Unfortunately, by then much of the artistry and workmanship of tartan making had been lost along with knowledge of family clan histories and relationships.[3]

Beyond this history, the Scottish clan system can help us understand the power of family identity in modern Western society. The Scottish clans continue to offer a sense of family belonging for many of Scottish descent throughout the world, and of course, they remain powerful in Scotland and the British Commonwealth today where wearing clan tartans is common.

The clan culture of Native peoples of North America is complex and varies from tribe to tribe and culture to culture. For example, the Cherokees of the United States have an ancient and complex system of clan relationships,[4] as do the Acomas of New Mexico. Clans are often tied to inherited positions and social standings within the tribe. Clans can also exemplify special talents or attributes that members of the clans are expected to exhibit and provide. In traditional villages such as some Acoma Pueblo, many of the ancient clan traditions, practices, and rights are still followed, including that of social standing and privilege.[5]

Another definition of clan that has modern impact is that a clan is a group united by a common interest or common characteristics, perhaps a social or political movement. In a negative sense, the American-based Ku Klux Klan (KKK) is an example of such a clan movement. In this sense, the "clan" is not related by kinship but by ideology. Using this definition of clan, we can include fraternities and social organizations.

Other terms related to family identity include the "extended family" and "families of choice." Extended family generally means biological family relationships that go beyond the primary family unit of parents and their children. Families of choice often arise when persons find that their biological families have rejected them or cannot or will not meet their social and psychological needs. For instance, Kate Weston writes about this in *Families We Choose*. She suggests that gays and lesbians often form social units that function much like biological families, giving them support that is often lacking within their biological families.[6]

The Social Roles of Families and the Library

The Western Family Model

Although the Victorian family is basically the model that is followed in Western cultures today where the primary role of the family is to raise, nurture, and support children as they grow into adulthood, at an earlier time, the family had an important economic role to play. Children as well as adults were economic commodities.

Economic consideration and child care still play a role in family life. Time when children and adolescents are available, as well as the time required of parents and other caregivers to connect with the services and programs, must be considered. This is especially important in areas that serve low-income persons.

Most library and school programs operate within the context of serving the overall mission of society for the betterment of families. As such, the library's programs are influenced by government policies. Laws and legal requirements also play a role in programs and services. This certainly applies to how health information is provided to youth and how it can be restricted. Sex information and family planning information is an example of such possible restrictions.

The family is an institution in society, but it also must relate to other institutions such as, schools, government, and religion. In terms of certain moral issues, some countries are more conservative than others. The U.S. government and society generally take a more reserved and conservative position regarding sexual information than some other Western countries. This view is influenced by religion and general social expectations. Currently, the official U.S. government policy about sex education is "abstinence only." This is interpreted by the government to mean that federal funding for sex education programs will be given only to programs that teach that sex before marriage is harmful to healthy development and is therefore unacceptable.[7] On the other hand, Canada supports "comprehensive" sex education programs that teach that there are several options to sexual conduct youth can consider within a framework of reliable and correct social and medical information. See Chapter 2 for more details. Youth librarians certainly need to be aware of such government policies, but they should consider these policies within the context of free discussion within a democracy, protected by legal rights as determined by laws, courts, and constitutional mandates.

Parenting as a Social Function

Parenting is most often associated with family, but parenting goes far beyond that. In very basic terms:

> Parenting comprises all the tasks involved in raising a child to an independent adult. Parenting begins even before the child is born or adopted and may last until the death of the parent or child. Parenting is a part of the relationship within a family.[8]

Attachment Parenting Theory

Attachment parenting theory helps us understand some of the basic rationale for many, if not all, health information programs, including library services and programs. Attachment theory suggests that infants seek "closeness to another person and feel secure when that person is present."[9] Attachment theory considers children to be social beings, needing social attachments to parents and others. Attachment is a part of normal child development. On the other hand, Freudian theory holds that children attach themselves to parents and others to satisfy needs and drives. Attachment theory justifies parent-child programs in libraries and schools in which both parent and child are allowed to share in activities with each other. Toddler programs are good examples of attachment-based programs.

Modern Demands on Parenting and Health Information

Over the years, parenting has become more complex as society and culture have developed. More choices for behaviors are available to both parents and children, and the consequences of choices are more immediate. Some hold that the benefits of being a parent are less now than before because of the social, legal, and economic responsibilities assumed by parents and demanded of them. These responsibilities are often enforced by laws and expectations. Both professional and public options now require parents to assume a large amount of the care and socialization of children that in the past might have been assumed by the extended family, the local neighborhood, religious associations and schools. In the nineteenth century, schools played an important role in teaching good manners, patriotism, and health and hygiene. Public schools were well suited for this role as more children from diverse backgrounds were enrolling in emerging schools systems.

Today the local community and the resources it offers still remain fundamental to successful parenting. In a study of parenting within challenged neighborhoods, family social researcher Robin L. Jarrett noted that "neighborhood conditions influenced how families organized, scheduled routines, and in general, reared their children."[10] She found that parents raising children in unstable neighborhoods showed commitment to good parenting and followed good parenting models. They relied more on parenting skills that they saw as successful, learned, from kin as well as their own experiences. They made great effort to separate their children from the local, threatening community, and they relied on family for protection and monitoring of activities. By necessity, they placed more restrictions on their children. They invested extensive personal effort in seeking resources and advocating for resources. For this, they paid a price in terms of cost, sacrifice of personal needs, and displacement of personal goals.

No matter what the race or ethnicity of the parents, among others, Jarrett noted that the following factors influenced successful child rearing[11]:

- Availability of extended kin networks

- Family-centered orientation

- Parental commitment to their role

- Efforts to seek out resources for their families

- Commitment to advocacy efforts

- Use of the parent role to counter "street" culture by providing examples of hard work, persistence, and family unity

- Emphasis on hard work and education

These same characteristics can be extrapolated to health care and health information resources needed by parents no matter what their social or economic backgrounds.

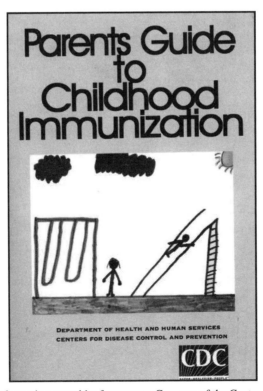

Figure 5.1. Health information pamphlet for parents. Courtesy of the Centers for Disease Control.

Youth librarians in both public and school libraries can play significant roles in helping parents learn how to access available health information resources in all communities. Librarians have opportunities to bring about change in many home environments through well-developed parenting programs that focus on health resources and good health-information-seeking behaviors. The programs used in libraries to help parents with the literacy training of their children are good models that already exist and that can be easily adjusted to accommodate health information and health information literacy.

Parenting Roles in Providing Health Information: Theory and Practice

The importance of the Jarrett research cited above is that it offers parents directions and opportunities to seek out and advocate for resources that will aid their families. These findings also suggest sound and effective ideas for program and service planning.

Families: Theories and Health Information

Theories about how families and society operate help us better understand our roles in planning health information services for children and youth and their parents and caregivers. The following theories are influenced by discussions that appear in Chibucos, Leite, and Weis's book, *Readings in Family Theory*.[12] Some of the major family theories are presented in the following discussion.

Basic Theory Glossary

Family systems theory contends that families operate much like a system with input, storage/operations, and output. In simple terms, when the nuclear family is formed by a couple, they bring certain values, resources, attitudes, traditions, and experiences into the family unit. After the family is formed, these aspects face the operational challenge of integration and the structuring of divergent values into a family unit that works to meet immediate and long-term needs. The family unit can be highly successful and highly dysfunctional, depending on how the family unit uses its assets and opportunities.[13] How the family understands and uses health information resources provided for them is an important aspect of the how the family operates as a successful system.

Life span family theory holds that families change over time and that they change when faced with both positive opportunities and negative challenges. Family life span theory contends that family development is continuous and is influenced by biological and age-determined factors, as well as by events that occur separately from biology and age influences.[14] Understanding this concept helps us plan health information services and approaches that are constructive in terms of serving individuals and families as they attempt to meet both immediate and long-term health needs and demands.

Social exchange theory is a theoretical construct built on the idea that we live in a complex world and that to survive, we must contribute to receive benefits from our society. The theory holds that social exchange is based on cost-benefit analysis. For example, "what will it cost me in terms of the benefits I will receive?" Social exchange theory is also built on negotiations, relationships, equitable exchanges, and the maintenance of rules that govern the exchange.[15] In developing and managing health information services, professionals in public and school libraries are involved in all of these aspects of social exchange. What benefit would the school library receive by having a local physician contribute a monthly newsletter for posting on the library's Web site? What benefit would the physician receive in terms of his or her time in contributing to this newsletter? What kinds of relationships would develop? What are the rules and responsibilities for maintaining the relationship?

Social conflict theory is a Marxist theory holding that conflicts in society are caused by power struggles between those who have resources and the means to use those resources to their advantage as opposed to those who do not.[16] These confrontations are played out in society in many ways, such as class, racial, and religious conflicts; power struggles; legislative directives and laws; court decisions; provisions for education and family life; strategies that reinforce acceptable models for families; the control of information; and the encouragement of approved social values. How resources are used is also a part of social conflict. In most societies, this conflict is continual, involving political and social disputes over how to use public and private resources. Institutions that offer a public service such as libraries and schools are constantly involved in these disputes because they compete with other service providers for limited resources.

The influence of social conflict theory on health care provision is apparent. The development of health information provisions in society at large as well as in libraries and schools is a progressive movement influenced by some of the major elements found in social conflicts. The movement is ideally designed to bring equity to a social situation in which there is a need for expensive information that has traditionally been controlled by and accessible only through experts. It is also in response to a change in public attitudes that place value on independent judgment by people involved in the management of their own lives, including their health care.

Values also play a large part in social conflict, and we can see this in health information for children and youth. What topics are allowed, and what topics are not allowed, what formats are allowed, what formats are not allowed? Values have an impact on issues such as parental rights to know the health decisions that affect their children, the rights of older adolescents for privacy concerning their health situations, and the rights of youth to receive information and to learn in an open society.

Feminist theory and *gender theory* seek to analyze and understand the role of women in society, especially in terms of politics, sexuality, power relationships, and women's rights, interests, and issues, including health issues. The foci of these theories are on studying discrimination, stereotyping, objectification, oppression, and patriarchy. Gender theory is a broader concept embracing the study of both males and females in social and cultural environments.[17,18]

Both these theories have strong implications for health information systems in libraries and schools. Both theories consider issues such as differences in health care information needed by both genders, equality of health information provisions, and equality in research funding and study of health issues faced by both males and females. On the other hand, feminist theory might place more emphasis on equality and special needs of women in terms of health care information and pointing out oversights and discrimination in funding and research, whereas gender theory focuses more on gender ideology and its application within health care and health information.

Symbolic interaction is a theory that seeks to help us understand how people and groups interact and how this interaction creates their personal identities. According to this theory, people develop meaning in terms of their social environments and the symbols that have meaning and power that exist there. People assess the situation and build and project personal images that will best help them to interact advantageously in this personal environment. Society, then, is a creation of individually perceived symbols based on individual experiences.

Symbolic interaction bases its analysis primarily on person-to-person interactive evidence, and pays little attention to larger demographic influences. People approach health care and health care information with an abundance of symbols that convey both negative and positive feelings and condition how people will react to health care needs and information. Authority, control, submissiveness, and helpfulness are just a few of the symbols that the client will use to build a personal relationship and identify with the library and school and professional helpers found there. Previous symbols from culture such as family, community, and traditions also play a strong role in how these symbols are integrated into an individual social view of the library, school, and health information. In designing health care information, the influence of such personal interaction symbols must be carefully considered.

At a basic level, *Behaviorism*, which previously had such a strong hold on the field of education, holds that our behaviors are triggered by cues that come to us from our environment, and our reactions are automatic and conditioned by previous experiences of reward or punishment.[19] Youth librarians can use this theory to better understand how their clients might interact with them. Some will come with negative expectations, and others will approach the library with positive feelings. These feelings will be based on previous experiences and behavior and environmental clues from earlier library and health experiences. Using behavioral principles, professionals can encourage positive interactions with patrons through positive personal interactions and by providing supportive services and programs.

As its name suggests, *Ecological theory,* as proposed by the late Cornell professor Urie Bronfenbrenner, is built around ecological concepts. Bronfenbrenner suggested that children live in broad and complex ecological systems that extend well beyond the immediate family. From these various systems, children acquire ideas of behaviors and values. Parents and caregivers are important, and they probably provide the most powerful influences, but they are not the only sources of information reflecting values and behaviors. A reciprocal interaction exists between children and all the environments they encounter.[20] Some social critics hold that this theory is now under challenge because of recent research in genetics that increasingly reveal how genes might influence and direct human behavior.

Nevertheless, the basic ideas of this theory are important to us as we plan health information services for youth. It implies that a strong, positive, and extensive ecological system is needed to help children develop and grow within supportive community contexts.[21] Health information services and health information literacy play important roles in these community ecological systems.

Helping Parents and Caregivers with Health Information

Parents and caregivers face a formidable task when seeking health information. With the advent of the Internet and the attention governments have shown to health needs, health information is now more readily available than ever. Youth librarians can help by identifying and providing access to international sources such as the World Health Organization (WHO); national government sources; state, regional, and provincial sources;

and local sources. Chapter 11 provides a list of selection tools and access points for health information, together with some basic suggestions for collection development.

In the United States, one of the major health information sources that librarians and school librarians can promote is MedlinePlus (http://www.medlineplus.gov). MedlinePlus, designed for the layperson, is a product of the U.S. National Library of Medicine and the U.S. National Institutes of Health. It offers a user-friendly approach to finding a wide variety of health information. In the words of its sponsors, MedlinePlus[22]:

> will direct you to information to help answer health questions. MedlinePlus brings together authoritative information from NLM, the National Institutes of Health (NIH), and other government agencies and health-related organizations. Preformulated MEDLINE searches are included in MedlinePlus and give easy access to medical journal articles. MedlinePlus also has extensive information about drugs, an illustrated medical encyclopedia, interactive patient tutorials, and the latest health news.

A useful source provided by this service is a link under "Other Resources" that points the way, although limited, to local community information libraries in the United States, Canada, and other countries. Because it is a free service provided by the U.S. government, many libraries already offer it through their local Web pages. Health departments in countries such as Australia and the United Kingdom offer links to similar information services.

Children's hospitals are especially aware of the information needs of parents and those who care for children and youth. Youth librarians can identify those of local and national interest and link to them through their local Web pages. A review of some of the postings of these hospitals offers insight into questions and concerns that parents and caregivers have. For example, the Children's Hospital and Regional Medical Center in Seattle, Washington, provides a service on its Web page called "Child Health Advice." It notes that

> These guidelines (topics) are intended to help you determine how sick your child is and if you need to call your child's doctor. Their second purpose is to help you treat your child at home when it is safe to do so.
>
> **IMPORTANT!** Your doctor's advice and your good judgment should always take precedence over information in these guidelines.[23]

Similar sites are available in the United States and other countries. For example, New South Wales' NSW+Health site offers "Life Stages." This venue offers extensively age-based information on a wide variety of issues, including those affecting children and youth.[24]

Institutional and Cultural Factors and Health Information

Institutions, Parents, and Caregivers

Acquiring health information is a learning experience, carried out or encouraged by institutions that have evolved specifically within community structures to facilitate learning and acquiring skills that are necessary or helpful for success. As discussed in previous chapters, health-focused institutions familiar to the public include organizations and foundations such as the Bill and Melinda Gates Foundation, hospitals, schools, libraries, and governments.

Health information services that libraries and schools provide operate within a mixture of social and cultural contexts, guided by rules and values of the societies in which they exist. As with professionals in all of society's institutions, librarians continually interact with their environments, constructing and redefining practices and actions that allow their libraries to function as legitimate social institutions. Often librarians find themselves networking with other institutions where boundaries become blurred and complex. Providing health information services and programs are examples of this complex web of networks that require continued changes, readjustment, and collaboration to meet demands of society. Parents and caregivers of children and youth, along with youth librarians, are players in these institutional settings where learning and acquiring information is the prevailing social mandate.[25]

Parent and Caregiver Constraints

Although institutional services are available and widely recognized by parents and caregivers, constraints often prevent parents and caregivers from taking full advantage of them. *Time* is a major constraint. Simply put, finding health information is time-consuming.

Institutional barriers are problems that caregivers and parents face. Sometimes rules and requirements are placed in the way of institutional support and access. Bureaucracies and institutional settings can evoke images of control and intimidation that discourage caregivers from approaching library-based health information providers.

Cultural and societal backgrounds often prevent parents and caregivers from approaching institutions such as libraries for help. This is closely linked to experiences with institutions connected to one's cultural background. Culture also affects what one expects from institutions and how one has been conditioned to approach those in authority within institutions, including schools and libraries. Culture also plays a role in how information is presented in terms of authority and authenticity. An important question must be asked: What symbols of authority and authenticity concerning health information will our users accept, and how can we provide those?

The needs of the handicapped can be considered as a cultural and social barrier. Policies and practices must be in place to address needs for physical access to equipment and facilities, as well as to a wide variety of health information.

Information seeking requires a certain level of *educational skill.* Reading and understanding cultural references are important. Lack of educational skills may prevent some people from attempting to approach a library or school for health information. Intervention on the part of the information provider is required in such cases. Perhaps it will be necessary to make provisions for reading the information to the client or having information translated into a language that the user can understand. Handouts, pamphlets, and Web sites should be created in such a way as to meet the needs of those with limited literacy and educational backgrounds. A commercial firm that produces low literacy materials for numerous organizations including governments is Clear Language Group (http://www.clearlanguagegroup.com).

Figure 5.2. Low-literacy health pamphlet produced for the National Cancer Institute by Clear Language Group. Courtesy of the National Health Institute.

Action Research and Planning Programs and Services for Families

Every family is different, and it is always difficult to make broad statements about what is needed and will work in individual community and family situations. In planning about family needs, some specific questions must be asked. Basic action research conducted at the local level can offer guidance. Answering and understanding the following questions or situations can aid in developing profiles of users, thus leading to better services and programs:

- Within a recent time period (e.g., the last six months) what medical situations requiring health information have parents and caregivers likely faced? In terms of medical situations, how might these occurrences be described (e.g., mild, expected with children of these ages, moderate, serious)?

- To whom are parents and caregivers likely to turn for health information?

- Other than to physicians, where or to whom are parents and caregivers likely to turn for health information (e.g., the Internet, friends, family members, etc.)?

- Are parents and caregivers likely to go to the local public library for health information? If not, what might prevent them from going there?

- If their children are in school, would they likely go to the school library for health information? If not, what might prevent this?

- Other than from physicians, how likely are they to perceive that adequate health information is readily accessible to them in their area?

- Do they have any feelings or opinions about how professionals such as teachers, librarians, and counselors can improve the availability of health information in their area?

Conclusion

Families, parents and other caregivers are crucial in a complex social network of providing health care information. Families are a fundamental institution in all societies. This chapter has presented a rationale for the role of parents and caregivers in providing health information for children and youth. Libraries and schools play major roles in inculcating values and attitudes of society, and they are major learning institutions in a community. They not only inculcate but also shape social values and behaviors, including positive attitudes and behaviors about health.

Improving the health of populations is one of the major concerns of modern life. As indicated by comments made in the family profiles of this chapter, to meet this responsibility, librarians in public and school libraries must

- Understand their roles in society and in their communities

- Appreciate the needs and attitudes of families

- Develop resources and collections that are accessible and reliable

- Collaborate with other agencies in the community

These attributes are fundamental to the role we must play as community advocates dedicated to improving the health and social well-being of families in our communities.

Notes

1. "Hatfield-McCoy Feud." Available at: http://en.wikipedia.org/wiki/ Hatfield-McCoy_feud, accessed January 11, 2007.

2. Michael Lynch, *Scotland: A New History* (London: Pimilco, 1992), p. 332.

3. *Clans & Tartans* (Glasgow: HarperCollins, 1991), pp. 7–8.

4. "Cherokee Clans." In *Wikipedia, The Free Encyclopedia*. Available at: http://en. wikipedia.org/wiki/Cherokee_Clans, accessed June 11, 2006.

5. "Acoma Pueblo." In *Wikipedia, The Free Encyclopedia*. Available at: http://en.wikipedia.org/wiki/Acoma_Pueblo, accessed June 11, 2006.

6. Kate Weston, *Families We Choose: Lesbians, Gays, Kinship* (New York: Columbia University Press, 1991).

7. "Abstinence-Only Education Policies and Programs: A Position Paper of the Society for Adolescent Medicine." *Journal of Adolescent Health* 38 (2006): 83–87. Available at: http://www.adolescenthealth.org/PositionPaper_Abstinence_only_edu_policies_and_programs.pdf, accessed January 10, 2007.

8. "Parenting." In *Wikipedia, The Free Encyclopedia.* Available at: http://en.wikipedia.org/wiki/Parenting, accessed June 13, 2006.

9. "Attachment Parenting." In *Wikipedia, The Free Encyclopedia.* Available at: http://en.wikipedia. org/wiki/Attachmentparenting, accessed June 13, 2006.

10. Robin L. Jarrett, *Indicators of Family Strengths and Resilience that Influence Positive Child-Youth Outcomes In Urban Neighborhoods: A Review of Qualitative and Ethnographic Studies.* (Baltimore, MD: Annie E. Casey Foundation, 1998), p. 8–21. See also "Poor Urban Communities Place Greater Demands on Parents, Regardless of Race." Available at: http://www.children. smartlibrary.info/NewInterface/segment.cfm?segment=1988, accessed June 13, 2006.

11. Jarrett. Available at: http://www.children.smartlibrary.info/NewInterface/segment. cfm?segment=1988f monitoring strategies, accessed June 17, 2006.

12. Thomas R. Chibucos, Randall W. Leite, and David L. Weiss, eds. *Readings in Family Theory* (Thousand Oaks, CA: Sage, 2005).

13. Esther Kane, "What Is Family Systems Theory?" Available at: http://www. estherkane.com/family_systems.htm, accessed January 10, 2007.

14. Helen Mederer and Reuben Hill, "Critical Transitions over the Family Life Span Theory and Research." *Marriage & Family Review* 6 (April 1983): 39–60.

15. University of Washington, "Social Exchange Theory." Available at: http://www.washington.edu/research/pathbreakers/1978a.html, accessed January 10, 2007.

16. "Social Conflict Theory." Available at: http://en.wikipedia.org/wiki/Social-conflict_theory, accessed January 10, 2007.

17. "Feminist Theory." In *Wikipedia, The Free Encyclopedia.* Available at: http://en.wikipedia.org/wiki/Feminist_theory, accessed January 10, 2007.

18. "Gender Studies." In *Wikipedia, The Free Encyclopedia.* Available at: http://en.wikipedia.org/wiki/Gender_studies, accessed January 10, 2007.

19. "Symbolic Interactionism." In *Wikipedia, The Free Encyclopedia.* Available at: http://en.wikipedia.org/wiki/Symbolic_interactionism, accessed June 14, 2006.

20. "Urie Brofenbrenner." Available at: http://www.psy.pdx.edu/PsiCafe/KeyTheorists/Bronfenbrenner.htm, accessed June 14, 2006.

21. M. Dean and W. Huitt, "Neighborhood and Community" (August 1999), citing R. Lewis and J. Morris, "Communities for Children." *Educational Leadership* 55 (1998), 34–36. Available at: http://chiron.valdosta.edu/whuitt/col/context/neighbor.html, accessed June 15, 2006.

22. U.S. National Library of Medicine and National Institutes of Health. "MedlinePlus: Trusted Health Information for You." Available at: http://www.nlm.nih.gov/medlineplus/aboutmedlineplus.html, accessed June 15, 2006.

23. Children's Hospital and Regional Medical Center (Seattle, Washington), Home Page. Available at: http://www.seattlechildrens.org/child_health_safety/health_ advice, accessed June 15, 2006.

24. New South Wales, "NSW+Health." Available at: http://www.health.nsw. gov.au/living/comm.html, accessed June 15, 2005.

25. Rodney T. Ogawa et al., "Linking Socio-Cultural Theories of Learning with an Institutional Theory of Organizations: Implications for Theory, Practice and Collaboration." Available at: http://www.exploratorium.edu/cils/research/ institutions.html, accessed June 15, 2006.

Chapter 6

Youth and Critical Health Concerns: Information for Parents and Caregivers

Introduction

This chapter looks at the special information needs of youth and their parents and caregivers as they face critical health issues. It also considers several models that might improve the way health information is provided to families. Critical health issues include life-threatening illnesses, terminal illnesses that are chronic and ongoing, and illnesses that are serious and episodic. The literature overwhelmingly suggests that critically ill youth and their parents and caregivers need supportive systems, including information networks, support groups, and specialized health information systems such as reliable sites on the Internet. Models of how people cope with critical illnesses are useful as we attempt to meet their information needs. The chapter also considers why health information is not always used.

An Overview of Useful Models and Theories

Health researchers have identified several models that are useful in helping families acquire and understand health information and how information can be applied to their unique situations. The Population Council, in its efforts to address the HIV/AIDS crisis, suggests that the following models are useful in understanding how people behave when faced with critical illnesses. By extension, these models are useful in this discussion[1]:

- **The AIDS Risk Reduction Model (ARRM).** This theory holds that change is a process and that individuals move from one step to the next as a result of a given stimulus (e.g., information) for healing or better adjustment to the illness to occur. Individuals must pass through these three stages: behavior labeling, commitment to change, and taking action.

- **Diffusion of Innovation Theory.** This theory explains how a new or innovative idea is considered, adopted, and spread throughout a given population. For example, what are the processes involved in how health information for families are adopted and spread? What is the role of a leader or gatekeeper in this process?

- **Ecological Systems Theory.** This theory involves families in the areas in which they live. It offers the idea of promoting better ways to deal with critical health situations centered on several social and political factors including changing individual behaviors and attitudes, promoting advocacy and organizational change to help families, giving attention to policy development, offering economic supports, encouraging environmental change, and providing multi-method programs.

- **Health Belief Model.** Dating from the 1950s, this theory suggests that people will change their health behaviors based on their knowledge and attitudes. The kinds of information and the availability of information are important in this model as is the premise that individuals can be effective in bringing about change in themselves (self-efficacy).

- **Social Capital Theory.** This theory suggests that most people in a common group have shared objectives and that they need structures that will allow them to pursue these objectives effectively. Among these structures are social cohesion, social inclusion, and community intervention strengths, involving interaction at both the sociocultural (social interaction) and the community organizational levels where organizations are able to act on behalf of the community. Information organized in a structured fashion with informed advocates ready to intervene for families in crisis is an important aspect of social capital.

- **Social Cognitive Theory (Social Learning Theory).** This theory posits that information alone, although important to effecting change in how individuals handle a health crisis, is not enough. For sustained change, an individual must be able to acquire skills and use these skills under changing and often difficult circumstances. Families with health crisis issues must acquire information and knowledge that will allow them to recognize and change their attitudes based on self-efficacy and positive social support systems. Librarians who offer information and provide a sense of community and social support for families help advance social learning.

- **Social Network Theory.** This theory considers the importance of relationships in how health crises and health care information might be managed in families. Aspects include understanding how families facing health crises select their relationship networks, how large these networks are, their relationship intricacies and communication patterns, who the reference people in the networks are, what the boundaries are within the networks, and what support or encouragement for appropriate behaviors and attitudes apply within the networks. For example, a family facing a health crisis is a social network; information becomes an important part of the network. Within this network, we must consider who has information, how it is shared and disseminated, who controls its flow and affirms it validity, and who is excluded from information within the social network.

- **Stages of Change Model.** This model was designed to illustrate stages in smoking cessation and revolves around six stages: pre-contemplation (e.g., no consideration given to changing behaviors), contemplation (thinking about changing behaviors), preparation to stop negative behavior, taking action to stop undesired behavior, maintenance of desired behavior, and relapse back to undesirable behavior. For a family in crisis, this model suggests that information must be presented or made available at appropriate stages as the family moves toward change. Information might initially focus on the family's desire to move in a positive way to face their crisis, but as the crisis continues, information might be needed with emphasis on how to enact and reinforce positive behaviors and attitudes. Rarely will these changes move in a linear fashion.

- **Individual and Social Change or Empowerment Model.** This model is both political and social. It emphasizes dialogue and encourages personal empowerment in solving social, cultural, political, and economic forces that individuals encounter in their lives. In this model, information is an empowering force that families facing a health crisis can use to provide a structure to their real lives and to take appropriate action to address situations that they might find oppressive or discriminatory.

- **Gender and Power Theory.** This model is a feminist look at power and gender equality. It holds that women have been socialized to be passive and even ignorant in terms of their roles in society, and it addresses relationships and societal definitions of role expectations of both males and females. For families facing health crises, this theory is useful in providing information that helps both mothers and fathers of critically ill children understand their mutually supportive roles that must go beyond what society might impose on them.

- **Reasoned Action Theory.** This is a useful theory in terms of health information in that it holds that most people are rational and make systematic use of the information available to them. On the basis of information, they consider the implications of their actions within the context of the time in which the behavior will likely occur. This theory gives special attention to personal intentions, attitude about a behavior, and "subjective norms," or what an influential peer or family group might expect. This suggests that with proper information and a positive social support system, a family facing a crisis with an ill child can be powerful in helping itself make sound decisions regarding the many issues that it faces.

All of these theories and models have implications for providing information to families of critically ill children, and various aspects of these are addressed later in this chapter. Because the ecological system model is inclusive of issues in most of these models, it is considered in more depth here than the other models. The ecological system model not only addresses medical needs, it also considers the emotional, sociological, and physical well-being of families and youth facing health crises.

Building Ecological Support Systems

Psychologist Urie Bronfenbrenner developed ecological theory. In his view, children and youth must be studied and understood within the context of their lives. His theory is known by several names including ecological systems theory, development in context theory, human ecology theory, and bio-ecological systems theory. It envisions four types of environmental systems in which the child develops; these environments do not stand alone, but influence each other. They include the following:

- **Microsystem:** A child's immediate environments: family, school, peer group, neighborhood, child-care environments, and the child's biology

- **Mesosystem:** Connections between immediate environments (i.e., a child's home and school)

- **Exosystem:** External environmental settings which only indirectly affect development (such as parent's workplace)

- **Macrosystem:** The larger cultural context (Eastern vs. Western culture, national economy, political culture, subcultures)

Within each of these systems expected roles, norms, and rules and support systems exist to inform and direct the child.[2]

Bronfenbrenner's book *The Ecology of Human Development: Experiments by Nature and Design* (1979) and his overall approach to the study of child development helped unify a number of diverse disciplines in the study of children. It has become one of the major theories of child and adolescent health care. This is especially true in recent years with the inclusion of biological elements into the microsystem in which health and health care maintenance by the family is often the first health care intervention made on behalf of children.[3] In recent years, biology has been expanded to include biopsychosocial factors in which the environment and physical, behavioral, psychological, and social elements all interact.[4]

Expanding on this mode, Neil Bracht wrote the following in 1978[5]:

- Health care and maintenance in families is influenced by social, cultural, and economic conditions.

- Negative behaviors associated with illness are disruptive to family stability and can interfere with good decision-making and coping skills.

- Medical treatment for family is often ineffective without social support and counseling services.

- Often health care services are fragmented, requiring community planning and institutional interventions and adaptation.

- Collaborative, multi-professional health care teams are increasingly necessary to provide effective solutions to complex social and medical problems facing families.

Information in various forms is essential for the families as they cope with critical illnesses in children and youth. Figure 6.1 illustrates how information underpins all the elements of the ecological family system. The information found in a system may be good and dependable, or it may be incorrect and even exploitive. Librarians as professional collaborators along with other professionals play important roles in providing good health information wherever it is needed in the ecological system.

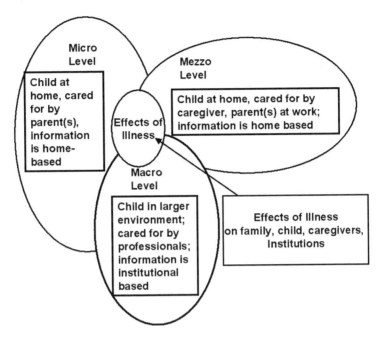

Figure 6.1. Information in an ecological family system.

Family Health Problems, the Helping Process, and Information Support

Although librarians are not counselors in the therapeutic sense, they are information counselors and benefit from the insights provided from the counseling process. An important aspect of counseling is the helping relationship. This concept means that those who counsel must assume a positive helping role with those they seek to counsel and therefore help. They become helpers to those who seek help. This aspect of counseling has a long and well-established history in many professions. These professions are often referred to as the helping professions. Among these are

- Teachers

- Physicians

- Ministers and priests

- Nurses

- Social workers

- Psychologists

- Psychiatrists

- Counselors of various types

Librarians are also helpers, but one factor hindering this recognition is that to be a legitimate helper within the helping professions, the helper must be deemed by society to help people change and grow.

This change and growth process is often enforced by laws or professional codes of conduct unique to various professions. For example, school librarians and teacher-librarians are generally certificated by governmental requirements, making them a part of the teaching profession with all of the expectations for helping their students change and grow that the teacher role implies. Public librarians serving children and youth perhaps have less of this social mandate, but they nevertheless are expected by social convention to play a constructive role in the life of those they help and serve. When librarians help people find and use information, they are indeed involved in a helping relationship.

Like most human relationships, the helping relationship is complex. Gerard Egan, in his book *The Skilled Helper: A Model for Systematic Helping and Interpersonal Relating,* provides the following basic steps in the helping encounter:

- **Attending.** This means giving the person who is being helped one's full attention, both physically and emotionally. Attention includes recognizing the social and psychological context in which the helping action occurs and the verbal as well as nonverbal actions that often define social and interactive contexts.

- **Clarification.** In many cases when families are in a health crisis, they are not sure what they need at a given moment; even if they have some idea about their needs, they are not always able to state them clearly. An important aspect of helping on the part of the helper-librarian is to facilitate a better understanding (clarification) of what is needed. This assists both the family and the librarian in their mutual search for information.

- **Problem Solving.** In this stage of the helping process, both the librarian-helper and the family or member of a family being helped become actively involved in solving the information-need problem. The active roles may pass back and forth between the librarian and client. At times the librarian-helper may assume a more assertive role, giving directions and structures about how to find and use information. At another point, the librarian may step back and allow the family member to assume this assertive and directive role. Collectively, they are actively involved in solving this information problem.

- **Action.** Action is the final stage of the helping process. Here family members or individuals with a family being helped assume more responsibility for the actions. In a therapeutic situation, they take action for changing their attitudes and behaviors for the better. This often involves risks. In an information-seeking situation, they likewise assume more responsibility for finding and using information. The librarian-helper is there to help and encourage, but the client must assume a certain level of responsibility for finding and using information and understand that risks may be involved. Risk may include time and inconvenience, expense, and even disappointment in not finding appropriate information. Throughout the action process in which the family is the more active participant, the librarian as information helper remains highly visible to give advice and encouragement and to set examples.

Figure 6.2 illustrates perception and clarification dynamics in the information-helping relationship.

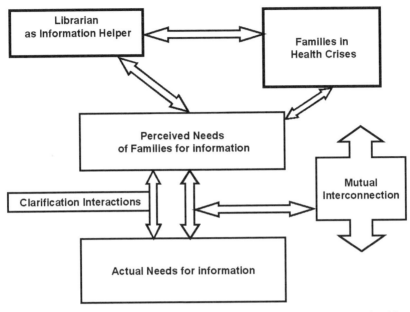

Figure 6.2. Clarification in librarian–family centered information-helping relationships.

Hilton Davis, an expert working with and counseling families of children who face critical health situations, outlines much of these concerns in terms of helping families with children in health crises in his discussion of the helping process. He especially says that the helper, and we include as helper the librarian-helper, must ensure that the following behaviors are adhered to[6]:

- Respect and hold families and their children in esteem

- Build a sense of self-efficiency (for both the helper and those he or she helps)

- Be realistic about what the helper can do

- As a helper, be open and genuine about experiences encountered, without distorting situations

- Show empathy and understanding of the families' situations; try to understand their situations from their point-of-view

- Display enthusiasm and willingness to be involved in the helping relationship.

- Use appropriate helping skills (many of which are used in the traditional library or information interview):

  – Attending behaviors

  – Active and involved listening

  – Encouragers to talk (prompters)

  – Empathy

    – Exploration and clarification

    – Encouraging mutual problem-solving behaviors

Davis explains that in the counseling interview, information given to the parents or caregivers have specific stages[7]:

- Stage 1—Giving information. Determine what is already known and ascertain a preferred communication style.

- Stage 2—Present the information. This includes giving information about diagnosis, pathology, causes, prognosis, and treatment. Often it is necessary to repeat the information in various ways so that retention and recall of important parts of the information is aided.

- Stage 3—Check the results making sure that the information is understood and that no misunderstandings linger.

- Stage 4—Ensure retention of the information discussed. Davis suggests several means of doing this: recording what has been said, giving out pamphlets, recording the interview for later review by the parents and their friends and families; and *referring the family to other readings and sources of information.*

As mentioned, most likely the clinical counselor will suggest that the parents or caregivers seek out other types of information. It is here that the youth librarians can play an important role in helping the families cope.

Like all helping relationship conferences, the information conference with the librarian should be well planned, or at least standardized models should be developed that will help guide the interview process. In this respect, the interview with the librarian has many of the same attributes of the interview with the counselor. For example, the location of the interview should be comfortable with good seating and privacy. At the beginning of the interview, small, traditional pleasantries are expected and necessary to establish the proper professional and emotional setting. The interview should have time limits that everyone understands. This is not to be abrupt but often, when finishing an interview involving ill children, all parties in the interview need time to compose themselves and to give attention to questions that come up at the last minute.

The Role of Information and Information Needs

The role of all librarians (e.g., public youth librarians, school librarians, librarians in a medical environment) must conform to professional models of help and conduct as just discussed. Research about information needs helps build such models.

A 1994 study by Joanne Zevenhuizen identified several important information needs of parents of critically ill children in Canadian hospital settings. "Assurance" was among the most frequently identified areas in which information was needed. Some needs that were not met included information about growth and development and educational information. Obstacles to obtaining information included extensive travel time to the hospital where parents might obtain information from experts. Pediatric specialists were the main sources of information for the parents in the study. Strong predictors of parents' information needs were their understanding of the seriousness of the child's illness, levels of parental education, and the area where the family lived.[8] These findings suggest that support information for parents can be supplied by libraries that are not necessarily found in hospital settings. Assurance and support information are often available in trade books and periodicals written for the consumer including information regarding growth and development and educational support services for children and adolescents. This information is not dependent on expensive medical experts for delivery.

Convenience and ease of delivery of information is also a factor. Public and school libraries are widely available in most communities. This information is not expensive, and it is not dependent on a hospital environment for accessibility. Librarians are trained (or can be trained) to provide consumer health information that supports and augments information of a clinical nature provided by medical experts.

The Center for Effective Parenting, Little Rock Center (http://www.parenting-ed.org/) strongly suggests that parents educate themselves about their child's illness. This knowledge certainly includes an understanding of the clinical nature of the illness, and this sound knowledge helps develop an understanding of reasonable expectations about the child's behaviors and limitations on behaviors. This knowledge also helps support children as they experience illnesses, begin to ask questions, and interact with others.

Of interest to youth librarians is the center's encouragement of parents and caregivers not only to ask for information from medical authorities but also to seek out books, videos, pamphlets, and other resources that are available at the local library.[9] An example of books that can be easily acquired by libraries includes those suggested in Terri Mauro's "Top 10 Books on Parenting Children with Terminal or Chronic Illness." She says this about her selection:

> Parents and family members of children with chronic or terminal illnesses need special support, advice and direction. These books can help you come to terms with tragedy, make meaningful contact with medical professionals, and provide your child and his or her friends and siblings with the care and compassion they need during a difficult time.[10]

Structures for Assurance, Community, and Networking

As Zevenhuizen noted in her interviews with parents of critically ill children in Canada, parents and their families need assurances and support. A number of support groups exist in various communities throughout the world. Health support and information groups are easily found on the Internet through such gateways as "Yahoo! Health Directory" (http://dir.yahoo.com/Health/.com) and "Google Directory—Health" (http://www.google.com/Top/Health/); nevertheless, one must be cautious in using some of these sites. Some come with high levels of authority, and others are testimonials of either success or failure of support and treatment. Building community, support, and networking is also a goal of these sites.

An example of the variety of information found in these sites is the Clubfoot Club (http://www.clubfootclub.org). This site described itself as

> the place to learn **About Clubfoot**—types of Clubfoot, treatment options, glossary of terms. There are **personal clubfoot stories**, helpful Clubfoot **links** to Clubfoot resources, parent support, and medical sites.

The overall design is positive and uplifting, but the authority for the site is hard to find. Its use of personal clubfoot stories is supportive in that it celebrates hope and encouragement.

Because the treatment and cure of clubfoot varies from individual to individual, many of these sites are devoted to personal stories of medical interventions and family relationships. In some of these sites, one finds a need for assurance, community, and sharing. The personal nature of these sites is often enhanced with family pictures and writings, as well as invitations for contacts.

One of the more authoritative sites that discusses the medical aspects of clubfoot is the Shiner Hospital in Los Angeles (http://www.shrinershq.org/Hospitals/Los_Angeles/conditions/Club_feet.aspx). Another clubfoot site written in consumer health terms for parents is provided by the Jackson Health System (http://www.um-jmh.org/chapter.cfm?id=9179).

A comprehensive and authoritative directory of health information and support sites and links in many areas of health and especially useful for parents and caregivers is DirectoryMedical.Com (http://www.directorymedical.com). In the words of the staff, this directory

> is designed to be your one-stop destination for anything you can think of that is about or related to health. We know that the Internet is an overwhelming space, and finding just the information you need can still be a frustrating and time-consuming process. Our editorial team makes great effort to evaluate the existence and accuracy of each web site.

As mentioned, information on the various suggested sites in the directory is broad-based including sites devoted separately to teen and child health concerns.

Health Information Literacy for Families in Crisis

As with any group or individual seeking health information, understanding how to use and evaluate information is necessary for families and caregivers of critically ill children. It may be that the librarian as health information provider will need to introduce basic concepts of how to use and evaluate health information. At best, the librarian may need to inform the family on how to approach the information they find independent of health experts. The National Library of Medicine and the National Network of Libraries of Medicine has developed instructional units on how to teach various aspects of consumer information especially tailored for public librarians. These instructions provide sound advice on how to help families better use information in understanding and adjusting to their unique problems (http://nnlm.gov/training/consumer/apple/ and http://nnlm.gov/gmr/training/classes.html#Con). Chapter 4 defines the basic aspect of health information literacy.

Problems Associated with Not Seeking Health Information

Although we have been primarily concerned with how people might seek information, we must also consider the real fact that many people do not and will not seek or use information in ways that health information providers might expect or wish of them. In his attempt to study why people do not use information, doctoral student Ronald D. Houston proposed a new taxonomy of information seeking theories. Much of his taxonomy can help us understand some of the inherent reasons why parents or caregivers of ill children do not seek out or even use health information. Although he considers many theories, the following seem most helpful to us in understanding why parents and other caregivers do not seek out and even use information that might be available to them:

1. **Anomalous State of Knowledge.** This has several characteristics—namely, the inability to verbalize or ask questions or even to have enough knowledge of the heath situation to know what and how to ask for information. Reference librarians often comment that this characteristic of communication behavior is common when working with the public.

2. **Barriers to Information.** Basically, this implies failures in communication patterns, and it can range from the inability to communicate in terms of cultural, social, and education expectations, as well as failures on the part of institutions to provide appropriate venues so that meaningful communications occur. Economic barriers relating to the cost of acquiring information can interfere with acquiring sound health information. All told, this suggests that some users will not seek health information simply because they lack knowledge about how information can be obtained within the context of their personal situations.

3. **Deference to Cognitive Authority.** The medical establishment in most countries over the years has acquired an enormous amount of respect and authority. This comes in many ways: extensive educational requirements for medical workers, governmental credentialing, professional oversight and control of practitioners, and political and social mandates given to the medical community. Faced with such authority, many parents and caregivers may simply defer to information provided directly by medical authorities and never feel the need go beyond that.

4. **Social Life and Social Capital of Parents and Caregivers.** The ability to seek information is very much tied to the social life and mores of individuals and how they have been conditioned to ask for and expect information. Those who have social capital are those who have been privileged through such positive characteristics as good education and good parenting to understand that information is readily available and can be obtained with proper social and negotiation skills. However, many who need health information lack this social capital.

5. **The Primary Reference Group.** Reference group theory is closely related to social life and social capital theory in that it basically holds that individuals are influenced by the social group to which they belong. This includes such elements as family, social class, religious and political associations, values from nationality, culture, economic standing, and how one views the role of government in personal lives. Not only does the primary reference group provide behavior guidance, it also offers the foundation for self-perceptions as well as how others are perceived. The reference group can determine how the parent or caregiver will seek information when faced with the illness of a critically ill child. For example, we often see this when religious convictions conflict with medical situations such as blood transfusions and other forms of medical procedures.

6. **Avoidance of Conflicting Information.** Most people seek a manageable comfort level in their lives. Health crises are attacks on these comfort levels. When health information may not preserve this comfort zone because it differs from what is wanted, that information may be avoided or rejected when it is presented.

7. **Support and Communication Networks.** Although conventional wisdom may hold that networks are essential for emotional and informational support for parents and caregivers with critically ill children, there are limitations that should be understood. Networks may discourage facing the unknown and relying on the network for information that only supports the network's goals and objectives but may not be sound in terms of health. Reliance on networks may offer a feeling of well-being for members, but it may support behaviors that encourage little effort to go beyond the boundaries of the network. Likewise, values within the network may support an unquestioning deference to the authority of the network and its values and information resources.[11]

Understanding Special Needs through Action Research

This chapter has attempted to outline and display the importance of youth librarians in helping families of critically ill children. Various models have been discussed that should provide focus on how people face illnesses and how they cope with its consequences. Although librarians are not therapeutic counselors, they have always been involved in helping people find information. This informational role and supporting techniques, together with their service orientations and social expectations, present a unique opportunity to help families as they face crucial information needs and decisions. Action research based on good questions can help in providing reliable and affordable health care information. The following questions can serve as benchmarks for action research:

• What major, critical health issues are children and their parents and caregivers facing in this area? Are parents and caregivers of critically ill children likely to turn to libraries for health information?

• What kinds of health information services might help with these needs?

• Understanding the major critical health issues faced by children and their caregivers, how might librarians in area libraries help meet some of these critical health information needs?

• Based on a standard list of health information services, what are professionally defensible ways of determining essential priorities?

• A gatekeeper is generally considered someone in a position of authority who controls access or has some manner of influence on how resources and information are dispersed to others. Are parents and caregivers of critically ill children likely to view librarians in their schools or communities in this role regarding health information?

Other suggestions for action research are discussed in Chapter 13.

Conclusion

The chapter has attempted to outline and display the importance of youth librarians in helping families of critically ill children. We have discussed various models that should provide focus on how people face illnesses and how they cope with the consequences. The informational role of librarians, information techniques developed over the years, and the profession's service orientations and social expectations present a unique opportunity to help families as they face crucial information needs and decisions.

Notes

1. Population Council, "AIDSQuest: The HIV/AIDS Survey Library Behavioral and Social Theories Commonly Used in HIV Research." Available at: http://www.popcouncil.org/horizons/AIDSquest/cmnbehvrtheo/reasact.html, accessed November 13, 2005.

2. "Ecological Systems Theory." In *Wikipedia, The Free Encyclopedia.* Available at: http://en.wikipedia.org/w/index.php?title=Ecological_Systems_Theory&oldid=80283371, accessed November 13, 2006.

3. "Ecological Systems Theory."

4. Christian Derauf, "Johhny Suzuki. Ecological Model and System Theory." Available at: http://www.hawaii.edu/dyson/Ecological%20model%20and%20systems%20theory%20web%201-21-01.htm, accessed November 15, 2006.

5. Derauf citing Neil F. Bracht, "Contributions to Comprehensive Health Care: Basic Premises." In *Social Work in Health Care: A Guide to Professional Practice* (New York: Haworth Press, 1978), pp. 19–33.

6. Hilton Davis, *Counseling Parents of Children with Chronic Illness or Disability* (Leicester: British Psychological Society, 1993), p. 76.

7. Davis, pp. 84–85.

8. Joanne Marily Zeyenhuizen, "Information Needs of Parents of Hospitalized Chronically Ill Children." Master's thesis, Dalhousie University, 1994, *Master's Thesis Abstract International* 34 (February 1996): 286.

9. Center for Effective Parenting, Little Rock Center, "How Parents Can Help Their Child Cope with a Chronic Illness." Available at: http://www.Parenting-Ed.Org, accessed November 17, 2006.

10. Terri Mauro, "Top 10 Books on Parenting Children with Terminal or Chronic Illness." Available at: http://specialchildren.about.com/od/medicalissues/tp/terminalillness.htm, accessed November 17, 2006.

11. Ronald D. Houston, "A Model of Compelled Nonuse of Information: A Dissertation Proposal." Austin: School of Information, University of Texas at Austin, 2006, pp. 87–92.

Chapter 7

Youth Health Information Needs: Theories, Products, and Designs

Introduction

In previous chapters, we considered many aspects of health care that affect society and youth. These include institutions, schools, public libraries, and various types of caregivers. In this chapter, we consider more specifically the health information needs of youth, the forces that drive those needs, and theories about information that help us understand how to respond to those needs. We also consider, in a broad way, some of the information products and designs that have been developed to bring information about health to youth.

Information and Health Information Literacy

Information is a difficult word to define because it has many different meanings in terms of the contexts in which it is used. *Merriam-Webster Online* dictionary provides several of these definitions. For the purpose of this discussion, we use two of these basic definitions. Information is:

- communication or reception of knowledge or intelligence

- knowledge obtained from investigation, study, or instruction.

In addition, we also use as a definition of information that asserts that information is conveyed by two or more reliable sources based on substantiated data and sources.

Closely related to these is the definition of information literacy. The Atlantic Canada Educational Foundation defined information literacy as follows:

> the ability to acquire, critically evaluate, select, use, create and communicate information in ways that lead to knowledge and wisdom. It encompasses all other forms of literacy—traditional literacy (the ability to read and write) and media literacy (the ability to critically evaluate and create media, such as television, advertising, news stories and movies) and numerical literacy (the ability to understand and solve problems with data and numbers).[1]

Health information literacy is similar, with the exception that its focus is on the many ways that health information is conceived, developed, presented, evaluated, and used. The Medical Library Association (MLA) notes that as people, including youth, become more responsible for making their own health decisions, they must be able to navigate and evaluate health information they encounter. MLA defines health information literacy as follows:

> the set of abilities needed to: recognize a health information need; identify likely information sources and use them to retrieve relevant information; assess the quality of the information and its applicability to a specific situation; and analyze, understand, and use the information to make good health decisions. It means knowing how to find, evaluate and use information about your health in all forms. It means knowing when you need information, where to find it and how to evaluate and use it in your everyday life.[2]

MLA suggests that the general public, the popular media, opinion leaders, and decision makers do not understand or appreciate how health librarians can help bring order to an ever-increasing mass of health information. MLA further suggests that health librarians, and we can add other librarians, can assist in helping people understand and use health information.[3]

Brief Notes on Theories about Information Needs and Information Seeking

As professionals who have responsibility for helping youth find health information, we need to understand how information is conceptualized and acted on. Social, psychological, information, and learning theories can help us in this understanding.

Interests and Needs Theory

Developing health information collections is highly dependent on our users' interests and personal needs. For youth, these interests or needs may arise from curiosity, school assignments, personal health situations, and developmental stages of growth.

Writing in 1979, James Dusek, a psychologist, described interests as serious and a highly engrained psychological and social process. Interests are internal because they satisfy or at least attempt to satisfy deeply held personal and psychological needs. Interests are social because they are often encouraged and even prescribed or discouraged by the society in which one lives. Interests often help determine social acceptability and prestige within specific social and cultural groups. If an interest is not supported by the larger groups, it is not likely to develop within the individual without special encouragement or individual determination.[4]

Needs are similar. Needs are often determined by how individuals recognize their needs and by the social support systems available to them. Needs are a part of an individual's perception of how to survive.

Interests in and need for health information are similar in that they can come from many sources: peer groups, mass media coverage, instruction and curriculum direction, and personal perceptions based on an individual's unique perceptions and needs surrounding an issue and the determination to seek out more information about a given topic for resolution. Needs may often arise from life's requirements for safety and survival. In youth this might include school assignments, sports participation, or even the illness of family, friends, and self.

Social psychologist Kurt Lewin believed that change in a group or an individual's life is based on a need for equilibrium. Although his model, "Force Field Analysis," was designed to help social groups understand and face change, it does have application for individuals. The model is based on the assumption that all of us want and need a sense of balance or equilibrium. Maintaining equilibrium is influenced by both positive (or driving) forces and restraining (or negative) forces in our lives. Positive information is needed to maintain a comfortable field in which to live. Both driving forces and restraining forces have various levels of power or energy (e.g., strong, weak, moderate). In this model, one seeks to encourage the power or energy of positive information and to lessen the effects of negative information.

For example, in health information, young athletes may seek information on how to improve their muscle strength and coordination while at the same time decreasing their information regarding vitamin regimentation because of expense. The illustration in Figure 7.1 shows how this might work for these athletes.

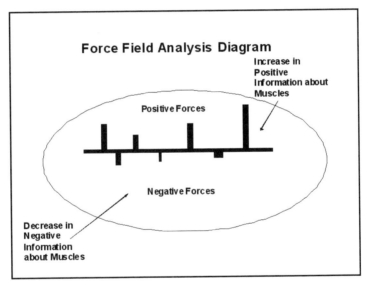

Fig. 7.1. Lewin's Force Field Analysis model.

Life-Space Theory

In 1957, vocational theorist D. E. Super proposed an idea that he called "life-space." This concept argued that careers were driving forces in modern life and that they often determined how we live our lives. Super suggested that individuals must seek a better integration of career and other roles that they play in life.[5] Psychologist Savickas titled this concept "life-role integration."[6] Super called these life roles "theaters." These various theaters for youth include those of the student, friend, and member of a team, a family and social networks.

Achieving life-role balance is central to this concept. Increasing cultural complexity and diversity in the lives of youth present a challenge to this balance in life. Cultural and personal issues such as health and health information are essential parts of achieving balance. Youth of all ages assume different roles as they move into various developmental stages. Health and health information play important roles in each of these life stages. Parents or caregivers provide health support and information to children, but as youth grow older and more integrated into school, friendship groups, and peer relationships, they assume more responsibility for their health care and the information they need to determine their health care needs. Libraries and other social and educational institutions play important roles in this aspect of the "life theaters" or life space of youth. Libraries are essential if societies are to provide the framework and support necessary for youth as they become more independent in their roles of seeking reliable health information.

Gestalt Psychological and Social Perceptions

Perception theories present two important views of how humans impose order on a world filled with stimuli. Gestalt psychology holds that in order for us to function in the world, we naturally impose order through mental processes. Gestalt theory "is a theory of mind and brain that proposes that the operational principle of the brain is holistic, parallel, and analog, with self-organizing tendencies."[7]

This theory suggests that perception is a complex process in which we seek a unified and holistic worldview. We therefore select, organize, and interpret sensory stimulation to establish a meaningful and coherent picture of our world. This theory maintains that as we seek to build a meaningful world, we require consistency for comfort and productivity. We seek common elements to reinforce this fundamental requirement. Our perceptions are influenced and based on prior experiences and information and are directed by our wants, needs, attitudes, and requirements for order, familiarity, reassurance, and, of course, consistency.[8]

Social perception is similar. It governs how we relate on interpersonal levels. We receive stimuli from those with whom we interact as well as other stimuli such as the mass media and other forms of information dissemination. These stimuli play a role in interpersonal situations. Sociologists say that we generally avoid information that might conflict with or contradict our perceptions of reality. Such avoidance behaviors make it difficult for us to correct perception errors, many times leading to problems of stereotyping or avoiding reality.

Perception of health care needs and health information reflect perception theory. Recent scandals involving the use of steroids among athletes demonstrate how some people dismiss medical knowledge and expert opinion regarding the ill effects of steroid use. Another example is overexposure to sun. Cancer related to sun exposure has significantly risen in the last few decades, yet many people still overlook these warnings in favor of the myth of the "healthy tan." Other readily available examples include illicit drug use, tobacco use, and unhealthy eating habits.

Psychological and sociological perception theories can help us understand how youth are likely to organize and manage the perceptual information coming to them and how that influences their use of health information. Librarians who work in public and school libraries are very much in the perceptional framework of youth. Accordingly, we as professional information providers need to formulate carefully professional and institutional behaviors in ways that will promote a positive perception of libraries as places to find reliable health information.

Information and Cultural Environmental Theories

A number of theories and approaches to understanding how people seek information within their cultural and social contexts are available for use as research methods and as observational tools. Brenda Dervin suggested through her "sense-making" theory and methodology that understanding how people seek and approach information in their everyday lives is necessary for the individual, as well as for information systems designed to provide information to them. Sense-making allows us to map situations, understand contextual tasks, and see how information is used or can be used within the life contexts of users and their needs.[9]

Marcia Bates used a forging metaphor to describe how people find online information. Calling her theory "berrypicking," she argued that people in their online searches hunt for the "ripe" and most appealing information that best fits their needs. The search is not linear but naturalistic, based on how the best information choices (the ripe berries) come into view.[10]

To earn spending money during summers, as an adolescent one of the authors of this book picked blackberries in several commercial fields. Bates's analogy is very much like the real world. The field is dirty, the sun is hot, and one must always watch out for snakes and stinging insects (environment and distractions); some berries are too ripe and decaying, and some are just right for picking. Still others are too green. And other pickers often push you aside for the better bushes (evaluation, selection of sources, and competition for resources). Finally, when you think you have picked enough and need to be paid, the field manager must weigh your work and decide whether you meet the criterion for payment or need to gather more for what he or she is willing to pay (evaluation and redesign).

Student researchers Benjamin Brigham and Justin Perron quote Bates this way:

> At each stage [of the information search process], with each different conception of the query, the user may identify useful information and references. In other words, the query is satisfied not by a single final retrieved set, but by a series of selections of individual references and bits of information at each stage of the ever-modifying search. A bit-at-a-time retrieval.[11]

Social Learning Theories

A number of social learning theories can help librarians shape health information systems by informing them of how youth in society learn to be members of a society and a group. Social learning theories[12] generally emphasize the role of modeling or observational learning. Parents and other caregivers can help in the social development of youth by modeling good and consistent health information-seeking behaviors and good health management.

Ethnology theories, based on evolutionary evidence, suggest that adaptation is necessary for survival in any society and that children are born with biological adaptive behaviors necessary for early survival. For example, with the development of psychological structures, the child soon acquires infant-caregiver attachments and other adaptive behavior patterns. The connection of ethnology theory to health care and health information is clear. Health is a part of the ethnological system, and both structural and psychological preparation must be afforded youth so that they can observe and participate in important health-based survival strategies.

Ecological systems theory is child-centered. It holds that children develop with complex systems of relationships ranging from their immediate environment of family and school to broader cultural situations having differing values and programs. Children's personalities and ways of thinking play important roles in how they develop as individuals. This may suggest that youth have a great deal of control over how they perceive health care and health care information based on personality characteristics and personal thinking behaviors. Because values found in their ecological systems help influence these characteristics, positive health care systems and health care information must be visible and easily available.

Socialcultural perspective theory suggests that children internalize important features of social dialogues and that they use these dialogues to structure psychological structures that guide their own behaviors. Cooperative dialogue with knowledgeable members of their society helps structure their thinking, informs them on how to behave, and contributes to a community's structure. The importance of this theory is obvious because it suggests that good health care and health care information is a form of social and cultural dialogue that when internalized and acted on can produce health-conscience communities and individuals.

Ethnomethodology theory is broad and contextually based. It sees all people in roles of creating social structures through their own actions and interactions, thus establishing their own realities. People, no matter what age, are continually trying to make sense out of their lives. Health crisis and the need for health information often call for a restructuring of people's views of their own life situation. Libraries and the Internet, often a first line of inquiry, are often called on to aid in this contextual struggle for a new life definition.

Structural functionalist theory may help underpin all of these theoretical concepts as this theory holds that society is made up of many parts, each of which contributes to the functioning of the whole. Good health care and good health information systems in libraries are just one part of the overall educational and social systems in a society. When they are available and function well, the whole society benefits.[13]

Legal Theories and Access to Information

The landmark decision *Board of Education, Island Trees, New York v. Pico* (457 U.S. 853,867 (1982), issued by the U.S. Supreme Court in 1982, set limits on how far a school board can go in removing books from school libraries. In recent years, *Pico* has been used in numerous cases involving the rights of youth to have access to information, especially information found in libraries. Examples include the fiction books *Daddy's Roommate* by Michael Wilhoite, *Heather Has Two Mommies* by Lesléa Newman, and the Harry Potter series. The ruling held that school authorities cannot remove books from libraries based on their own dislikes but must justify any removal based on sound educational reasons. Their reasons must be sound enough to stand up if challenged in court.

Nevertheless, censorship and legal theory often revolve around circumstances that are difficult to resolve within the context of a pluralistic society. Legal theorists regularly ponder these regarding First Amendment rights of underage youth. Have First Amendment rights been violated when

- certain materials and information have been systematically excluded from library collections?

- school authorities insist that excluded materials are available elsewhere in the community, such as public libraries and bookstores?

- materials are acquired but access is limited by age or by special permission?

- courts assume the right to determine what is permissible in a school library collection?

- information is not made available in library collections when requested or expected?

- school authorities have the right to insist that they have the legal right and social expectations to inculcate traditional values in students through library collections?

- mature youth are excluded from information they need to plan and make decisions about their lives and their health?

For a more detailed discussion of these issues, see Chapter 12.

Basic Information Needs

Concerns of Youth

What do children and adolescents really want to know about health? Often a way to find out is to visit a reliable Internet site such as TeenHealth, sponsored by the Nemours Foundation and review some of the questions that teens pose to the experts (http://www.teenshealth.org/teen). Following is a sample of questions that have been asked:

- Skin Care

  – Can I pierce my own eyebrow?
  – Should I pop my pimple?

- Nutrition and Dieting

  – How can I lose weight safely?
  – What is cholesterol?
  – What is the right weight for my height?

- Periods

  – Can a girl get pregnant if she has sex during her period?
  – My periods are irregular. Is something wrong with me?

- Emotions

  – Am I in a healthy relationship?
  – How can I become less shy?
  – How can I deal with my anger?
  – How can I get my grandparents to stop frustrating me?
  – How can I help someone who's being bullied?
  – How can I improve my self-esteem?
  – How can I stop my nightmares?

       – My boyfriend and I broke up. How can I feel better?

       – What can I do about my anger?

       – Why do I fight with my parents so much?

- Health basics

       – How much sleep do I need?

       – Is exercise safe for teens?

       – What is it like to have surgery? To stay in a hospital?

- Hygiene

       – Why do I sweat so much?

Other concerns on this site involve illnesses and infections, getting help for problems, and questions asked specifically by either boys or girls. Generally these questions centered on maturation issues. Other useful online sources are the Teens' Page available at MedlinePlus (http://www.nlm.nih.gov/medlineplus/teenspage.html), the University of Arkansas Health Science Library's "Teen Health Information and Resources for High School" (http://www.library.uams.edu/resources/TeenResourcesandHealthInformation. aspx), and the Arkansas Children's Hospital Library (http://www.archildrens. org/resources).

Smoking and tobacco use by children and adolescents is a pressing national and international concern. In responding to this problem, the Centers for Disease Control and Prevention through its National Center for Chronic Disease Prevention and Health Promotion has developed a number of information campaigns targeting young smokers or youth that are likely to become smokers. These products include posters, booklets, pamphlets, and audiovisual products. A list of these is available at the Centers' Web page (http://www.cdc.gov/tobacco/index.htm). Celebrities are often used to promote good health information. Figure 7.2 is a poster from the Center's Celebrities against Smoking series.

Figure 7.2. Model Christy Turlington appearing in the "Celebrities against Smoking" series. Courtesy of the Centers for Disease Control and Prevention.

Concerns of Parents and Caregivers

The Internet is a good source to access the concerns of parents and caregivers. KidSource Online (http://www.kidsource.com/kidsource/pages/Health.html) is just one example. This site provides information on a variety of issues including childhood obesity and cholesterol in children, gymnastics, tetanus, winter safety, medications, holiday management, common colds, recalls of unsafe toys and play equipment, and even back-to-school shopping advice.

Kids on the Street and Their Special Needs

One of the most difficult situations to address is adolescents who live on the streets in many of the world's cities and towns. According to Lynn Rew of the University of Texas School of Nursing, this is one of the least addressed groups in the health literature. In a study to better understand the sexual health needs of street youth, she and her colleagues, with a grant from the National Institute of Nursing, studied a group of adolescents who lived on the street near the University of Texas at Austin. She and her cohort of researchers were particularly interested in learning if brief interventions with information about better ways of dealing with sexual health issues could improve the attitudes and behaviors of these youth. After questioning and selecting youth for the program, the research team focused on an intervention strategy that considered the following:

- Group dynamics because they learned that these youth did not know how to communicate within larger social groups

- Knowledge of sexually transmitted diseases and infections

- Decision-making skills

- Assertive communication skills

- Self-care skills

- Sexual health

Once they learned the basic needs of their research subjects, the team concentrated on an instructional approach that emphasized AIDS knowledge, future time perspective (teaching these youth to think into the future, not just the day-to-day experiences of their lives), self-efficacy (e.g., self-confidence), condom use, assertive communication training, sexual self-care behaviors, and knowledge of safe sex and sexual risk behaviors. Three intervention sessions were used to give information and instructions separately to both male and female participants. Comparisons of the intervention group and the comparison group where no information was given showed that only a small increase had occurred in reported behaviors of the youth. For example, knowledge about AIDS remained stable in the intervention group but actually decreased in the comparison group; there was a significant increase in the intervention group concerning self-efficacy. Interestingly, both groups showed a decrease in assertive communication, self-care behaviors, safer sex, and control issues with no change in sexual risk behaviors. Based on gender, female participants showed an increase in AIDS knowledge, better use of self-efficacy in condom use, higher assertive communication skills and self-care knowledge, and safer sex behaviors. Male participants continued to show greater sexual high-risk behaviors. From this, the researchers concluded that gender-specific intervention is supported.[14]

Similar to nursing, the library and information literature in how to reach street youth is not extensive. Librarians can learn much from this in that information intervention, like health instruction intervention, is complicated and generally must be ongoing within the context of a supportive environment. Although not labeled as such, the skills that Rew and her colleagues attempted to teach are essential information literacy skills. Reflecting information skill needs, the Rew study suggests that better designed information products such as pamphlets and brochures are needed for this special youth group. These products need to give special attention to graphics and the likely low reading levels and specialized vocabulary of potential users.

Rew and her colleagues advise that work with street youth must develop in concert with stakeholders (e.g., other agencies and individuals that are interested in street youth). Interveners in this work must be persistent and always remember the underlying values of their professional mission. She concludes with these remarks about what she and her colleagues learned from street youth that will offer encouragement to youth librarians as we too seek to help street youth:

> To the hundreds of homeless youth who have taught us about their lives, who have inspired us with their myriad strengths and for whom we should show deep respect through our willingness to care about, to care for, and to connect with them.[15]

A Library Profile: The Aurora Public Library

In 1994–95 the Aurora Public Library, under a Library Services and Construction Act (LSCA) grant and in cooperation with Aurora (Illinois) area public libraries, schools, community agencies and higher education, created the Teen Health Information Network (THINK). The librarians and staff in the cooperating agencies surveyed adolescents in the schools regarding a number of health information questions.[16] One aspect of the survey asked where they obtained their health information. Adolescents noted the following:

- Parents
- Television or radio
- Magazines

- Books
- Doctors
- Classroom instruction

Eighteen percent never used print sources such as books, magazines, or newspapers. Certain topics held the highest interest for adolescents. These topics included:

- Violence
- Personal safety and self-protection from attack
- AIDS/HIV
- Bodybuilding
- Physical fitness
- Rape

- Child abuse
- Drugs and teen drug users
- Alcohol and teen drinking
- Diseases
- Marijuana
- Teen suicide

The researchers admit that they overlooked some important information areas including homosexuality, guns, and premarital sex and relationships. This research was conducted before the Internet became such a powerful force in information delivery. Newer research would certainly reflect its impact.

When asked what kinds of information formats they preferred, adolescents noted:

- Videos to check out from the library
- Speakers and demonstrations
- Magazines and newspapers
- Books
- Pamphlets
- Audio cassettes to check out from the library
- Computers and CDs with printing capabilities

Based on this information, the library established a Teen Advisory Group (TAG) and revised its collection policy to include more inexpensive paperbacks, recent books on diseases and social issues surrounding health, and information on puberty and sexual development. It also took measures to improve access to health reference sources. The revised policies also included more fiction regarding health and multiple copies of popular titles in areas such as AIDS/HIV, abortion, drugs, and gangs and other related issues. Resources suitable for parents and professionals, including selected research journals, were increased. The library also decided to survey a wide array of service agencies in the area regarding health needs regarding AIDS/HIV, sexually transmitted diseases, substance use and abuse, teen pregnancy, violence prevention, gang awareness, sexuality issues, nutritional needs, and mental health topics.

The library developed outreach programs that included speaker programs, parent programs, and the ordering or creating of training materials for professionals. They held sponsoring workshops for local professionals and created and supported wellness fairs.

A library-based public relations program was initiated. This included appearing at library professional meetings; visiting schools, improving community contacts, and creating displays of materials at appropriate community locations.

The project survives as the Teen CARE Network, basing "much of its planning on the previous experiences and information gathered by the Teen Health Information Network (THINK)."[17] At one time during its operation, the CARE Web site included an active link with e-mails to school and public libraries in the area, and visitors were encouraged to "ask a librarian" if they had questions.

The National Library of Medicine and Its Guidance

The National Library of Medicine (NLM) has identified several strategies that help promote health information through public libraries.[18] These include activities such as

- Offering bookmarks and brochures
- Holding children's storytime with topics on community health concerns
- Providing computer/Internet training with a health focus
- Conducting classes on wellness
- Enhancing library and community Web sites
- Suggesting local and national resources regarding breast cancer screening and detection
- Educating community workers on health resources available at the local public library

- Exhibiting at local health fairs

- Networking with supporters throughout the community

- Sending press releases to local papers and radio stations

- Holding a teen night with a speaker on kids' health topics

In addition, NLM points out that libraries can become involved with other community agencies in projects associated with community outreach, consumer health collections, cultural and bilingual information efforts, education endeavors, and health information projects for teens.

A Profile of Youth Health Needs

Health Information Literacy

As mentioned throughout this book, health literacy is necessary to help youth find and evaluate health information regarding a wide range of topics. Among others, these include the following:

Food and Diet

- Child and teen nutrition

- Food allergies

- Food safety

- Vegetarian eating

- Reading food labels

- Healthy snacks

- Weight management

Growth and Development

- Sleep problems

- Dysfunctional school environments

- School performance

- Unstable homeschooling

- Puberty

- Early puberty

Social and Cultural Issues and Conflicts

- Parent relationships

- Homework issues

- Teen driving and starting to drive issues

- Bullies, violence, harassment
- Short or tall stature
- Talking about sex
- Drug use
- Smoking
- Staying home alone for younger youth
- Getting a job/working
- Lying and stealing, honesty
- Making friends
- Building self-esteem
- Peer pressure
- Separation and loss
- Death and dying
- Conflict resolution

Youth Safety

- Gun and weapon safety
- Fireworks safety
- Swimming and water safety
- Sports participation and injuries
- Sun and skin safety
- Legal and safe use of motorized vehicles

Diseases and Related Issues

- Acne
- Asthma and/or allergies
- Depression
- Eating disorders
- Eczema
- Gynecomastia experiences by some males
- Knee pain related to growth, exercise, or recreation
- Mononucleosis
- Scoliosis
- Sexually transmitted diseases and infections

- Suicide thoughts and attempts

- Dysfunctional mental health of friends and family

- Warts and other skins problems

Guidance from a School Expert

School librarian and author Juanita Buddy suggests that we need to address the broad range of health issues through our contacts with parents, teachers, and students.[19] Of course, resources are important, but she emphasizes that approach and delivery strategies are also important. She suggests that school librarians can play several roles and already possess many strategies to use in providing health information. First of these is the *role of the teacher*. In this role, we can promote project-based and independent learning and research, always emphasizing information skills in finding health information. The sharing of health care experiences is also a useful strategy within this role that involves talking about health issues with students and faculty. In this way, resources regarding exercise, nutrition, and useful Web sites can be provided.

School librarians also perform the *role of instructional partner*. Here they become a collaborator in planning health-information-based teaching units. Collaboration is possible with a variety of teachers and staff including health and physical educators, school food services, and home economics teachers. This offers the school librarian the opportunity to help integrate national, state, and local health education standards and expectations into the overall instructional program of the school. This also gives the school librarian the opportunity to celebrate special observances such as National Nutrition Month and National School Lunch Week.

The *information role* of the school librarians as information specialists is paramount. Here they share knowledge and expertise about resources available in print and nonprint, as well as resources available at national, state, and provincial governmental levels. This offers opportunities to introduce concepts of the virtual reference library and "ask a librarian."

The *role of the school librarian as administrator* is important. In this capacity, the school librarian manages collection development and resources. As funds decrease for the school library program, school librarians can seek alternative funding such as grants from private, commercial and governmental sources.

Sexual Health: Problems and Prospects

Sexual health is of fundamental importance in providing adequate health care for youth. Yet in the United States considerable debate is occurring concerning the appropriate ways to present and the proper content of sexual health information. The major approaches used today include the following[20]:

- **Abstinence only** in which students are encouraged to refrain from sexual intercourse until marriage and abstinence accomplishes the prevention of sexually transmitted diseases and pregnancy.

- **Abstinence until marriage** in which students are taught that sexual activity outside of marriage is harmful.

- **Abstinence plus** in which abstinence is stressed but information about birth control and condom use for the prevention of sexually transmitted infection and disease are included in overall instruction.

- **Comprehensive sexual education** in which a wide range of topics are covered including birth control methods and sexual responsibility. More specifically[21]:

> Comprehensive sex education stresses abstinence and includes age-appropriate, medically accurate information about contraception. Comprehensive sex ed [is] also developmentally appropriate, introducing information on relationships, decision-making, assertiveness, and skill building to resist social/peer pressure, depending on grade-level.

Since 1996, the U.S. federal government's official policy through congressional mandate is to support abstinence-only sex education programs in schools that receive federal aid for such instruction.

Government policy in Canada is determined by provincial education ministries, and these programs vary. The "Canadian Guidelines on Sexual Health Education" is issued by the Public Health Agency of Canada. The document is intended to offer direction and assistance to local, regional, and national groups and organizations, as well as government bodies such as schools to develop and improve sexual health education policies and programs concerning the diverse needs of people in Canada. The guidelines do not mandate content or approaches, but are based on

> the concepts of community participation and individual choice-hallmarks of a health promotion philosophy. Sexual health education is defined as a broadly based, community-supported enterprise in which the individual's personal, family, religious and social values are engaged in understanding and making decisions about sexual behaviour and implementing those decisions.[22]

The United Kingdom endorses comprehensive sexual education with some limiting configurations. For example, in England, "information about contraception and safe sex is discretionary."[23]

A 2004 conference titled "Hit and Miss: A Consensus Conference on Sexual Health Education in BC" considered some of the pressing issues involved in sexual health education in British Columbia. Most of their conclusions and recommendations are of value to anyone considering sex education resources and services. Briefly summarized, the report stated that[24]

- Sex education should begin in the primary grades.

- A more consistent knowledge base for instruction should be created and delivered consistently.

- Social marketing campaigns must be conducted and associated with larger health issues.

- Sexual health information must be linked to broader issues of society, relationships, and decision making.

- Better communication patterns must be established between school and community.

- Educators' skills must be standardized.

- Faculties of education must become more involved in the training of sex educators.

- Parents must become more involved through formal and informal structures.

- Youth must have a voice in content and instruction.

- Better resources must be provided.

- Community shareholders must be involved in sexual health education.

- Sexuality must be embraced, not merely accepted.

- Role models that personalize and personify the diversity and expressiveness of sexuality must be found and presented.

The conference noted four major themes that emerged from the discussion:

1. Knowledge and values linked to values of community and reflecting cultural sensitivity

2. Content including power relationships, gender identity, self-efficacy, helping youth feel positive about themselves, and contrasting media images with reality

3. Accountable delivery systems and content linked to other curricula

4. Youth emphasized as consumers of sex health information, as well as the role of parents and community in supporting the role of the school in providing sex health education and information.

A 2007 study in Washington State indicated that most schools there focused their sex health education programs on HIV/AIDS education and tended to present their curricula based on KNOW HIV/AIDS Prevention and Family Life and Sexual Health (FLASH). Seventy percent of the schools that responded to this survey reported that they followed an Abstinence Plus or comprehensive program, meaning that they stressed abstinence but also included information on condom use mainly to prevent the spread of AIDS and other sexually transmitted infections. Twenty percent reported that they used Abstinence Only or Abstinence Only until Marriage, indicating that abstinence was the only sure way to prevent pregnancy and the spread of sexual infections.

The six major topics covered in the schools' curriculum included abstinence (91%), refusal skills (86%), information about sexually transmitted infections (86%), finding help and referrals/resources of sexual health (70%), condom use and effectiveness (56%), and pregnancy options (38%). Only 27 percent indicated that their curricula included sexual identity and orientation.[25]

These figures and approaches are probably reflective of the United States. A news article in the May 16, 2006 issue of the Washington Post reported that in 1999:

> A ... Kaiser Family Foundation study found that about a third of U.S. public high schools have sex education programs that advocate strict abstinence until marriage. Experts at the Sexuality Information and Education Council of the United States say the number has since grown, with some states not only accepting federal funds for abstinence education, but also including federal government language in their sex education guidelines.[26]

Youth librarians are very much involved in sex health education programs in that they often are the only easily available sources for comprehensive sex education materials if their schools follow an official abstinence educational program. Federal restrictions do not apply to materials purchased for school library collections with nonfederal funds. A First Amendment constitutional question may even be raised if comprehensive sex education materials are acquired for school library collections with federal funds.

Information Products: Design, Evaluation, and Delivery

Culture and Society

Good health information products that are designed to convey important information must consider the intended audience, including the culture and society from which the audience comes. At the beginning of the AIDS/HIV health crisis, authorities learned that selected symbols and ways of expressing vital information using those symbols is paramount to success. Cultural systems such as family, friends, relationships, and institutions must be carefully considered. In some cultures, the family plays an important role as authority and providers of information; in others, the peer group may have greater import. Institutional authority is important, but institutions and their supporting bureaucracy are sometimes suspect and equated with control and punishment. Good health information design recognizes these issues, and providers develop products that avoid harmful symbols, while using others that are likely to promote acceptance of the information.

A Health Instructional Model and Product

Many health instructional models and products are available, and many of these provide different philosophical and medical points of view. Frances Meiser is a learning and behavior specialist and consultant located in Austin, Texas. Among other interests, she has a desire to promote better health education programs for children. Her center is called the Brain Train Center, and she advocates "promoting health habits for minds and bodies." Her philosophy is spelled out in her book *The Brain Train: How to Keep Our Brain Healthy and Wise*, published by Safe Goods in 1997. She emphasizes the brain and how the brain must be fed wisely so that it can ensure healthy living. This is not a metaphor but a guide to good eating that will nourish the brain. She advocates that certain foods are good for the brain and that the right types of exercise can influence the brain in terms of promoting cell connectivity. Water, she feels, is very important for brain development and further, that certain activities promote and ensure the brain's healthy functioning. She strongly cautions against the negative effects of electromagnetic energy on brain development. This includes electromagnetic energy found in computers, and she offers advice on how to reduce the harm that can come from these forces in computers. She is especially happy to talk to teachers about her ideas and offers her services as a consultant to teachers and educational institutions. She does caution that the advice she gives in her publications and consultations is not of a medical nature and is written for educational and informational purposes only.[27]

Figure 7.3. *The Brain Train: How to Keep Our Brain Healthy and Wise* by Frances Meiser. Published by permission of Frances Meiser. Copyright 1997 by Frances Meiser.

Basic Factors in Evaluation

All health information products must stand up to credible evaluation. Printed materials, including books, reference items, and pamphlets, must be judged according to many criteria:[28]

- Purpose

  – What is the product's overall goals and objectives?

  – Is the purpose fulfilled?

  – Who is the audience?

- Authority

  – Who is the author or contributors?

  – What credentials or signs of qualification and authority do they present? Do the authors and/or contributors have established reputations?

  – What is known about the publishers or producers? Do they have established reputations?

- Authenticity and Accuracy

  - Are the facts accurate as presented?
  - Are points of view clearly labeled?
  - Is the material dated?
  - Is documentation provided in a logical manner for the intended audience?
  - Are illustrations used appropriately in terms of the intended audience and purpose of the item?
  - Are depictions of social and cultural groups realistic, avoiding stereotypes?

- Format Constructs

  - Is the binding or packaging suitable for typical use?
  - Is it constructed well (e.g., binding and good-quality paper and a high-quality and reliable medium?)
  - Does it use design features well (space, captions, placement of items, etc.)?
  - Does it use appropriate fonts, suitable for the intended audience?

Evaluation of Health Information on the Internet

Many of these criteria can be applied to evaluating health information that is found on the Internet. The Health Information Technology Institute of Mitretek Systems, Health Summit Working Group, developed the following criterion for health information on the Internet:[29]

- **Credibility:** includes the source, currency, relevance/utility, and editorial review process for the information

- **Content:** must be accurate and complete and an appropriate disclaimer provided

- **Disclosure:** includes informing the user of the purpose of the site, as well as any profiling or collection of information associated with using the site

- **Links:** evaluated according to selection, architecture, content, and back linkages

- **Design:** encompasses accessibility, logical organization (navigability), and internal functionality (see discussion on design in this chapter)

- **Search Capability:** includes use of keywords, Boolean logic

- **Interactivity:** includes feedback mechanisms and means for exchange of information among users

- **Caveats:** clarifies whether site function is to market products and services or is a primary information content provider

Readability and Usability of Materials including Web Sites

Preparing and designing health information materials is a complex process involving readability, computer usability, and information architecture. Materials must be readable for the intended audience, whether in print, visual, or Web sites. Studies as far back as the late 1940s and 1970s have indicated that pamphlets and other similar materials developed for distribution at community health clinics and help centers often are too advanced for the reading skills for many who need the information.[30] In situations in which reading and language skills inhibit receiving good information, well-conceived graphics, using only keywords or well-recognized icons or symbols, often help.

Usability is a word coined by computer experts who are concerned that products such as Web sites are easily understood and used by their intended audiences. A simple definition of usability is as follows[31]: "The ease with which visitors are able to use a Web site.... Web site usability is not just about making sure everything on the site works, but how quickly and easily visitors are able to make use of the site."

Usability basics involve understanding the users, information architecture, navigation design, how writing for the Internet differs from writing for print page design and layout, and testing the product for usability. Usability testing considers the effectiveness of Web design by testing it with its intended audience. Included here are types of usability testing procedures available, how to identify usability questions and issues, how to gather and interpret data, and how to redesign the product based on the testing results.[32]

Briefly stated, information architecture involves organizing content, navigation, design, and overall structure. Writing involves the good use of composition skills, understanding typeface and fonts, and determining legibility and line structures. Page design considers the artistic and visual effects of the Web site such as page layout, grid systems, groupings, use of colors, functional graphics (e.g., icons and symbols), controls, and application of acceptable standards.

Commercial Online Products

Popular and easy-to-use commercial databases are now available to libraries of all types. These include commercial companies such as EBSCO and Gale Research. Popular databases include *Alt HealthWatch* (EBSCO), *Consumer Health Complete* (EBSCO), *Health & Wellness Resource Center* (Gale), *Health Organization Directory* (Gale), *Health Reference Center* (Gale's Infotrac), *Health Source: Consumer Edition* (EBSCO), *Medline* and *MedlinePlus* (NLM), and *Natural and Alternative Treatments* (EBSCO). As many of the titles indicate, their contents reflect consumer information needs and interests, such as alternative treatments.

Online Resources

The Internet and its many Web sites provide free and easy access to a number of information resources. These include chat rooms, columns by experts, "frequently asked questions," and "ask the librarian" services. Some of the major search engines also provide easy access to health information such as "Yahoo! Health" (http://health.yahoo.com).

Chat rooms are often included in youth-orientated sites, and in recent years, authorities have voiced concern about some of those available to children and adolescents. The major concern is that they offer potential for abuse by sexual predators and others who seek to victimize youth. *U.S. News & World Report* outlined some of the dangers of youth-based venues such as MySpace. This special report outlined how parents can offer protection as well as discussed ways to make these sites "predator-proof."[33]

Health Information for Special Needs

Often people find themselves in need of special and often highly technical information about special and catastrophic illnesses that affect the lives of families. This information may be medical in character, but often it is information that requires emotional support and the sharing of experiences. The Internet offers a wide variety of information venues for support. For example, the U.S. Department of Health and Human Services provides a directory of such organizations through its Healthfinder Web site. Listings here range from "Abdomen" to "Youth-At-Risk" including diseases such as childhood diabetes and multiple sclerosis (http://www.healthfinder.gov/organizations).

The online commercial resource, *Health Organization Directory* (Gale), mentioned previously, lists agencies, organizations, schools, journals, newsletters, publishers, Web sites, hospitals and health care facilities, programs, and special care providers. These listings can be accessed by topics, names, and state and provincial locations. Information provided is brief, generally consisting of name, address, and phone and fax numbers. No descriptions of services are given. Chapter 11 provides more information on resources.

Outreach, Collaboration, and Social Marketing

As endorsed by the NLM, outreach and collaboration are necessary and important elements that youth librarians can use in promoting health information. Outreach programs in libraries have a long and successful history, and collaboration has been emphasized in recent years as a necessary strategy for school librarians. Collaboration, according to the *Merriam-Webster Online Dictionary,* is "to work jointly with others or together especially in an intellectual endeavor" (http://www.m-w.com/dictionary/collaborate).

Social collaboration is similar, but in professional terms, it generally means that individuals in organizations must form social networks to share their ideas, values, and work responsibilities. It is a move away from individualism and management through hierarchical directives.[34] In 1992, Paul Mattessich and B. R. Monsey surveyed the available literature on collaboration and identified the following attributes that comprise collaboration[35]:

- Efficiency of the operation

- Negotiation skills of participants

- Social, professional, and personal benefits that occur through collaboration

- Power to help make decisions

- Social and administrative support for collaboration

- Skill and expertise of participants

- Territoriality and its protection and/or sharing

- Authority and control as accepted by participants

- Initiation of contact by participants and/or leaders

Most if not all of the attributes are self-explanatory. Nevertheless, one more element can be added to collaboration: *social marketing.* Social marketing is important for youth librarians who wish to promote their health information services and programs within a collaborative framework. Social marketing is social intervention that uses standard commercial marketing techniques to promote positive social and individual changes in behaviors and attitudes or to reinforce existing positive behaviors and attitudes. The elements of social marketing include *Action* to promote a service or product, *Interest* to create or increase interest in a service or product, *Desire* to ensure a wish for the product or service, and *Action* to act in a collaborative way.[36]

The model in Figure 7.4 places both social marketing and social collaboration attributes within an associational context. Marketing expert Alan Andreasen believes that to bring about a real change in social structures, social marketers need to recruit important players including competitors, lawmakers, regulators, the media, and members of the health care community.[37]

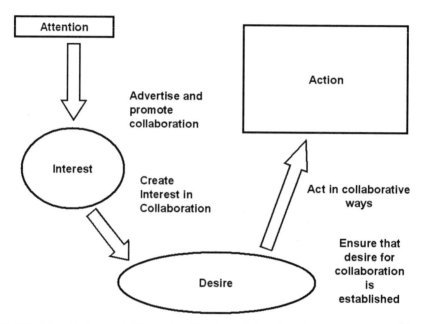

Figure 7.4. Social marketing model for teacher-librarian collaboration. A version of this model appeared in B. Immroth and W. B. Lukenbill, "Teacher-School Library Media Specialists Collaboration through Social Marketing Strategies: An Information Behavior Study," *School Library Media Research* 10 (2007).

Libraries as Health Information Gatekeepers

Social collaboration theory suggests that youth librarians in small and rural communities can play important gatekeeper roles in the dissemination of health information. Research by Gilda B. Ortego conducted in the sparsely populated area of the Big Bend region of West Texas found that medical doctors were the primary sources for health information used there. Beyond that, she found a "diversity and complexity of health information seeking behavior among the rural inhabitants of Big Bend" and that residents felt a need for a health information center.[38]

Can the library be that center? The concept of the "librarian as gatekeeper of health information" needs future research and development. Chapter 13 continues this discussion.

Conclusion

Health information in society is crucial. Youth, because of their general inexperience in life, are especially vulnerable to bad health information, leading to bad health behaviors. This chapter has looked at some of the major health information needs of youth and considered the social and psychological forces that drive those needs. Included in this discussion have been basic theories about information that can help us understand and respond to the needs and behaviors of youth. Information in this chapter has included library and instructional models, products and resources, and evaluation of resources and services. Although there are problems to be faced, youth librarians have the will and expertise to face them with force and determination.

Notes

1. Atlantic Canada Educational Foundation, "Information Literacy." Available at: http://www.upei.ca/fac_ed/tlit/info/whatis.htm, accessed September 9, 2006.

2. Medical Library Association, *Communicating Health Information Literacy* (Chicago: The Medical Library Association, 2005). Available at: http://www.blueline.mlanet.org/pdf/healthlit/hil_comm_plan.pdf, accessed September 9, 2006.

3. "Health Information Literacy." Available at: http://www.mlanet.org/resources/healthlit, accessed September 9, 2006.

4. James B. Dusek, "The Hierarchy of Adolescent Interests." A Social Cognitive Approach," *Genetic Psychology Monographs* 100 (August 1979): 41–72.

5. Spencer G. Niles, Edward L. Herr, and Paul J. Hartung, *Achieving Life Balance: Myths, Realities, and Developmental Perspectives: Information Service no. 387* (Columbus, OH: ERIC Clearinghouse on Adult, Career, and Vocational Education, 2001), p. 15, citing D. E. Super, *The Psychology of Careers* (New York: Harper and Row, 1957). ERIC document no. 458 420. Available at: http://www.call.tamu.edu/erica/docs/niles/niles4.pdf, accessed September 10, 2006.

6. Niles, Herr, and Hartung, citing M. L. Savickas, "Career Development and Public Policy: The Role of Values, Theory, and Research." Paper presented at the International Symposium on Career Development and Public Policy: International Collaboration for National Action, Ottawa, Canada, May 1999, p. 29.

7. "Gestalt psychology." In *Wikipedia, The Free Encyclopedia*. Available at: http://en.wikipedia.org/wiki/Gestalt_psychology, accessed September 21, 2006.

8. Malcolm Fleming and W. Howard Levie, *Instructional Message Design: Principles from the Behavioral Sciences* (Englewood Cliffs, NJ: Educational Technology Publications, 1978), pp. 3–98.

9. "Reports of the Demise of the 'User' Have Been Greatly Exaggerated: Dervin's Sense-Making and the Methodological Resuscitation of the User—Looking Backwards, Looking Forward: Panel Discussion." Panel session, American

Society for Information Science & Technology Annual Meeting, 2005, Charlotte, NC. Available at: http://www.asis.org/Conferences/AM05/abstracts/59.rtf, accessed September 11, 2006.

10. Marcia J. Bates, "The Design of Browsing and Berrypicking Techniques for the Online Search Interface," *Online Review* 13 (October 1989): 407–424.

11. Benjamin Brigham and Justin Perron, "Information-Seeking Behavior in Recreational Planning; An Exploratory Study of Recreational Travelers Conducted in Seattle, Washington." Unpublished paper, School of Information, University of Washington, Seattle, p. 4, citing Bates. Available at: http://www.ischool.washington.edu/informatics/capstones/2004/brigham_perron.pdf#search=%22information-seeking%20behavior%20in%20recreational%20planning%22, accessed September 11, 2006.

12. Jennifer Bothamley, *Dictionary of Theories* (London: Gale Research, 1993).

13. More information about social learning, as well as learning theories in general, is available on the Internet at "Learning Theories," http://www.emtech.net/learning_theories.htm and at "Exploration in Learning & Instruction: The Theory into Practice Database," http://tip.psychology.org, accessed September 14, 2006; see also David C. Leonard's book, *Learning Theories A to Z* (Phoenix, AZ: Oryx Press, 2002).

14. Lynn Rew, Elizabeth Abel et al., "A Sexual Health Intervention for Homeless Adolescents." Lecture presented by Lynn Rew, University of Texas at Austin, Texas, February 14, 2007. Based on research funded by the National Institute of Nursing, Research/National Institute of Health, Grant No. R01-NR04820.

15. Rew et al.

16. Judith Kuze and Sue Erickson, "The Teen Health Information Network (THINK)," *Illinois Libraries* 77 (Fall 1995):157–82. Available at: http://www.lib.niu.edu/ipo/1995/il9504157.html, accessed September 15, 2006.

17. "Welcome to the Teen CARE Network, Aurora, Illinois, USA," 2001. Available at: http://www.aocn.aurora.edu/teencare/index.html, accessed September 15, 2006.

18. National Network of Libraries of Medicine, "Resources for Members of the National Network of Libraries of Medicine (NNLM). Guide 4. Plan Activities to Reach Project Goals." Available at: http://nnlm.gov/outreach/community/services.html#teen, accessed September 17, 2006.

19. Juanita Buddy, "Keeping Current Library Media Specialists: Addressing the Student Health Epidemic," *School Library Activities Monthly* 22 (October 2005): 56–58.

20. Alison Peters, *Sex Education in Washington Public Schools: Are Students Learning What They Need to Know?* (Np.: Alison Peters Consulting, 2007), pp. 5–6.

21. Advocates for Youth, "Comprehensive Sex Education." Available at: http://www.advocatesforyouth.org/sexeducation.htm, accessed February 16, 2007.

22. Iconocast, "Canadian Guidelines for Sexual Health." Available at: http://www. iconocast.com/dinner-movie/Canadian_Sexual_Health.htm, accessed February 16, 2007.

23. "Sex Education." In *Wikipedia, The Online Encyclopedia*. Available at: http://en.wikipedia.org/wiki/Sex_education, accessed February 16, 2007.

24. Options for Sexual Health, "Hit and Miss: A Consensus Conference on Sexual Health Education in BC, Vancouver, May 29–30, 2004, Report on Proceedings, June 28, 2004," pp. 7–10. Available at: http://www.optionsforsexualhealth.org/about/advocacy/hitandmiss.pdf, accessed February 16, 2007.

25. Peters, *Sex Education.*

26. "In the United States." *Washington Post*, May 16, 2006. Available at: http://www.washingtonpost.com/wp-dyn/content/article/2006/05/15/AR20060 51500826.html, accessed February 16, 2007.

27. Interview with Frances Meiser, December 18, 2006.

28. Based on criteria suggested by the Montgomery County Maryland Public Schools, "Guides to Evolution of Media Materials."

29. The Health Information Technology Institute of Mitretek Systems, Health Summit Working Group, "Criteria for Assessing the Quality of Health Information on the Internet—Policy Paper." Available at: http://hitiweb. mitretek.org/docs/policy.html, accessed September 18, 2006.

30. Iddo Gal and Ayelet Prigat, "Why Organizations Continue to Create Patient Information Leaflets with Readability and Usability Problems: An Exploratory Study," *Health Education Research* 20 no. 4 (2005): 485–93.

31. "Web Site Usability," Available at: http://www.marketingterms.com/dictionary/web_site_usability, accessed September 18, 2006.

32. Human Factors International, "Essentials of Usability Seminars." Available at: http://www.humanfactors.com/training/essentials.asp, accessed September 18, 2006.

33. Michelle Andrews, "Special Report—Decoding MySpace." *U. S. News & World Report* (September 18, 2006): 46–60.

34. Ron West, "Reflections on Collaboration," *GSC Quarterly* (Winter 2003). Available at: http://www.ssrc.org/programs/gsc/gsc_quarterly/newsletter7/content/west.page, accessed September 19, 2006.

35. Paul W. Mattessich and B. R. Monsey, *Collaboration—What Makes It Work: A Review of Research Literature on Factors Influencing Successful Collaboration* (St. Paul, MN: Amherst H. Wilder Foundation, 1992).

36. Philip Kotler, Ned Roberto, Nancy R. Lee, *Social Marketing: Improving the Quality of Life,* 2nd ed. (Thousand Oaks, CA: Sage, 2002).

37. Alan R. Andreasen, *Social Marketing in the 21st Century* (Thousand Oaks, CA: Sage, 2006).

38. Gilda Baeza Ortego, "Health Information Seeking Behavior of Rural Consumers in the Big Bend Region of West Texas." Ph.D. dissertation, Texas Woman's University, 2001, abstracted in *Dissertations Abstracts International*, 62-A (October 2001): 1258.

Chapter 8

Planning Health and Fitness Programs and Services

Introduction

This chapter considers the important elements of planning health information services and programs for public and school libraries. Included are discussions regarding some of the elements, strategies, and theories for basic planning. The chapter closes with action research questions regarding leadership roles in providing health information to children and youth.

Planning for Health Care Information: Basic Leadership Strategies

Leadership is fundamental to good planning in both school or public library environments. K. D. Benne and P. Sheats wrote in 1947 that good leaders must be able to handle both tasks and maintenance functions. Stated in broader terms, task functions mean the ability to achieve goals that are rational and well planned. Maintenance tasks are more emotional and directed at encouraging satisfaction necessary to maintain organizational and community structures that lead to success. Examples of task functions include the following:[1]

- Initiating activity
- Information seeking and information giving
- Opinion giving
- Elaborating
- Coordinating
- Summarizing
- Testing feasibility

- Evaluating

- Diagnosing

Maintenance functions involve the following:

- Encouraging

- Gatekeeping

- Setting standards

- Following and expressing group feelings

- Consensus taking

- Harmonizing

- Reducing tensions

Although Benne and Sheats wrote these in reference to group work, they certainly apply to the overall processes involved in planning health information services for youth.

In 1965, scholar F. C. Mann added these skills to leadership: technical, human relationships, administration, and institutional (e.g., understanding the structure and operations of bureaucracy and institutions). These skills are especially important as one moves into higher executive levels of management, including skills related to human relationships, administration, and institutional framework.

Technical skills become less important at higher levels of leadership.[2] Such skill sets have been reiterated in numerous writings since the 1940s. For example, a 1973 U.S. Army training manual echoed many of these same principles of leadership. Advising military leaders to[3]:

- Cultivate knowledge of self and readiness for self-improvement.

- Be technically proficient.

- Seek responsibility and to take responsibility for actions.

- Make sound and timely decisions (based on good problem solving, decision making, and planning tools and techniques).

- Set the example (through good role modeling).

- Know staff and colleagues and look out for their well-being (through knowledge of human nature, behaviors, and motivation strategies).

- Keep staff and coworkers informed (communicate with those with whom you work).

- Develop a sense of responsibility in your staff and coworkers.

- Ensure that tasks are understood by staff and then supervised and accomplished (communicate expectations and standards).

- Train as a team (as a leader, do not remove yourself from training).

- Use the full capabilities of your organization (through teamwork, communication, and networking).

In her book *Leaders in Libraries: Styles and Strategies* (1991), Brooke E. Sheldon, former dean of three American schools of library and information science, noted similar characteristics of leadership that she found in national and international library leaders. She wrote that library leaders exhibited leadership traits such as the ability to communicate effectively, to network well, to take risks, and to be visionary.[4]

Organizations and Operational Theories

Cultural theories. Planning health information services involves an understanding of cultural diversity. Cultural theories help explain how various cultures operate and interact with other cultures. Cultural theories are many and complex, but this discussion briefly reviews only organizational culture and general social culture.

Culture has many meanings, but based on a standard dictionary definition, culture is how a group of people who are associated with one another in some manner of membership. With time, a culture forms unique characteristics of "beliefs, social forms, and material traits"[5] In 2002, the United Nations Educational, Scientific and Cultural Organization (UNESCO) defined culture as "a set of distinctive spiritual, material, intellectual and emotional features of society or a social group, and that it encompasses, in addition to art and literature, lifestyles, ways of living together, value systems, traditions and beliefs."[6]

In its mission of promoting health, the National Library of Medicine (NLM), through the National Network of Libraries of Medicine (NNLM), has commissioned a series of guidelines and instructional units that address issues of understanding and addressing cultural aspects, especially minority cultures. One unit in the series is *Planning and Evaluating Information Outreach among Minority Communities: Model Development Based on Native Americans in the Pacific Northwest.*[7] The many contributions and resources of NLM are mentioned throughout this book, including Chapters 2, 3, and 11.

Organizations develop cultures that are unique and that set them apart from other organizations, no matter how similar. *Organizational cultures* embrace both material and nonmaterial attributes. Material aspects might be design of facilities and furnishings, expected dress of workers, and policies and operating procedures that give direction and guidance. Nonmaterial elements include core values, attitudes, and a belief system that embraces and promotes a constructed, shared and promoted image of the organization.[8]

Understanding the library or school culture is necessary not only in forming internal health information programs and services, but also in reaching out to colleagues and users in the community through networking, promotion, and collaborative efforts. No matter how similar, all groups with whom we interact bring their own cultures to the table.

Change and Innovation

Planning for new services and programs means change, and it also provides opportunities to be innovative and to introduce new ideas. Change can also invigorate both staff and library users. In their guide to planning, the NNML suggests two theories, *social learning* and *diffusion and innovation,* that it believes promote both change and innovation.

Social learning theory. Social learning is a behaviorist-based theory that is practical and understandable. It was introduced by professor Albert Bandura in an effort to explain how people learn behaviors, particularly aggressive behaviors. He theorized that learning is caused by both the learners and what they bring to the situation, as well as what the environment provides the learner in various ways. He also suggested that mass media play a strong role in learning both appropriate and inappropriate social roles and skills. His 1977 book, *Social Learning Theory,* offers a readable explanation of his ideas.[9]

Health care information is based on providing resources that allow people to learn from information and to integrate that learning into appropriate behaviors. As noted, NNML suggests that social learning theory is a viable theory for both staff and library users. The illustrations below are learning theory concepts suggested by NNML and adapted for public and school library media center situations[10,11]:

- Behavioral Capability. Have knowledge and ability to use it and to act appropriately with that knowledge.

  - Staff Action: Offer the client a service (e.g., a reference citation or an Internet resource) that will likely answer his or her question(s).

- Expectations. Believe that something tangible and concrete will come from that knowledge.

  - Staff Action: Walk the client through an Internet search of reliable resources, explaining how they are useful.

- Self-Efficacy. Have confidence in self to take action and to be persistent.

  - Staff Action: Provide health information literacy instructions that will build confidence.

- Observational Learning. Understand that beliefs are reinforced by observations of persons similar to oneself.

  - Staff Action: Offer examples and demonstrations based on others who have experienced successes with health resources.

Diffusion of Innovations Theory. NNML also recommends diffusion of innovation theory as a useful concept to bring about change when initiating a new health information program. Diffusion of innovation theory was first introduced by Everett Rogers in the 1940s. He describes how new ideas are introduced and accepted into environments.[12] One of the key elements in this theory is that most people do not accept new ideas based on logical, scientific evidence but on the weight given to it by opinion leaders, innovators, and early adopters. Innovators and early adopters test out, endorse, and either accept or reject new ideas and methods. Critical mass or a collection of persons who accept the innovation is necessary for a new idea or new program to be generally accepted. Acceptance by innovators and early adopters in a school or public library system is crucial for acceptance and eventual success of a health information program. At the planning stage (and perhaps at the early initial implementation stage), acceptance by innovators and early adopters is an absolute necessity and involves the public library's and school's formal (administrators) and informal (influential faculty and staff) leaders. Planning will require that innovators and early adopters in the system be identified and addressed with special care. Once the program has been accepted by these leaders, the same attention can be given to potential users.

According to this theory, new ideas are generally accepted by innovators and early adopters if the new ideas or concepts meet these challenges[13]:

- *Relative Advantage.* Offers advantages over existing programs and services.
  - Staff Action: Provide examples, evidence, and benefits of new program and services in relation to current program (how existing problems in health care can be influenced by reliable health information).
- *Compatibility.* Considers compatibility in relation to values, habits, experiences and needs of users.
  - Staff Action: Promote resources and services that will meet immediate and known health information needs.
- *Complexity.* Answers the question: is the idea or concept easy to understand and use?
  - Staff Action: Make sure that training experiences and information is provided that meet with known levels of expertise and successful experiences in health care information.
- *Trialability.* Offers innovators and early adaptors opportunities to try out the concept or idea before accepting it.
  - Staff Action: Plan to bring these persons together for a briefing about the program and perhaps offer some hands-on opportunities to experiment with some of the resources to be offered such as MedlinePlus.
- *Observability.* Requires that the new idea offer tangible and visible results.
  - Staff Action: Provide proven examples of how the program will benefit the community, for example, its potential for reducing children's accidents both in school and in the community.

Major Steps in Planning Health Information Programs and Services

Community Awareness, Needs, and Assessment

The Internal Environment. One of the significant questions to ask is, "do we need health information programs and services in the library?" The first step is to determine the level of awareness at the local and building level among the staff and administration. Observation might indicate whether the idea of health information has been discussed, formally or informally, by the staff and administration. A survey of the staff and administration might also reveal existing policies and services regarding health information. In schools, curriculum guides and discussions with teachers about their needs and experiences should provide useful background information. Of course, a review of the library's collection and collection development polices should be reviewed to provide information about how systematically the library has collected health information.

It may be that the idea of a specialized health information service operating from the library may be so new that few people have given it much thought. If this is the case, some information marketing may be in order. Information marketing is simply placing an idea forward in the hope that it will be considered thoughtfully.

Social marketing, although related to information marketing, is a process that can help encourage the use of health information. Social marketing differs from information marketing in that it goes beyond providing information about services and resources. Social marketing uses many of the techniques of commercial marketing, although its approach is not to create monetary profit but to promote social good and well-being of citizens. Generally, social marketing revolves around services and programs that are available and that will be of benefit to a great number of people. Social marketing also promotes a desirable idea or positive changes in social behavior, and it has been used widely in health fields to encourage less smoking and periodic medical examinations and doctor visits for health conditions related to a variety of health problems and diseases. Using one's professional judgment, it might be necessary to use social marketing to encourage the administration and staff to entertain and accept the idea that a library-based health information program for youth is necessary.

The External Environment

Many of the attributes mentioned above involve assessing the community external to the library. What is the level of awareness in the wider community? (The wider community might be limited to the service area of the school or public library.) Will a health information program for youth be supported? What resources already exist in the area? How are health information resources already in the community being used and promoted? Will the proposed program be a duplication of existing programs and services? What are the groups or agencies that exist in the community that would likely support this program? Who are the community leaders that might look favorably on a health information program for youth in neighborhood schools or libraries? What types of personal contacts are necessary in the community based on its demographics and history? Again based on demographics and community history, how can this idea be presented (marketed) to community leaders and opinion leaders?

The NLM Guidelines for Development

As mentioned in several places in this book, the NLM is dedicated to supporting and making available health information to the general public through various venues. The NLM has been very active, with the help of the American Association for the Advancement of Science (AAAS), in encouraging public libraries to provide appropriate community health information services and programs. On the basis of this objective, the NLM has developed a number of guides to help facilitate their agenda. The following discussion is based on some of the major principles stated in these guidelines.

Know the Community and Develop a Profile

Planning of programs and services requires an understanding of the community to be served. The NLM suggests that these factors must be determined:

- Who is the target audience?

- What are the major health information needs?

- What access problems exist?

- What are the highest priorities to address?

In school situations, the primary target audience will naturally be the local school and the school area or boundaries that it serves. Knowledge of this can be obtained from existing records, observations, and conversations with administrators and staff.

Public libraries can define their targeted youth populations in much the same way. The targeted youth population may be the entire city or governmental units served by the library, or it may be the local neighborhood or region. Documentation will be available from observation, conversations with knowledgeable persons, interviews with community leaders and government officials (planning agencies, departments such as parks and recreation, neighborhood centers, government-sponsored clubs), and, of course, demographic studies published or posted on the Internet by government and other agencies and associations. A useful source of information about the target audience is organizations and government agencies that already serve the target audience within the framework of their own missions.

Youth librarians can gain useful information about the target audience by questioning "stakeholders." Stakeholders are persons who have or will have a vested interest in the programs and services. These include students, teachers, staff, parents, and various users of the public library.

Once the data are collected, a community profile can be compiled. Basically this is a picture of the community as it now exists, but at this point, the profile in only a preliminary picture, more still needs to be done.

Determine Needs and How to Meet Those Needs

The NLM suggests several means of obtaining information about health information needs. Perhaps the most obvious is to establish a relationship with existing health providers and discuss in depth their perceptions of health information needs for children and adolescents. This is an excellent means to determine gaps in the health information system that the library and school might fill.

Focus groups, mailed questionnaires, personal interviews, and telephone interviews are means of obtaining information about health information needs. Some of these techniques have been used by libraries and offer models for others to emulate and expand on. Don A. Dillman, in his *Mail and Telephone Survey: The Total Design Method*[14] and its update, *Mail and Internet Surveys: The Tailored Design Method,*[15] offers some useful guidance for questionnaire development. The focus group technique is now widely used by various groups, organizations, and researchers, including the NLM. Richard A. Krueger and his colleagues, Mary Anne Casey[16] and David L. Morgan,[17] provide guidance on how to use focus groups.

Develop Goals and Objectives

After the program staff members have developed a clear understanding of the community and its needs, specific goals and objectives for programs and services can be developed. Goals and objectives generally focus on these attributes:

- What are the major problems to be address?

- What intervention strategies are possible and likely to improve the situation?

- What effects will the program and service produce?
- What improvements to health care information will programs and services bring about?
- What are the goals and objectives of the audience?
- How will the goals and objectives produce a better understanding of health information resources (health information literary)?
- How will the goals and objectives be measured for stated accomplishments?

Especially for schools:

- What kinds of goals and objectives will increase student learning and performance?
- How will the goals and objectives articulate with the curriculum?
- How will the goals and objectives improve information literacy skills?
- How will the goals and objectives improve the health care awareness of the school community (parents, students, teachers, administrators, staff, and the target community)?

Obviously, desired outcomes play an important role in formulating goals and objectives.

Outcome measures. Outcome measures will be essential not only in evaluating the effectiveness of the program but also in planning specific services. Outcome measures, directed at changing behaviors and attitudes about health information sources and how to find them, form the foundation of solid goals and objectives. The NLM suggests the following measures that can influence positive behavior changes[18]:

- Increase the awareness of health information sources
- Increase specific knowledge about health information sources
- Influence positive attitudes about health information sources
- Influence beliefs about health information sources
- Facilitate technology access and willingness to use information technology
- Develop skills necessary for the better use of health information resources
- Reinforce existing positive behaviors and attitudes
- Build community and institutional support for programs and services

Especially for schools:

- Increase teachers' and staff members' awareness of the importance of health information in curriculum and other areas of student life
- Increase positive parental attitudes and behaviors about health information
- Make health information easily accessible

- Increase the participation of health providers in the community in contributing to the school's health information program

- Increase students' health information literacy performance

Methods helpful in determining the impact and outcomes of goals and objectives are discussed in the evaluation section of this chapter.

Plan Activities and Strategies

Activities should grow from established goals and objects. Earlier chapters discuss possible activities and program strategies in more detail. Overall, activities and strategies address the needs of the target populations and generally fall into these areas:

- Exhibits and bulletin boards increase awareness of

    - Health information and resources in the library
    - Community health information located elsewhere in the community
    - Emergency contact information regarding health issues

- Internally produced publications increase awareness and include

    - Brochures
    - Fact sheets
    - Pathfinders
    - Finding guides and subject bibliographies

- Equipment and databases make health information accessible and include

    - Free databases such as MedlinePlus
    - Commercial databases such as the Thomson Gale Health Reference Center Academic Service
    - Computer and audiovisual facilities
    - Internet access (connections; areas for access and privacy; assistance)

- Collection development provides easy access to information by giving attention to

    - Policy and selection issues and policies
    - Collection access and improvement
        - Books
        - Periodicals
        - Nonprint resources
        - Reference materials
        - Parent information
        - Selected technical medical resources
        - Document delivery
        - Interlibrary loan support
        - Membership in library-sharing networks

- Health information literacy instruction improves access through
  - Tutorials, seminars, demonstrations
  - Curriculum development and support
- Information consultation by staff facilitates health information awareness among
  - Parents
  - Students and library users
  - Staff and faculty
  - Community leaders and contributors
- Special collections for parents address special needs through
  - Special resources
  - Web site presence with parent information

Barbara Casini and Andrea Kenton offer good advice for planning services and programs for public libraries in their book *The Public Librarian's Guide to Providing Consumer Health Information.*[19] Lynda Baker and Virginia Manbeck's book, *Consumer Health Information for Public Librarians* offers similar advice as well as giving considerable information on resources.[20]

Plan for Evaluation and Gather Data

Evaluation takes many forms, and it can be expensive. Therefore, an evaluation process must be based on what is logical and affordable. These factors to be considered include limitations of staff time, funds, time frame of the program, access to computer facilities if needed, agency restriction on how subjects can be approached, record accessibility because of privacy policies and laws and difficulty in designing instruments that can adequately measure results.[21] Evaluation can be conducted internally by the program staff or by an external evaluator.

The Internal Evaluation

Several evaluation procedures are available for program managers who conduct internal evaluation. Some of the major approaches are given in the paragraphs that follow.[22,23]

Formative and summative evaluations. Formative evaluation occurs before the program is placed in operation. It is designed to discover any problems that might interfere with the effectiveness of the program either before or while it is operation. Formative research is widely used in testing advertisement and in educational products before they are released. Methods generally used in formative evaluation include interviews, focus group sessions, and performance testing.

In theory, summative evaluation comes at the end of the program when the data are analyzed and changes are made before the program is offered again. In practical terms, for long-terms programs, summative evaluation can be made at discrete intervals as the program proceeds, and the incoming data indicate changes are needed. Summative evaluation is useful because it helps focus on whether goals and objectives are met and the effects the program had or is having on participation.[24]

Process evaluation. Process evaluation is concerned with how the program is implemented. Time frames, program checklists, and their relationship to the overall program are monitored. Process evaluation can be an administrative (external) audit of the activities and plans to make sure they are in accordance with legal, financial, and policy directives of the institution.

Outcome-based evaluation. Outcome evaluation seeks descriptive data to document a program's immediate and long-term effects. In libraries, evaluation has generally meant attendance counts, new library cards issued after or during a program, increase in materials circulated by the library, and increase in reference questions related to a program. For health information programs, it might result in more use of health-related databases and Web sites, more specific information or reference questions regarding health issues directed at the staff, and more interest from teachers in incorporating health information into instruction. Documentation for outcome measures are based on administrative records kept for the duration of the program (e.g., library cards issued, reference inquiries and types of questions logged during the time of the program, observation and logs of Web site use, electronic counts of Web site visits, anecdotal evidence provided to staff or collected by staff, and informal observations and conversations with users about programs and services). Anecdotal evidence is that which is not scientifically controlled, and it is not based on results coming out of a research protocol.

Outcome evaluation is also directed at determining effects of the program, particularly how the program and services change people's behavior, attitudes, and belief patterns regarding good health practices and health information. Librarians, as well as personnel in other institutions, often find data that indicate behavior and attitude changes hard to collect and measure.

Standard methods used for impact evaluation include survey methods such as telephone or Internet surveys, logs of self-reported behaviors and attitudes, and studies of public behaviors (e.g., data on use of health information resources, reports on visits to doctors and clinics and follow-ups on recommended health tasks (e.g., children's vaccinations), and long-range changes in the target audience's health information-seeking behaviors.[25]

In recent years, the Institute of Museums and Libraries (IMLS) has instructed programs that it supports through its funding to report results of their program activities using impact results. The institute has supported a number of studies concerning how libraries can successfully implement outcome evaluations. One of these is Joan Durrance and Karen E. Fisher-Pettigrew's book *How Libraries and Librarians Help: A Guide to Identifying User-Centered Outcomes* (2005).[26] Their book offers guidance on how libraries can gather data that show impact results of their programs and services. IMLS offers excellent resources at http://www.imls.gov/applicants/resources.shtm. State libraries, such as those in Texas and Florida, likewise offer additional resources. Eliza Dresang and her colleagues, Melissa Gross and Leslie E. Holt, give additional advice concerning outcome measures for youth services in their book *Dynamic Youth Services through Outcome-Based Planning and Evaluation.*[27]

Analyze the Data

Data are customarily analyzed using several approaches. Quantitative data such at those coming from coded instruments (e.g., questionnaires, and structured interviews), will require statistical analyses. Appropriate statistical programs and methods are available for this. Qualitative data from focus group discussions or open-ended questionnaires will require analyses of texts for important themes. Strict adherence to coding measurements will be required to ensure validity. Computer-based content-analysis programs can be used to help with these types of analyses. Depending on the evaluation team's level of knowledge, comfort with statistics and the sophistication of the statistics being gathered, statistical experts are often used to process and help analyze the data.[28]

Whatever the methods of analysis used, care must be taken that biases do not enter into the development or application of the initial research instruments or the ways in which the data from those instruments are analyzed. Cultural perceptions either in the original instrumentations or their analyses may also affect the validity of the final results. Cultural values and perspectives are often embedded in such attributes as language and language translations, symbols of respect and authority, and traditional ways of coping and solving problems.[29] Beverly Scot's *Consulting on the Inside: An Internal Consultant's Guide to Living and Working Inside* is useful in the evaluation of such data as she highlights cultural problems and barriers.[30]

The External Evaluation

As mentioned, legal and funding requirements may necessitate that the program be evaluated by an external evaluator. This must be understood early in the planning process so that funds can be budgeted for it and the external evaluator can be selected. The techniques used for this type of evaluation are much the same as for an internal evaluation process. External evaluation requires that an experienced consultant be placed under contract. This contract is legally binding, and it clearly states expectations, dates, deadlines, and fees to be paid the consultant, methods to be used in the evaluation, and the nature of the final report. The evaluator often requests that he or she be given access to management documents and allowed contact with a variety of participants in the programs (e.g., staff, administration, clients, community members). Sometimes an evaluator may wish to be an active participant in the program. Numerous popularly written books are available for consultants, and the American Society for Training and Development is a professional organization supporting professional consulting (http://www.astd.org/astd). Alexander and Elaine Cohen provide useful advice on selecting an external consultant for a library project.[31]

Report and Use Findings

Evaluation findings based on well-conceived and administered procedures conducted internally by the staff or by an outside consultant may be used in several ways. First of all, they are used to assess the overall effectiveness and outcomes of the program findings.[32] They can:

- Help determine how well the program met established goals and objectives

- Serve as keys to making needed changes in the program

- Identify specific activities and strategies that were effective as opposed to those that were not

- Uncover unexpected outcomes and results

- Help staff reflect on lessons learned

A written report is generally expected from an evaluation process. This may be formal or informal, depending on the organizational culture of the parent organization, its supporters and funders, and community. Advantages of written reports are many. They[33]

- inform managers, administrators, and sponsors of the successes of the program and serve as guides to advocating for needed funds and resources.

- increase understanding of the program in the organization, the target audience, and externally to those found in the wider community.

- increase the likelihood of cooperation and collaboration with other agencies, as well as with staff members in the parent organization, such as teachers in a school.

As mentioned, the written report can be very formal, consisting of an executive summary, statement of purpose, background of the program, methodology used in developing the program as well as how it was evaluated, summary of results, highlights of major findings, and recommendations for improvements. Attachments such as profiles of the target audience(s), copies of data collection instruments, and other items that offer insight into the program can be added. External consultant reports generally follow this formal approach.

A less formal approach, but nevertheless an important one, is to abstract major findings from the formal report and shape these into different formats suitable for distribution to various groups. These may take the form of Web site summaries with links to full reports, news releases, brochures, announcements, and reprints of sections of the formal report (e.g., executive summary, major findings, and recommendations). The idea is to reach interested groups with information that has immediate and obvious appeal to them.

Other Options for Planning

Of course, options other than those just discussed must be considered in planning programs and services. Many of these have already been discussed in various chapters of this book.

Program design configuration is a planning option and raises the question, what levels of services are to be offered: basic, mid-range, or extensive? Planning options and choices will be made on the basis of various economic and social circumstances.

Procedures and strategies for marketing the health information program and services are options to be planned and are absolutely necessary for success. Marketing procedures are discussed elsewhere in this book.

Leadership in the Medical Field

Historically, the medical field has been well served by outstanding leaders from ancient times to the present. Some of the more modern leaders have become household names, such as Clara Barton, Florence Nightingale, and Walter Reed. Without going into excessive detail in this discussion of leadership, it seems proper that we recognize some of these persons in celebrating their roles in medicine and in recognizing our indebtedness to them as leaders. Among others, these include the following:

- Clara Barton, organizer and first president of the American Red Cross

- Florence Nightingale, influential pioneer and theorist in nursing and public health

- Lina Rogers Struthers, first American school nurse

- Crawford Long, first surgeon to use general anesthesia

- Harvey Cushing, leader in modern brain surgery

- Paul Dudley White, cardiologist and founding member of the American Heart Association

- Charles Drew, a physician who perfected blood transfusion techniques

- Walter Reed, army physician who confirmed that yellow fever was transmitted by mosquitoes rather than by person-to-person contact

- Mary Edwards Walker, Union Army surgeon and first woman to receive the American National Medal of Honor for her work with the military during the American Civil War

- The Mayo Brothers and their pioneering work in establishing the Mayo Clinic, known throughout the world

- Elizabeth Blackwell, the first woman to earn a medical degree in the United States

Without question, both public and school libraries must include both biographical information about medical leaders and technical and scientific medical information. Clara Barton holds a special place in U.S. history for her work in helping the sick and those suffering from disasters. Figure 8.1 is an artist drawing of her based on a 1907 picture taken in Russia while attending an international conference of Red Cross organizations. All persons from around the world who have advanced health care and medicine deserve a place in library collections. Figure 8.2 shows other famous leaders associated with medicine and health care.

Figure 8.1. Clara Barton, first president of the American Red Cross.
Line drawing by Richard H. Hendler.

Crawford Long

Mayo Brothers

Elizabeth Blackwell   **Mary Edwards**   **Walter Reed**
Walker

Figure 8.2. Leaders in medicine. Pictured left to right are Crawford Long, the Mayo Brothers, Elizabeth Blackwell, Mary Edwards Walker (center), and Walter Reed. Images from U.S. postage stamps honoring medical leaders and archival materials from the U.S. Dept. of Health and Human Services.

Action Research and Leadership

Innovators and leaders in many areas can provide necessary and timely information on various elements in the planning process. Leaders such as librarians, teachers, parents, staff members, administrators, community leaders, and government agents and officials offer avenues for good advice on planning health information structures. Some basic questions to ask are the following:

- What is the leadership role of libraries in offering health information?

- Assuming that libraries have a leadership role to play, how can that role be better defined?

- How can the leadership role of the library as a vital and dynamic source of health information be articulated to the public and to librarians?

- What are some internal and external social and governmental structural changes needed to better facilitate this role?

- What are some ways and means of broad-based collaboration with other parties who have a vested interest in better health information for children and youth?

A useful guide to action research is Lesley Farmer's *How to Conduct Action Research* (2003). She discusses the action research process, how to use data, application of appropriate statistics, and how to use action research once it is available.[34] Action research questions and suggestions are discussed in Chapter 13 and Appendix A.

Conclusion

Planning information health programs and services for children and youth in libraries and schools involves a number of elements. This chapter looked at some of the vital factors considered necessary for program success by experts and organizations. The chapter relied heavily on prior work conducted by the NLM and by Mary Ellen Wurzbach, professor at the College of Nursing, University of Wisconsin at Oshkosh. Both of these sources emphasize the importance of community involvement, effective activities and strategies in programs and services, sound leadership, and systematic evaluation. A fundamental principle is that good health care information influences positive behavior regarding how people manage their health and that of their families. This principle lies at the heart of all successful health information programs and services.

Notes

1. W. Bernard Lukenbill, *AIDS and HIV Programs and Services for Libraries* (Englewood, CO: Libraries Unlimited, 1994), p. 217, citing K. D. Benne and P. Sheats, "Functional Role of Group Membership," *Journal of Social Issues* 4 (1948): 41–49. From William R. Lassey and Marshall Sakhkin, *Dimensions of Leaderships* (San Diego, CA: University Associates, 1983).

2. Lukenbill, citing Floyd C. Mann, "Towards an Understanding of Leadership's Role," in R. Dubin et al., *Leaderships and Productivity* (San Francisco: Chandler, 1965), pp. 251–259, citing William R. Lassey and Marshall Sakhkin, *Dimensions of Leaderships*.

3. Donald Clark, "Concepts of Leadership: Performance, Learning, Leadership's and Knowledge," citing United States, Dept. of the Army, *Military Leadership* (Washington, DC: U.S. Government Printing Office, 1973). Available at: http://www.nwlink.com/~donclark/leader/leadcon.html, accessed June 21, 2006.

4. Brooke Sheldon, *Leaders in Libraries: Styles and Strategies* (Chicago: American Library Association, 1991).

5. *Webster's Ninth New Collegiate Dictionary* (Springfield, MA: Merriam-Webster, 1983), 314.

6. "UNESCO Universal Declaration on Cultural Diversity," February 21, 2002. Available at: http://www.unesco.org/education/imld_2002/unversal_decla. shtml, accessed June 21, 2006.

7. National Network of Libraries of Medicine, *Planning and Evaluating Information Outreach among Minority Communities: Model Development Based on Native Americans in the Pacific Northwest*. Available at:

http://nnlm.gov/archive/pnr/eval/projdes.html and http://nnlm.gov/archive/pnr/eval/index.html, accessed June 21, 2006.

8. Gary Hutchinson Stewart, "Large Corporations, the Research University and Factors of Technology Transfer: The Austin, Texas Study." Ph.D. dissertation, University of Texas at Austin, 1992. Abstracted in *Dissertation Abstracts International* 53-A (June 1993), part 1, 4288. Gary Hutchinson Stewart, "Corporations, the Research University and Factors of Technology Transfer: The Austin, Texas Study." Unpublished Final Oral Defense Document, University of Texas at Austin, 1992.

9. Albert Bandura, *Social Learning Theory* (Englewood Cliffs, NJ: Prentice Hall, 1977).

10. Catherine Burroughs, *Guide to Planning, Evaluating and Improving Health Information Outreach*. Draft December 17, 1999 (n.p.: National Network of Libraries of Medicine, Pacific Northwest Region, 1999), pp. 21–22. See also NNLM's Planning and Evaluating Health Information Outreach Projects series. "This 2006 series presents step-by-step planning and evaluation methods. Along with providing information about evaluation, each booklet includes a case study and worksheets to assist with outreach planning. The booklets are designed to supplement *Measuring the Difference: Guide to Planning and Evaluating Health Information Outreach* and to support evaluation workshops." Available at: http://nnlm.gov/evaluation/booklets/booklet1.html, accessed June 22, 2006.

11. Albert Bandura, *Self-Efficacy: The Exercise of Control* (New York: W. H. Freeman, 1997).

12. Everett M. Rogers, *Diffusion of Innovation* (Glencoe, IL: The Free Press, 1962).

13. Burroughs, pp. 26–28.

14. Don A. Dillman, *Mail and Telephone Surveys: The Total Design Method* (New York: Wiley, 1978).

15. Don A. Dillman, *Mail and Internet Surveys: The Tailored Design Method*, 2nd ed. (New York: Wiley, 2000).

16. Richard A. Krueger and Mary Anne Casey, *Focus Groups: A Practical Guide for Applied Research,* 3rd ed. (Thousand Oaks, CA: Sage, 2000).

17. David L. Morgan, *Focus Groups as Qualitative Research,* 2nd ed. (Thousand Oaks, CA: Sage, 1997).

18. Burroughs, p. 12.

19. Barbara Casini and Andrea Kenton, *The Public Librarian's Guide to Providing Consumer Health Information* (Chicago: Public Library Association, 2006).

20. Lynda Baker and Virginia Manbeck, *Consumer Health Information for Public Librarians* (Lanham, MD: Scarecrow Press, 2002).

21. Mary Ellen Wurzbach, ed., *Community Health Education and Promotion: A Guide to Program Design and Evaluation,* 2nd ed. (Gaithersburg, MD: Aspen, 2002), p. 587.

22. Burroughs, pp. 36–53.

23. Wurzbach, pp. 583–602.

24. Burroughs, pp. 41.

25. Wurzbach, p. 586.

26. Joan Durrance and Karen E. Fisher-Pettigrew, *How Libraries and Librarians Help: Guide to Identifying User-Centered Outcomes* (Chicago: American Library Association, 2005).

27. Eliza T. Dresand et al., *Dynamic Youth Services thorough Outcome-Based Planning and Evaluation* (Chicago: American Library Association, 2006).

28. Burroughs, pp. 54–65.

29. Burroughs.

30. Beverly Scot, *Consulting on the Inside: An Internal Consultant's Guide to Living and Working Inside* (Alexandria, VA: American Society for Training & Development, 2000).

31. Alexander Cohen and Elaine Cohen, "How to Hire the Right Consultant for Your Library," *Computers in Libraries* 23 (July–August 2003): 8–10.

32. Burroughs, 66.

33. Burroughs, 67.

34. Lesley S. J. Farmer, *How to Conduct Action Research* (Chicago: American Association of School Librarians, 2003).

Chapter 9

The Rio Grande Valley of Texas: Highlighting Issues and Models for Health Information

Introduction

Health care and health care information are of critical concern to societies around the world. As a model for consideration, this chapter describes some of the health-related issues and problems faced in the Rio Grande Valley of Texas, outlining a unique school system in Texas that seeks to address some of these concerns. The chapter concludes by suggesting research that might help youth librarians assume gatekeeper roles in providing health information in rural and small towns and in other isolated communities. Some elements of this discussion will be useful in urban areas as well, where libraries are not used for basic health information.

Health Issues in the Rio Grande Valley of Texas

The Rio Grande Valley of Texas lies just across the border from Mexico.[1] In Texas, the area is often referred to simply as the "Valley." This area includes eleven Texas counties with large Hispanic populations. It is one of the poorest and, by many accounts, most underserved areas in the United States. Like all of Texas and much of the western United States, it was once a part of Mexico. The United States' annexation of Texas in 1845 facilitated the Mexican-American War of 1846–58 (known in Mexico as La Intervención Norteamericana). At the end of the war, most of what was then northern Mexico became part of the United States. Many long-term residents of the Rio Grande Valley can trace their families back to when the area was Mexican. Politically and socially, the area continues to reflect much of this background.

Always in flux, in recent years these changes have been exacerbated by large population growth and the impact of the North American Free Trade Agreement of 1993 (NAFTA). This trade agreement has brought with it both positive and negative socioeconomic influences including political and financial changes.

Although health care coverage for many low-income children and adolescents has increased in recent years, both in the Valley as well as nationally, because of federal and state funding, there are still large numbers of people living in the region who are uninsured. In 2000, 34 percent of area residents were uninsured compared with 14 percent in the rest of the United States.

Many assume that those without funds and health insurance can turn to public hospitals for health care. This is not generally the case; laws and regulations often prevent this. For example, citizenship or proof of legal residency is often required, and hospitals are mandated to provide care for only the poorest (e.g., 21 percent below the federal poverty level). The lack of public-supported hospital facilities in the Rio Grande Valley further exacerbates this.

Language and education play large roles in health care and health care information. This eleven-county region is heavily bilingual with both English and Spanish spoken widely. Nevertheless, many residents speak only Spanish. In 2000, government statistics reported the Hispanic population for the region to be 88.2 percent, and indications are that by 2020, it will reach 93.3 percent.

Education levels are generally low in the area. The 2000 U.S. Census reported that 33 percent of the area's adults, aged twenty-five years or older, had less than a ninth-grade education compared with 11 percent for the United States.

Poverty levels for the region are high. In 2000, some 35 percent of the population lived below the federal poverty level, compared with 12 percent for the United States. Hidalgo County has the highest poverty levels in the entire United States, with 40 percent of all residents living below federal poverty levels in 2000.

The Texas-Mexico border is one of the most heavily crossed borders in the United States. Texas alone has sixteen border crossing points with millions of people crossing each year. This binational crossing and mobility introduces the dangers of communicable diseases and places stress on health care facilities of both countries. Communicable diseases that are of special concern in the region are tuberculosis, waterborne gastrointestinal diseases, sexually transmitted diseases, dengue fever (a mosquito-transmitted viral disease), and HIV/AIDS. In addition to these concerns, the Valley must also deal with issues such as oral health, maternal and child health care, mental health, chronic diseases such as diabetes (including childhood diabetes), and childhood obesity. In recent decades, asthma has become serious, affecting youth in a growing numbers.

Health care resources are limited. In 2000, nineteen hospitals located in the eleven-county area served a population of 1,301,053. Local public health departments operated by various governments in the area appear to provide only limited services. A 2003 survey showed that only three agencies offered indigent services, one provided HIV/AIDS care, two treated sexually transmitted diseases (STDs), three attempted to address tuberculosis (TB) needs, three offered vaccinations, and three provided health education. The United States-Mexico Border Health Commission created in 1994 also offers support to various health agencies in both countries. Various foundations and Valley medical institutions such as medical schools also offer support.

Professional health care workers are also limited in the eleven-county area. In 2000, only 1,362 physicians practiced in the area, with Kinney County having only one and Zapata County only two. Nurses in the area in 2002 numbered 7,440 (full-time equivalent [FTE] nurse equivalents) in the area surveyed, compared with 193,019 (FTE) in Texas.

Only 239 dentists practiced in the eleven-county area in 2002, serving a per dentist population of 5,726 compared with 1,722 per dentist population in the United States.

Health Information Services in the Valley: A Pilot Study

The United States National Library of Medicine's (NLM) "Health Disparities Plan 2004–2008" emphasizes public health information and community outreach. Among its core values are beliefs that good, affordable, easily accessed health information and health information technologies are key components in lessening the effects of poor health care and poor or inadequate health care information available to underserved populations. In the early 2000s, a team of researchers lead by medical librarian Virginia M. Bowden conducted a federally funded pilot study of four counties located in the southern tip of Texas, commonly called the Texas Lower Rio Grande Valley. The study tested the assumption that providing access to health information found in NLM's MedlinePlus in both Spanish and English could address some of these disparities found in underserved populations.[2] Their study focused on Hispanics. The pilot study included a survey of physicians about their information needs and practices including the use of MedlinePlus. In addition, the study placed MedlinePlus facilities in several other venues including the following:

- One teaching site at the High School for Health Professionals, located in Mercedes, Texas, provided training for peer tutors to help students understand and use MedlinePlus.

- Two health clinic sites (one urban and one rural) had basic staff training on how to use MedlinePlus, how to make appropriate referrals to the system, and generally how to use the system as a health information resource.

- One community center located at the Cameron Park *colonia* in Brownsville. (As used in Texas *colonia* refers to a neighborhood that developed along the border without basic services such as water or sewer.) Training was offered to local *promotoras* or staff officials to help residents use the Spanish version of MedlinePlus.

- Four focus groups of Hispanics who used health information in their professional roles were trained to use MedlinePlus and to offer feedback about their experiences to the investigators.

A number of useful insights were found from all of these situations, and many are useful to youth librarians in planning health information services and programs. These included the following:

- Physicians showed an increase from a similar 1990 study in their competency to use computers for information, and they also showed an increased awareness of MedlinePlus, but they generally lacked the time to spend searching for information.

- Librarians in established health information centers serving the area, such as the Circuit Librarian Health Information Network and the Regional Academic Health Center, did not feel that their services would be less needed with increased use of MedlinePlus.

- Overall, the investigators ranked the high school instruction situation and the community center placements as the most successful and the rural and urban health clinics the least successful.

The high school situation was successful because students and faculty had need for the information, and the faculty was assured that MedlinePlus was a more reliable source compared with information that their students might find on the Internet. Librarians there were also appreciative of new information sources that they could provide for their students and faculty. This training program is more fully described in a report by Debra Warner and her research colleagues published in the April 2005 *Journal of the Medical Library Association*.[3]

The community center operation was successful because it offered a new service with new content that helped invigorate the center. The *promotoras* who were in charge of offering and managing services within the center found it useful in fulfilling their roles of providing health and social service information to the residents.

As noted, the less successful operations were the health clinics. The need for health information there took on different dynamics with the staff not seeing the need or reason to promote MedlinePlus. They had developed other means of health information delivery and were content with those methods, and they felt that they did not have the time to attend to personalized health information needs through information technology systems such as MedlinePlus.

The research team concluded that the best approach to offering health information and lessening disparities found among various underserved populations regarding good health information is through educational settings.[4] Although libraries were not the primary focus of this study, youth librarians, working in educational institutions, can learn from these findings. Figure 9.1 places some of these findings in a school and library context.

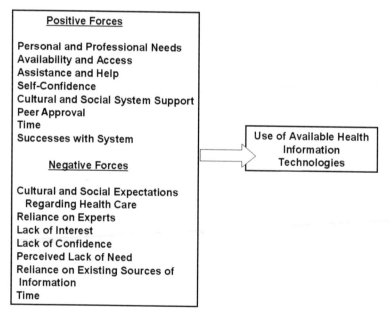

Figure 9.1. Positive and negative forces influencing the use of available health-information technologies. Rio Grande Valley Secondary School Education for Health Workers: models and examples.

The South Texas Independent School District

As previously discussed, the Rio Grande Valley of Texas faces many health, social, and economic problems. Providing health care personnel for the area and offering employment for health providers are critical to the area. The South Texas Independent School District attempts to address some of these educational concerns. This publicly funded district, South Texas Independent School District, located in San Benito, was originally established by the Texas Legislature in 1964 specifically "to provide education to disabled youth who were then excluded from public education."[5] It was known as "Rio Grande Rehabilitation District." In 1973, it was renamed South Texas Independent School District, and it now serves three South Texas counties: Cameron, Hidalgo, and Willacy. It augments the services of twenty-eight other school districts in these counties by offering special magnet school opportunities for students with special interests. Originally the legislature intended the district to offer vocational training, but in recent years, it has redirected some of its focus to include vocational and academic education.

In 2006, the magnet schools included the South Texas Business Education and Technology Academy located in Edinburg, the South Texas High School for Health Professions (Med High) in Mercedes, the South Texas Academy of Medical Technology (Med Tech) in San Benito, and the Science Academy of South Texas, also located in Mercedes. School libraries have always been a part of the development of the magnet schools. All campuses are served by newly constructed library facilities, and in 2006, the centers collectively reported library holdings of 70,000 books, 5,000 videos, and 50 Web databases.[6]

The South Texas High School for Health Professions (Med High)

The South Texas High School for Health Professions was the first magnet school in the Rio Grande Valley. The school offers open admission, but prospective students must attend an advisement session and a full-day "New Scholar Academy" in the summer. The school's mission is to provide "rigorous academic training and advanced technical skills that will allow students to pursue careers in allied health careers and/or post secondary education." The school offers both a standard high school curriculum along with intensive health-related courses. Emphasis is placed on academic study, practicums in health-related fields, and outreach services in the community. Students take a series of health, science, and technology classes that include medical terminology, medical technology, and introductions to various medical environments (e.g., dental assistance, medical laboratory, clinical nutrition, rehabilitative service, veterinary assistant, maternal health, gerontology, and pharmacology). Electives include scientific research and design, research in environment health, psychology, sociology, sports medicine, and weight training. The school was recognized in 2006 by *Newsweek* as among the 100 top high schools in the United States.[7] As a part of its offerings, the district also maintains the highly regarded Science Academy of South Texas (Sci Tech). The academy provides an academic program for secondary grades in math and science career fields supporting architecture, engineering and computer science. Sci Tech is associated with Project Lead the Way, Inc., a national preengineering program in which students can receive college credit beginning their freshman year. In their senior year, students research "a real-world problem and develop a solution." The academy also has partnerships with a number of universities including Rice University, Rochester Institute of Technology, University of Texas—Pan American, and

South Texas College.[8] The school also offers a number of technician-level certification programs that provide employment for students in various medical fields upon successful completion of the certification program.[9]

Biblioteca Las Américas

The library media center is called Biblioteca Las Américas (BLA),[10] and it serves the students of Med High and the Science Academy. The library was one of three 2006 National School Library Media Program of the Year Award winners designated by the American Association of School Librarians (AASL). In its award announcement, AASL said this about the programs:

> La Biblioteca Las Américas is a 33,000 square foot facility serving over 1,300 students from two magnet schools in the South Texas Independent School District. Although a freestanding facility, the library media program at BLA is a model of curriculum integration. The program is also a model for student inquiry, with over 40 opportunities for research, inquiry, and presentations for grades 9–12. Extended hours provide additional time for student research.

The awards committee said this about all three winners:

> In each of the schools and districts, the school library media specialists are acknowledged as curriculum leaders…. Administration, fellow teachers, and students acknowledge that role, and provided examples of ways in which they depend on the school library media program as the central focus of teaching and learning in the school.[11]

BLA opened in 1998. It has a staff of three librarians, five assistants, one secretary, and a three-person custodial staff. Its book collection includes more than 38,000 titles, and it provides students and staff with extensive periodical and newspaper subscriptions and retrospective microform periodical collections, videos/DVDs/CDs, art prints and framed artworks, and networked computers. Online resources include MedlinePlus, full-text services from Proquest and eLibrary, EBSCO services including its Health Source files, GALE Infotrac containing its Health Module, and a variety of online reference resources including Facts on File. Interlibrary loan services are also available through local and regional institutions such as the Hidalgo County Library System, Rice University, Valley Medshare, and the Regional Academic Health Center of the University of Texas Health Science Center at San Antonio. The library is also a member of Amigos.

Programs and services include research assistance, reading encouragement programs, satellite recording facilities, video editing and production facilities, and rotating displays of student work and art exhibits. Special collections include a Spanish language collection, the Rice University Professional Collection, Rice University Patent Collection, and the Baylor University Medical Collection. In addition to these, BLA offers a lunchtime concert series by student performers, German classes (taught by the lead librarian who has extensive knowledge and education in German), Valley community information, and information on wellness activities in the school and community.

The school provides numerous programs including outreach into the community and a peer tutor program in which the library is highly involved. One of the school's successful events is the health fair. This is a program of exhibits showcasing community organizations. The fair includes demonstrations, activities, and door prizes. Although the fair is held in the library, it is organized by peer tutors and the Physical Education Club. The professional staff members are also involved with the Medical Library Association and are often invited to speak and present at various conferences held throughout the United States.

Figure 9.2. Biblioteca Las Américas in the evening hours of operation. Photo by Sara Reibman; courtesy of the South Texas Independent School District.

South Texas Academy of Medical Technology

The South Texas Academy of Medical Technology,[12] which opened in 2003, is also a part of the South Texas Independent School District and is also located in San Benito. Known as Med Tech, much like Med High, this magnet school provides a college preparatory curriculum with hands-on course work in medical technology. Students who plan professional careers are encouraged to apply.[13]

Principal Harry Goette gives this message to prospective students:

> Our mission is to educate future medical professionals in the health sciences through the integration of rigorous academic, medical and technological education. Med Tech offers a curriculum that prepares students for careers in health care such as a doctor, pharmacist, nurse and medical researcher. Students spend three years on campus taking health science courses as well as completing stringent academic requirements. In their senior year, students put this health science background into practice as interns at hospitals, pharmacies, doctors' offices and assisted living centers.

He continues:

> The combination of strong academic skills and the use of advanced technologies are present in every aspect of medicine in the 21st century. If you want to be a doctor, pharmacist, nurse or researcher, strong academic and technological skills are required. Med Tech provides a strong foundation for both.[14]

The school offers a curriculum that leads to the "National Health Care Foundation Skills Standard Certification." A certification program is also offered in food preparation and management. These certification programs are offered as options to students. The curriculum is coordinated with other area universities such as Baylor College of Medicine, Harlingen Medical Center, Regional Academic Health Center, Texas State Technical College, Valley Baptist Medical Center, and University of Texas at Brownsville.

A general high school curriculum is provided, supplemented with four courses that introduce students to medical technical skills and environments. For example, its health science technology curriculum begins with medical terminology and an overview of medical fields followed by three other courses that introduce students to various aspects of medical laboratory experiences and clinical practices at more advanced levels. The school encourages, but does not require, 75 hours of community outreach service for every student.

Med Tech is supported by its Med Tech Library. This facility strives to meet the needs of curriculum and research requirements. It also plays a role in encouraging reading and creativity and multimedia learning. It offers access to well-selected Internet resources, and its collection is further expanded through its online catalog connection with BLA.[15]

Impact on Valley Communities

Both of these magnet schools serve the needs of students who want employment in the medical field after graduation, but they also prepare students for further academic study. Important, too, is the service they provide in helping to alleviate some of the severe health problems that Valley communities now face. Field experiences, practicums and outreach activities are among the highlights of these two schools. However, the actual impact of these schools on health care and health care information has not yet been studied extensively.

The Librarian as Gatekeeper: Bringing Health Information to the Valley

Research in Texas and in other parts of the United States and the world clearly shows that health care information is sadly lacking in rural communities and small towns. This is not a new problem, but it continues as a growing, unsolved social policy issue. The NLM has recognized this, and through its various programs and grants has sought to address some of the issues that cause these problems.

In Canada, rural health care has been the focus of the Canadian Population Health Initiative (CPHI),[16] Canadian Institute for Health Information (CIHI),[17] the Public Health Agency of Canada (PHAC),[18] and the Centre for Rural and Northern Health Research (CRaNHR) at Laurentian University.[19] In Australia, the National Rural Health Alliance Inc.[20] and the Australian government's Institute of Health and Welfare[21] have similar directives and interests.

In the United Kingdom the Institute of Rural Health seeks to

> inform develop and promote the health and well being of rural people and their communities through its three main academic programme areas: research and projects (contributing to the evidence base), education and training (developing a workforce fit for purpose), and policy analysis (including rural proofing).[22]

In Scotland, a similar mission is undertaken by the Centre for Rural Health Research and Policy.[23]

All of these countries and the various groups that have interest in rural health reveal common elements regarding health care situations similar to research from the Rio Grande

Valley of Texas. Common to these are populations that face shortages of medical personnel and facilities, large populations of native peoples with health issues, environments that are often hazardous, and work that is difficult and often dangerous and subject to accidents. Can public and school libraries play a role in helping to alleviate some of these health information problems and conditions not only in the Texas Rio Grande Valley, but elsewhere as well?

One element that is often overlooked in research concerning this problem is the role that rural and small town librarians might play in helping their communities have better access to good health information. Libraries and community information centers are often found in rural and small towns; with the growing availability of Internet network connections in these libraries, reliable health information is increasingly available. MedlinePlus is an excellent example of health information that is now available online and free of charge throughout the world. Beyond that, rural and small-town public and school librarians can play a part in their communities by taking on a "gatekeeper" role based on the following definition as "gatekeeper." A gatekeeper is generally considered someone in a position of authority who controls access or has some manner of influence on how resources and information are dispersed to others. We can extend this question to urban areas where libraries are not used for basic information needs.

Of course, social and community research is needed to address this question. By using the Rio Grande Valley of Texas as a purposeful research sample, some basic research questions regarding the health information role of librarians as gatekeepers in isolated areas can be considered. Findings from such studies are likely to be applicable in urban areas as well. If such research is successful in helping to define a health information gatekeeper role for youth librarians, it might well offer strategies for a better defined role for librarians as community developers and leaders in providing health information for rural and small town communities. See Chapter 13 and Appendix A for more discussion of the gatekeeper role.

Conclusion

Education is one of the primary solutions to health care and health care information in all parts of the world. Questions of how to create and prepare health care information, how to distribute it, and how to help people use it are critical concerns reflected in the literature and discussions of many professions. Youth librarians play an important role in this dialogue because they perform significant educative roles in today's society. As such, they are increasingly called on to assume a forceful role in providing health information to their publics. Effective models and practices are available to youth librarians and are discussed in this and other chapters in this book. Nevertheless, more research and reporting of good practices are needed now and in the future to advance this important social and education role within library environments.

Notes

1. David C. Warner and Lauren R. Jahnke, *U.S./Mexico Border Health Issues: The Texas Rio Grande Valley* (San Antonio, TX: Regional Center for Health Workforce Studies, Center for Health Economics and Policy, the University of Texas Health Science Center at San Antonio, April 2003). Much of the descriptive materials in this section are based on this report. Available at:

http://www.uthscsa.edu/RCHWS/Reports/NAFTA2.pdf, accessed December 27, 2006.

2. Virgina M. Bowden et al., "Health Information Hispanic Outreach in the Texas Lower Rio Grande Valley." *Journal of the Medical Library Association* 92 (April 2006): 180–189. Available at: http://www.pubmedcentral.nih.gov/articlerender.fcgi?artid=1435849, accessed December 27, 2006.

3. Debra G. Warner et al., "High School Peer Tutors Teach MedlinePlus: A Model for Hispanic Outreach." *Journal of the Medical Library Association* 93 (April 2005): 243–252. Available at: http://www.pubmedcentral.nih.gov/articlerender.fcgi?artid=1082942, accessed December 27, 2006.

4. Bowden et al.

5. "San Benito, Texas—Education." Available at: http://www.sbedc.com/relocation/education, accessed August 10, 2007.

6. "South Texas Independent School District." Available at: http://www.stisd.net/, accessed December 30, 2006.

7. "Med High. South Texas High School for Medical Professions." Available at: http://medhigh.stisd.net/, accessed December 30, 2006.

8. South Texas Independent School District, "Sci Tech." Available at: http://www.stisd.net/scitech, accessed March 28, 2007.

9. Interview with Lucy Hansen, Lead Librarian, Biblioteca Las Américas, April 25, 2007.

10. "Biblioteca Las Américas." Available at http://medhigh.stisd.net/, accessed December 15, 2006.

11. "AASL Selects 2006 NSLMPY Award Winners." Available at: http://www.flr.follett.com/intro/pdfs/nslmpy06.pdf, accessed December 23, 2006.

12. "South Texas Academy of Medical Technology (Med Tech)." Available at: http://medtech.stisd.net, accessed December 22, 2006.

13. Letter and editorial comments from Lucy Hanson, Lead Librarian, Biblioteca Las Américas, March 26, 2007.

14. South Texas Academy of Medical Technology (Med Tech), "Principal's Message." Available at: http://medtech.stisd.net/p_message.htm, accessed December 22, 2006.

15. "South Texas Academy of Medical Technology (Med Tech), "Med Tech Library." Available at: http://medtech.stisd.net/dudleym, accessed December 22, 2006.

16. Canadian Population Health Initiative. Available at: http://secure.cihi.ca/cihiweb/dispPage.jsp?cw_page=cphi_e, accessed December 30, 2006.

17. Canadian Institute for Health Information. Available at: http://secure.cihi.ca/cihiweb/splash.html, accessed December 14, 2006.

18. Public Health Agency of Canada. Available at: http://www.phac-aspc.gc.ca, accessed December 13, 2006.

19. "Centre for Rural and Northern Health Research." Available at: http://cranhr.laurentian.ca, accessed December 13, 2006.

20. "National Rural Health Alliance, Inc." Available at: http://nrha.ruralhealth.org.au/?IntCatId=14, accessed December 14, 2006.

21. Institute of Health and Welfare, Australia. Available at: http://www.aihw.gov.au/ruralhealth/faqs.cfm, accessed December 13, 2006.

22. "Institute for Rural Health." Available at: http://www.rural-health.ac.uk, accessed December 30, 2006.

23. "Centre for Rural Health Research and Policy." Available at: http://www.abdn.ac.uk/crh/about.shtml, accessed December 30, 2006.

Chapter 10

Global Health, Health Information, and Education

Introduction

The preceding chapters have considered many health information problems, and although most of these issues are Western European, the British Commonwealth, and North American examples, we cannot overlook the global impact of health on children and youth. In fact, a global look at health issues is an excellent tool for us to use as we consider our own public school library situations. With this in mind, this chapter briefly reviews some of the major health themes and solutions suggested by UNESCO. It reiterates some of the ways that youth librarians might respond to these issues through information and educational programs and services. It gives attention to the selection of materials and collection development. Materials and collection building become even more important as globalization increases. Globalization brings heightened awareness to health information, coupled with a demand for it.

Important Major Global Health Themes

Since the nineteenth century, great strides have been made in the health of children and youth; yet much still needs to be done to make the world a safe and comfortable environment. The United Nations Educational, Scientific and Cultural Organization (UNESCO) has identified these youth-related global issues that must be seriously addressed in the twenty-first century:

- Hunger

- Micronutrient deficiencies and malnutrition

- Intestinal infections

- HIV infections and other sexually transmitted diseases

- Malaria

- Violence

- Drug and alcohol abuse

UNESCO states that if these health problems are not solved or reduced, children and youth can never have a psychologically supportive environment in which to learn and develop. UNESCO further states that improving health is based on skills-based health education, good health policies developed for individual schools, and on-site school health care.[1]

The European Commission recognizes these as problems but also adds emerging health concerns such as influenza, West Nile virus, rabies, bioterrorism, and respiratory diseases caused by environmental pollutants.[2] The World Health Organization (WHO) also presents an extensive list of health issues facing youth and their caregivers around the world. Among others, these include teenage marriage and pregnancies, honor killings, female genital mutilation, age of sexual consent issues, family planning services, reproductive health education, and adequate and correct sex education. WHO also suggests that health education involves changing harmful gender norms and practices throughout the world.[3] Although these health issues may not affect each school or even every country, information about them needs to be readily available for research, instruction, and personal enlightenment.

School Health Policy, Skills-Based Health Education, and Health Information

Health Policies

UNESCO states that for children to learn and develop, educators must maintain a healthy and protective school environment. To do this, a school's health policy must address many important issues that play major roles in the health of children and youth in schools. These basic issues include hygiene and nutrition, but they must go beyond that and specifically consider emotional, physical, and sexual abuse; discrimination against children with handicaps and diseases such as AIDS; harassment; drug, alcohol, and tobacco use; and violence and bullying. A policy must consider health education and how it is to be taught and integrated within the total curriculum.[4] We can add here that health education must include good, reliable health information and its adequate use and distribution.

Policies must also encourage good health attitudes of students, staff, faculty, and parents. UNESCO suggests that faculty can act as models for good health behaviors for students by demonstrating in their personal lives proper hygiene, refraining from smoking (or not smoking in the presence of students), and healthy eating habits.[5] Fortunately, in some schools around the world, we see these concerns already addressed (e.g., discouraging of teachers from smoking on school property, breakfast and lunch programs, health and physical education courses, school library media health collections, and policies that address major issues such as violence and harassment).

Curriculum and Skills-Based Learning

UNESCO's guidelines suggest that in addition to health courses, concepts of good health should be integrated in many areas of the curriculum. Their suggestions certainly have implications for health information acquired by youth librarians for their public and school libraries. The following is not an inclusive list of how health can be promoted throughout the curriculum, but it can serve as a beginning checklist both for curriculum and collection development. These include[6]:

- HEALTH AND SCIENCE

  Encourages students to:

  - Observe and record
  - Measure and make comparisons
  - Ask questions, hypothesize, and predict
  - Make experiments and interpret the results

- MATHEMATICS

  Promotes the following skills and knowledge in students:

  - Use of numbers
  - Weights and measurements
  - Estimating and recording data
  - General applications to healthy living (e.g., medication measurements and time frames for medicine use, body and weight monitoring, water and sanitation, nutrition and food intake calculations)

- SOCIAL STUDIES

  Develops in students analytical skills related to:

  - Ideas about social living and cooperating
  - Living together and social and group dependency
  - Health and environment and responsibility to preserve a healthy environment
  - Rights and duties of citizens to encourage healthy living
  - Responsibility to respect differences in health conditions
  - Developing skills to understand the geography and history of health
  - Studying the health of a community through demographic surveys and other basic research methods
  - Sharing information and promoting understanding of various views about lifestyles
  - Sharing information and customs regarding food and food practices
  - Developing empathy for others who suffer health problems
  - Considering one's immediate environments (e.g., home safety driving and driving responsibilities

- LANGUAGE AND INFORMATION LITERACY

  Promote health and health information through communication and understanding by:

  - Using language correctly, through grammar and correct usage
  - Listening, speaking, reading, and writing effectively
  - Using language as a tool for thinking and doing: finding, interpreting and working with information and ideas

– Writing used in observing, describing, and recording

– Promoting information literacy skills in finding, understanding and using information

Skills-Based Learning

Skills-based learning as promoted by UNESCO is both cognitive and psychosocial, designed to increase knowledge about health and to promote the critical use of information. It helps students grow socially and psychologically so that they will be able to understand situations that can influence their health and lives and be able to make good decisions regarding those situations. These skills include learning to respect others, learning to negotiate, developing refusal skills when faced with adverse situations, and having the self-confidence to make decisions independently from their peers and significant others in their lives. Skills-based learning reflects many of the current, widely accepted social, psychological, and learning theories of today.

Skills-based learning also reflects the natural ways in which children and youth learn. It is participatory and uses direct observations, modeling, and social interactions.[7] As just mentioned, skills-based learning reflects independent learning and judgments, and as such, it must be based on critical use of good, reliable health information.

School Libraries and Global Health Information

The International Federation of Library Associations (IFLA) through its two sections concerned with children and youth (Children and School Sections), underscored its understanding of the crucial need for health information in the 2007 program titled "Libraries in Good Health: Resources and Practices Designed to Support Community Development and Outreach in Health-related Issues." The general theme of the program highlighted[8]:

> [T]he library's role in supporting community health-related topics, programmes and services. The community may be the primary or secondary school or the local community or district. The support may come in the form of resources and materials, programmes and services designed to meet the health and medical needs of particular members of that community: mothers, families, youth who have left school, the elderly, for example. This theme is linked to the overall theme of the 2007 World Library and Information Congress: "Libraries for the Future: Progress, Development and Partnerships" and to President Byrne's theme of "Partnerships."

The primary goal of the conference was to address these concerns:

• Collections, services, and programs related to health, in its broadest sense

• Needs and interests of African libraries and librarians in serving schools and the community

• Good resources and practices in supporting community health from around the world, recognizing the context and cultural sensitivities of the health and medical fields

• Social and cultural role and impact of collaboration and partnerships in community development and outreach

The call for papers identified specific objectives that reflected some of the broader issues associated with health information in public and school library environments. Potential presenters were asked to consider[9]:

- The audience for programs and how audiences and their needs can be identified

- Planning for community development and cooperation

- Partners for health care initiatives

- Materials and formats (print, audio, visual, etc.)

- Staff training in materials and information use

- Marketing and promotion

- Measurements for success and improvement

- Strategies for continuation of successful programs

The central idea behind this program reflects much of what has been discussed in this book and puts health information into its rightful global context. The program's emphasis is well placed on important elements of health information: selecting and providing good health information, knowing the general state of health in communities, understanding health information needs, gaining community support, offering outreach services, marketing and promoting health information, and continued evaluation and improvement of good, proven services.

Collection Development, Services, and Programming

Collection Development

As we see from the IFLA conference of 2007, health information materials and resources concern librarians and school personnel in all parts of the world. Good collection development for health information follows good collection development procedures in general. There is no need for us to go into the logistics of how collections are developed because many excellent books and guides are already available. Selection of health information must be a part of any library's or school library media center's official selection policy.[10]

At a basic level, the emphasis on health information in public and school libraries can be placed on consumer health information, general health care, and social issues relating to health and society. The historical, psychological, and cultural aspects of health and disease should also be represented in a basic collection. Because some aspects of health care and health information are controversial, a good collection development plan and policy will help in the defense of topics that might come under challenge. This type of information is often the most needed and thus must be defended. Subjects relating to certain diseases such as HIV/AIDS and topics including sexuality, family planning, and cultural manifestations of sexual behaviors and sexual norms are often subject to censorship.

What is significant about health information is that it is available from many sources, some of which are outside of the general venues used by libraries to acquire materials. These, too, must be considered for inclusion in collections or made accessible in some way. In recent years, the Internet has become a major supplier of health information, and, as we have noted in several previous chapters, these sources can be used after careful review. Fortunately, some of the world's most respected medical institutions, organizations, and governmental establishments maintained authoritative and reliable health information. An example of a professionally managed collection of Web sites is the "Fun Educational Website for Teachers and Kids." This is a cooperative Web site with multi-participants, all having individual URLs. Many of them provide health materials appropriate for children.

In addition to the Internet, other electronic formats are popular with youth, and these should be carefully considered. DVDs, CDs, and newer communication technologies such as podcasts and social networking are becoming the format of choice for many of the world's youth today. Major commercial information producers such as Thomson Gale, Facts on File, and others also provide vast amounts of health information in electronic forms. MedlinePlus, produced by the United States National Library of Medicine (NLM), must not be overlooked as a fundamental electronic source of reliable health information constructed especially for use by the general public.

Books and other printed materials such as periodicals and pamphlets are still needed and will be used. Some commercial publishing companies such as the Hippocratic Press specialize in health information for youth. This company promotes itself as producing "age-appropriate stories for children that entertain, educate, and reassure both parent and child about the medical issues they face together." Visit their Web site at http://www.hippocraticpress.com/about-hippocratic-press/index.shtml.

Print materials are produced by many sources, with some being readily available through traditional library channels, while others are less accessible. For example, governments of all types produce health information, but these are often difficult to obtain. Pamphlets and brochures are especially popular with youth. This type of material is frequently created and distributed by local, state, provincial, and national organizations and governments. Again, identifying and locating these materials require special sources and knowledge. The review journal *VOYA: Voice of Youth Advocates* is a good source for locating such items, as is *The Vertical File Index*, produced by the H. W. Wilson Company. See Chapter 11 for other sources.

A variety of sources within communities produce health information, and librarians and school library media center specialists should canvas their communities for this type of material. As mentioned, pamphlets and brochures are popular, but other types of informational formats are also useful, such as meeting announcements, information postings about medical and health services, and available online directories. This information can be evaluated according to standard selection procedures and added to the collection as appropriate through community bulletin boards, the vertical or information file, and Web sites. Lukenbill's *Community Resources in the School Library Media Center: Concepts and Methods* gives advice on how to select and organize community information.[11]

The health information collection need not only contain medical information but can also include fiction, biographical and works of poetry, drama, and art. These types of materials help humanize health and health care information. Figure 10.1 illustrates these elements in developing a health information collection.

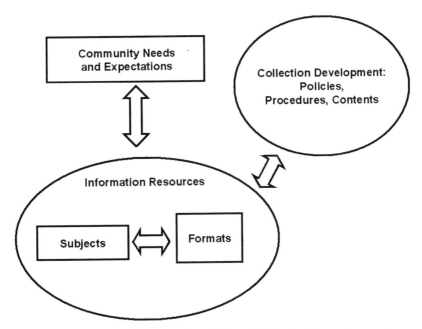

Figure 10.1. Basic health information and the collection development process.

Programming and Services

Programs and services lie at the heart of any good health information management plan. In addition to building collections, services and programs can include knowledge about health resources in the community so that effective contact and referrals can be made. Distribution of free materials produced by other agencies is also a good service to offer. Health information programs such as speaker programs made available through both public libraries and the school library media centers are good, fundamental programs to offer. Outreach activities to the community are also vital services. In public and school library environments, outreach can include visiting classrooms and giving out information about health care and health issues, as well as presenting booktalks, book reviews, and showing films on health issues.

Outreach services can also include providing services and programs to juvenile detention centers, hospitals, recreational halls, and other places where youth are found. Offering useful programs in cooperation and coordination with medical and health organizations, as well as with professionals who maintain private practices, are significant outreach activities. Outreach not only provides good information to those who might need it, but it demonstrates to the community at large that public and school libraries and their services and programs are vital to good, strong, and continued community and social development.

Conclusion

Health care and health care information are historic elements in human history that have perplexed humanity for eons and in all parts of the world. Since the nineteenth century, great advancements have been made in health and in information and knowledge about health; several useful models for health care delivery have developed over the years. Health care has been more successful in the developed countries of Europe and North America. The rise of globalization illustrates the inequality and disparity of health care around the world. At one extreme, we have a system of experts and institutions that offer the finest health care available in history. Traditionally, in these systems the "expert" medical authority makes most of the important decisions. In recent years in developed countries, a newer model has assumed a respected level of influence. This model asserts the idea that patients are participants in their health care management. They have a duty and responsibility to play an important role in management of health care at the individual level and at the group and family levels. This model requires that each person know how to acquire, evaluate, and use health information wisely. In countries where health care and information have been scarce and difficult if not impossible to obtain, this model may offer hope.

This newer model requires that public libraries and school library media centers play a positive role in supplying health information and in helping people understand how to better use it. As globalization takes root, a great many resources and procedures will be widely available, but with these growing resources come individual responsibility to use them wisely. Public and school librarians can help globalization become a positive influence on human society.

Notes

1. UNESCO, "Focusing Resources on Effective School Health." Available at: http://portal.unesco.org/education/en/ev.php-, URL_ID=35168&URL_DO=DO_TOPIC&URL_SECTION=201.html, accessed December 30, 2006.

2. European Commission, "Public Health." Available at: http://ec.europa.eu/health/ph_threats/com/emerging/emerging_en.htm, accessed December 30, 2006.

3. World Health Organization. Available at: www.un.org/esa/socdev/unyin/documents/ch04.pdf, accessed December 30, 2006.

4. UNESCO.

5. UNESCO.

6. UNESCO. "Focusing Resources on Effective School Health. Skills-Based Health Education Tools." Available at: http://portal.unesco.org/education/en/file_download.php/2fe2615e6d609a593d8516bd0b56f411FINAL+cc3-gpt02health cur.doc, accessed March 11, 2007.

7. UNESCO. "Youth and Health Issues." Chapter 4 in *World Youth Report 2003*.

8. IFLA, Public Libraries, Reading, and School Libraries Sections, "World Library and Information Congress: 73rd IFLA General Conference and Council, Call for Papers." Available at: http://www.ifla.org/IV/ifla73/calls-en.htm, accessed December 31, 2006.

9. IFLA.

10. Carol Ann Doll and Pamela Petrick Barron, *Managing and Analyzing Your Collection: A Practical Guide for Small Libraries and School Media Centers* (Chicago: ALA Editions, 2002). W. Bernard Lukenbill, *Collection Development for a New Century in the School Library Media Center* (Westport, CT: Greenwood Press, 2002). Phyllis J. Van Orden and Kay Bishop, *The Collection Program in Schools: Concepts, Practices, and Information Sources* (Westport, CT: Libraries Unlimited, 2007). Phyllis J. Van Orden, *Selecting Books for the Elementary School Library Media Center* (New York: Neal-Schuman, 2000).

11. W. Bernard Lukenbill, *Community Resources in the School Library Media Center: Concepts and Methods* (Westport, CT: Libraries Unlimited, 2004).

Chapter 11

Selection and Collection Development for Health Information: A Bibliographic Approach

Introduction

Collection development is an integral part of health information care and management, but it requires an eclectic approach because health care and health information cannot be narrowly defined. Health care and health information involve most aspects of society. With the expansion of information technology and the Internet, health information is abundant and ever-expanding, so much so that this richness can be overwhelming. This richness places demands on the limited resources that most youth librarians face. This chapter discusses some of these issues and provides a list of selection aids that can help in this important process.

Holistic Health Principles and Collection Development

Holistic health is a nonmedical term related to well-being that considers the physical, mental, and spiritual aspects of life as closely interconnected and balanced. (See http://www.destinationspa.com/travel_pros/spaGlossary.htm). Its principles can be used to help build health information collections.

Because it is a nonmedical philosophy, some of its methods are not always accepted within the medical community. Many of its approaches and treatments are not evidence-based but emphasize the spiritual. Nevertheless, its basic idea of wholeness and interrelatedness can be used to help in the development of a viable health information collection. This type of approach encourages us to look at health and health issues broadly as it emphasizes the interconnections between health and society.

Questions and Problems in Selecting Health Materials

In making selections regarding health information, some major criteria to consider are the following:

- Accuracy, authority, up-to-datedness, and usability within its format and intended audience

- Availability when ordered and ease of acquisition within the usual procedures

In recent years, commercial selection and acquisition programs and services such as *Books in Print,* Baker and Taylor, Follett Library Resources, and Brodart have become available to librarians. Although based on professional recommendations, we must ponder how precise or relevant these programs are in helping to identify and acquire health information materials. Related to this are questions about selection sources and items outside the mainstream review sources that librarians generally use to make selections. These include publications or productions by educational specialists, doctors, institutions, foundations, and hospitals, among others. Items produced by such individuals or groups are rarely included in standard acquisition and review systems. Ephemeral materials such as pamphlets, brochures, and some electronic materials are rarely covered by standard selection aids, although the situation regarding electronic materials has certainly improved in recent decades. We might ask the following:

- Within mainline selection aids, how well or often are health-related items covered?

- Can librarians rely on these alone for selection guidance regarding issues such as the authority of health materials and the verification of revisers' qualifications?

- Are suggestions for uses provided for curriculum and programming?

- Are comparisons made with other similar items?

Hundred of publishers and producers exist in the world, some of whom specialize in health materials such as the children's publisher, Hippocratic Press. Are these publishers and producers easily identified, and if so, are their products easy to acquire?

- Are their items regularly reviewed by standard selection aids?

- Do special selection aids exist for health information? If so, what are some special selection tools in the area of health that are currently in print and up to date?

Governments at all levels—federal, provincial, and local agencies—produce health information. Many of these are aimed at the consumer, but how easily are these identified, described, and reviewed, and what special acquisition procedures must librarians use to procure these? A good source for information on how to manage health and medical information libraries and centers is Frank Kellerman's *Introduction to Health Sciences Librarianship: A Management Handbook.* This is part of Greenwood Press' well-regarded Library Management Collection series.

Another useful guide is the Medical Library Association's *Consumer Health Reference Service Handbook* by Donald A. Barclay and Deborah D. Halsted. This is written to help librarians understand consumer health information and to better meet the demands of health information. It annotates "hundreds of sources for consumer health information and illustrates the principles and practice of consumer-health librarianship." The book's accompanying CD-ROM provides templates for developing effective consumer health Web sites and for designing in-house consumer health information brochures.

Basic Subject Guides for Health Information Collection Development

The central characteristics to all collection developing approaches is policy formation and direction, consistency, user information needs, and good selection and review procedures ensuring accuracy, legitimacy, diversity of views, currency, and usability. A fundamental understanding of interests, needs, health subjects, and topics is essential to good selection. The following is a broad list of subjects and categories that can offer a means of helping to develop and maintain viable health information collections. These topic suggestions and the following list of selection aids have been developed around some of the major health care issues.

- Alternative and homoeopathic medicine
- Anatomy
- Biology and physiology
- Biographies (persons who have advanced health care; true medical stories and adventures)
- Biomedical approaches (engineering, materials, methods, personnel, careers, etc.)
- Community information (selected local community information featuring health care and health care information)
- Consumer education for youth, parents, and caregivers (materials in various formats that offer well-presented information for the layperson)
- Cultural and social aspects of health care (e.g., impact on cultural norms and expectations; sociology of medicine)
- Dentistry (tooth care and hygiene)
- Diseases and treatment (descriptions of diseases and their treatments)
- Ethics and responsibilities (legal and professional ethics expected of the health care system)
- Fiction and the fine arts (with medical and disease themes)
- Financing health care (procedures for determining the cost of health care)
- Emergency care and first aid
- Environment and environmental issues
- Globalization of health issues (impact of government, economic and social factors on the spread and control of diseases)

- Governmental responsibilities for health (history of governments in health care, role of government in health care, political and economic systems as determents of health care and information)
- History of diseases in society
- Holistic medicine (mind-body connections)
- Hygiene and person care (e.g., grooming and skin care)
- Institutions and groups involved in health issues
  - Hospitals
  - Research centers
  - Regional and national health centers
  - Advocacy and consumer groups
- Insurance and cost control (problems of the health insurance cost, the uninsured, universal health coverage; constraining health care cost)
- Journals (selected technical and consumer health information journals)
- Laws, legislations, and ordinances (the role of laws, legislations, and local ordinances in determining health care)
- Medical care and delivery systems
- Medical geography (the location and spread of diseases in a worldwide context)
- Medical information literacy (includes medical quackery and malpractices)
- Medicinal information technology
- Medical personnel, education and employment, careers
- Medical technology
- Medicines and pharmacology
- Mental health issues (mental illnesses, government and social support systems as well as how to adjust to and/or cope with mental illness on a personal level)
- Microbiology
- Mind and body (e.g., health-related issues, holistic health)
- Nutrition, dieting, and food
- Private industry and enterprises (the role of private industry and enterprise in health care)
- Public policies (how policies affect health care and access to health care)
- Safety issues (e.g., driving, home and workplace safety)
- Self-care (health issues)
- Sex education and sexuality
- Social roles and responsibilities for health care (policy and action)

- Sports medicine
- Veterinary medicine
- Web sites (selected international, national, and local Web sites)

Selection Aids and Finding Guides

The following is a highly selected list of selection aids and finding guides that can help in building and maintaining a viable health information collection for both school library media centers and public libraries. Most of the titles listed date from 2000, but several older aids have been included because they offer needed retrospective coverage of health-related items still available in print or available in library collections.

Selection Aids and Sources Offering Access to Health Information

Sources for selections of materials are abundant. This array of available sources contains both print and electronic sources. The three listings that follow attempt to highlight both types. Part A is devoted largely to print, with some nonprint and electronic sources included. Part B contains electronic sources, including Web sites. Part C discusses a variety of other sources including foreign-language materials and special care needs.

Part A. Combined Print and Electronic Review Sources

ALA's Guide to Best Reading (frequent editions). Chicago: American Library Association. Lists and annotates books in an ongoing series. These are considered "best" for the given year under review. Includes the best in fiction, nonfiction, and poetry books for all ages listed in Notable Children's Books, Notable Books, Editor's Choice, and Best Books for Young Adults.

ALAN Review (periodical). Offers reviews of fiction and nonfiction books of interest to young adults three times a year. It is published through the auspices of the National Council of Teachers of English with the interests of English and literature teachers keeping their students in mind (www.english.byu.edu/resources/alan).

Association for Library Service to Children. *Notable Books for Children*. Chicago: The Association for Library Service to Children, annual. Lists books considered by a committee of professionals to be the best published during the preceding year. Lists include fiction and nonfiction. The association also publishes annually its *Notable Films and Videos for Children* (http://www.ala.org/alsc). Often its listings include items related to health and society. See also Young Adult Library Services Association listed later.

Barr, Catherine, and Gillespie, John T. *Best Books for Children: Preschool through Grade 6*, 8th ed. Westport, CT: Libraries Unlimited, 2005. Includes more than 25,000 in-print titles for children in grades K–6. Arranged by themes, the concise annotations provide bibliographic information and review citations.

Beers, Kylene, and Lesesne, Teri. *Books for You: An Annotated Booklist for Senior High,* 14th ed. Urbana, IL: National Council of Teachers of English, 2001. Presents a thematic listing of more than 1,000 books for high school students. Arranged by themes, readers (teachers, librarians, students, and parents) are encouraged to explore many areas. Award-winning books are highlighted in an appendix.

The Book Report (periodical;). Continued as *Library Media Connection* Reviews print and multimedia material including online resources, software, and hardware. It considers the needs of curriculum development and highlights social themes and issues that have curriculum and information appeal. In addition to reviews, it offers advice about how to integrate books into curriculum and instruction (http://www.linworth.com/ bookreport.html).

Book Review Digest (periodical). Provides bibliographic citations and digests of reviews of books as they appear in the professional and literary press. First published by the H. W. Wilson Company in 1905, it includes children and young adult reviews along with bibliographic and acquisition information. Its electronic format is *Book Review Digest Plus,* with links to reviews it cites (www. hwwilson.com/databases/brdig.htm).

Booklist (periodical). Presents reviews of recommended books, and nonprint items, and computer programs for use in school library media centers and public libraries. Essays and reviews cover special topics such as easy-to-read and foreign language materials. Through its *Booklist Publications* imprint, it issues bibliographies, lists, and special monographs designed to help in the selection of materials (http://www.ala.org/booklist).

Books in Print (periodical). Offers convenient access to information on the availability of books within the book trade market. First published by the R. R. Bowker Company in 1948. *Subject Guide to Children's Books in Print* followed in 1970. In recent years, *Books in Print* has become more useful as a selection aid through its publishing of abstracts of reviews of selected items. Its electronic version, *Book in Print Plus,* has expanded this to include reviews of children's and young adult books as well as special services such as award books and guides to materials according to grade, reading, and special interest needs (http:// www.bowker.com).

Brown, Jean E., and Stephens, Elaine C. *Your Reading: An Annotated Booklist for Middle School and Junior High,* 11th ed. Urbana, IL: National Council of Teachers of English, 2003. Offers a variety of books, fiction and nonfiction, for the middle and junior high school child. This source is intended to be used by teachers, students, and parents in selecting good and interesting books to read.

Bulletin for the Center for Children's Books (periodical). Offers reviews of children's books and books for adolescents. Reviews are brief, but rating scales offer recommendation suggestions as well as suggested audience and uses (e.g., R for recommended, NC for those not recommended; SPC indicates that subject matter or treatment tends to limit the book to specialized collections). Reading levels for each book are also provided (http://bccb.lis.uiuc.edu).

Cassell, Ann, and Hiremath, Uma. *Reference and Information Services in the 21st Century: An Introduction.* New York: Neal-Schuman, 2006. Although this text provides only limited health information, it is a good basic source for print and electronic media most frequently used in reference work (http://www. neal-schuman.com/reference21st/index.htm).

Coping series. New York: Rosen Publishing. Intended for adolescents and addressing some of their major concerns, this series of well-reviewed books is described by the publisher as providing up-to-date information many teens need to help them make informed choices and get the support they need to control these sometimes alarming situations (http://www.rosenpublishing.com).

Dillon, Martin, and Shannon Graff. *ARBA In-depth: Health and Medicine.* Westport, CT: Libraries Unlimited, 2004. "Provides focused help for … health and medicine collection development needs. Critical reviews of quality reference titles by subject. Experts cover general and specialized titles in the areas of: Medicine, Nursing, Pharmaceutical sciences, and Nutrition." For advanced collections. http://lu.com/ showbook.cfm?isbn=9781591581222).

Gillespie, John T., and Barr, Catherine, eds. *Best Books for High School Readers: Grades 9–12. Supplement to the First Edition.* Westport, CT: Libraries Unlimited, 2006. Includes more than 2,600 highly recommended titles published from June 2004 to June 2006. Arranged thematically, this resource provides, in the words of the publisher, "state-of-the-art reading guide and selection tool for teen reading material, both fiction and nonfiction."

Health Reference Series. Detroit, MI: Omnigraphics, various dates, (http://www. omnigraphics.com). Contains a number of consumer health information titles. Some examples include:

Shannon, Joyce Brennfleck. *Adolescent Health Sourcebook: Basic Consumer Health Information about the Physical, Mental, and Emotional Growth and Development of Adolescents,* 2nd ed., 2006.

Judd, Sandra J. *Complementary and Alternative Medicine Sourcebook: Basic Consumer Health Information about Complementary and Alternative Medical Therapies,* 3rd ed., 2006.

Sutton, Amy L. *Dental Care and Oral Health Sourcebook: Basic Consumer Health Information about Dental Care, including Hygiene, Dental Visits, Pain Management, Cavities, ... Dental Implants,* 2nd ed., 2003.

The Horn Book Guide to Children's and Young Adult Books (periodical). Attempts to list and comment on all children's and young adult books published in the United States. Although comments are brief, the guide provides a rating scale indicating the quality of the book and includes a guide to genre and subject areas (http://www.hb.com/guide).

The Horn Book Magazine: About Books for Children and Young Adults (periodical). Devoted to promoting reading and culture through the reviews and critical analysis of books for children and young adults, this fine literary review and discussion journal has various sections or departments including reviews of newly published books, recommended paperbacks, new editions and reissues, and science books. Special columns are devoted to discussing young adult books, re-reviewing older books, and reviewing Canadian books. It also publishes *The Horn Book Guide,* which is a listing with annotations and brief reviews of children's and young adult books published in the United States (http://www.hbook.com). (See following description.)

Kirkus Reviews (periodical). Offers long and detailed reviews of fiction and nonfiction books for adults, adolescents, and children. Reviews are intended for booksellers and librarians and appear before the books are published, allowing librarians and bookstores to stock in anticipation of demand. The children's section that must be subscribed to apart from the basic subscription, offers special lists such as holiday books (http://www.kirkusreviews.com).

Klatt (periodical). Publishes reviews of paperback books, young adult hardcover fiction, audio books, and educational software appropriate for young adults in classrooms and libraries. Reviews cover most fields of interest including fiction, literature and language arts, biography and personal narratives, education and guidance, social studies, history and geography, sciences, the arts, and recreation. Newsletter supplements are provided (http://www.hometown.aol.com/kliatt).

Lancet (periodical). Intended primarily for physicians and other medical personnel, *Lancet,* by most accounts, is one of the oldest peer-reviewed and important international medical journals. It is important to consumers of health care information because of its international coverage of medical events and situations and its editorial approaches to important medical issues affecting society. Book reviews are included. (http://www.elsevier.com/wps/find/journaldescription. cws_home/31066/description#description).

Lester, Ray, ed. *The New Walford, Volume 1: Science, Technology, and Medicine.* New York: Neal-Schuman, 2005. Classifying more than twenty types of print and electronic reference resources, including general introductions; dictionaries, thesauri, and classifications; associations and societies; libraries, archives, and museums; digital data, image, and text collections; directories and encyclopedias including more than 150 subject areas with the guidance of over a dozen subject specialists (http://www.neal-schuman.com/db/9/519.html).

Lima, Carolyn W., and Lima, John A. *A to Zoo: Subject Access to Children's Picture Books,* 7th ed. Westport, CT: Libraries Unlimited, 2005. Includes information on fiction and nonfiction picture books for children. This has become a standard reference resource for collection development and reader's advisement that includes more than 4,000 titles published since 2001. Subject and bibliographic guides are provided along with title and illustrator indexes.

McClure, Amy A., and Kristo, Janice V. *Adventuring with Books: A Booklist for Pre-K–Grade 6,* 13th ed. Urbana, IL: National Council of Teachers of English, 2002. Lists more than 850 books published between 1999 and 2001. Entries are suitable for children for research, learning, and pleasure reading.

Nature (journal). This is one of the premier scientific journals in the world. Includes both articles and reviews. This is a necessary journal in most health information collections. It is available both in print and electronic form (archived back to 1987). http://www.nature.com/nature/index.html.

Parents' Choice Foundation (electronic resource). Provides an online source for written reviews and discussion intended for parents and educators, including librarians. Covers all areas of children's media including books, television, home video, recordings, toys, music, recordings, and computer software. (http://www.parent-choice.org).

Publishers Weekly: The Book Industry Journal (periodical). Offers broad coverage of events in the book trade including children's and young adult publishing. This trade journal covers current books just released by various publishers (http://publishersweekly.reviewsnews.com).

Rees, Alan, ed. *Consumer Health Information Source Book,* 7th ed. Westport, CT: Greenwood Press, 2003. Includes newsletters, pamphlet titles, health information clearinghouses, toll-free hotlines, health-related resource and referral organizations, online services and CD-ROM products, selected Web sites, and a listing of supportive professional medical textbooks, monographs. This is an impressive guide to popular print and electronic health information for general consumers.

School Library Journal (periodical). Serves children and young adult public librarians and school librarians as a dependable review source. It contains review sections on computer software, audiovisual media, and fiction and nonfiction books. Reviews are written by professionals knowledgeable about the needs of youth and their education (http://slj.reviewsnews.com).

Science Books and Films (periodical). Reviews are published by the American Association for the Advancement of Science in six print issues per year. It covers print, film, and software materials in all areas of the sciences for all ages. Reviews are directed at all types of librarians and educators. *Science Books and Films Online* is its companion that is included in a subscription to the periodical (http://www.sbfonline.com).

Sexuality Information and Education Council of the United States (SIECUS). *Guidelines for Comprehensive Sexuality Education*, 3rd ed. (New York: SIECUS, 2004). Outlines the council's approach to sexual health (http://www.siecus.org/pubs/guidelines/guidelines.pdf).

Teacher Librarian: The Journal for School Library Professionals (periodical). Addressing the needs of professionals who work with children and young adults, this independent school library journal reviews books and nonprint media. It also features articles on current issues and trends. Reviews cover children and young adult books, new nonfiction, best-sellers, video materials, computer software, and Internet resources. It also profiles authors and illustrators (http://www.teacherlibrarian.com).

Voice of Youth Advocates (VOYA) (periodical). Reviews films, video games, and fiction of all kinds. This hard-hitting review and discussion journal is intended to help librarians who work with adolescents. It provides good coverage of nonfiction items including health related issues.(http://www.voya.com).

H.W. Wilson Co. *Wilson Core Collections* offers several basic guides to collection development. These include *Children's Core Collection. Middle and Junior Core Collection*, and the *Senior High Core Collection*. Guides in this series present "standard" or "core" collections of titles based on expert recommendations for elementary, middle, junior high, and senior high school library media centers. In keeping with the company's philosophy of service, all recommendations made by this series are based on professional, expert opinion. Yearly supplements are published for each title in the series listing new materials as well as newer editions of older works. In 2000, all titles in the Core Collection series became available in electronic format.

H. W. Wilson Co. *Vertical File Index* (periodical). Provides specialized subject index to pamphlets issued by a broad range of public and private sources features information on important topics (such as health and health care) often unavailable in book form (http://www.hwwilson.com/print/vfi.html).

Young Adult Library Services Association (YALSA). *Best Books for Young Adults.* Chicago: YALSA, annual. This list offers a well-selected listing of titles including both fiction and nonfiction, with an abundant selection of fine biographies (http://www.ala.org/ala/yalsa/booklistsawards/outstandingbooks/ outstandingbooks.htm). The association also issues *Best Films and Videos for Young Adults* annually. Other titles published by YALSA include *Outstanding Books for the College Bound* (2004), *More Outstanding Books for the College Bound* (2005), *Best Books for Young Adults* (2005), *Popular Paperbacks for Young Adults, Selected Audiobooks for Young Adults*, and *Selected DVDs & Videos for Young Adults*.

Part B. Electronic Sources

AIDSinfo. This is a service of the NLM, offering information on a variety of topics concerning HIV, the virus that causes AIDS. Major categories include clinical trials, translation tools, live help, HIV/AIDS glossary, drugs, vaccines, and health management topics (http://www.aidsinfo.nih.gov).

Alternative Medicine Homepage. Falk Library of the Health Sciences, University of Pittsburgh, Pittsburgh, Pennsylvania. Offers "a jumpstation for sources of information on unconventional, unorthodox, unproven, or alternative, complementary, innovative, integrative therapies" (http://www.pitt.edu/~cbw/ altm.html).

Alt HealthWatch. EBSCO. "[I]ndexes over 140 full-text journals concerning complementary, holistic or alternative healthcare and wellness. 28 of these journals are peer reviewed.... In addition, the database includes full-text pamphlets and reports" (http://library.boisestate.edu/reference/help/althealthwatch. htm).

American Medical Association Home Page. Provides information on American medicine and concerns for medical care; includes list of the association's publications, most of which are technical in nature (http://www.ama-assn.org).

Anderson, P. F., and Nancy Alleen, eds. *The Medical Library Association Encyclopedic Guide to Searching and Finding Health Information on the Web.* 3 vols. New York: Neal-Schuman, 2004. Provides Information on how to search the Web for health information, as well as information on illnesses and other aspects of health care.

BBC. Offers a number of useful Web sites dealing with health. Its "BBC Schools: Learning Resources for Home and School," along with other topics, provides useful health and socially related information associated with the British national curriculum (http://www.bbc.co.uk/schools). An abundance of health information is found throughout its postings, including "BBC Health" (http://www.bbc.co.uk/health).

"CAPHIS Top 100 List" is a list of 100 recommended high-quality health information Web sites. These sites are evaluated by CAPHIS according to currency, credibility, content, and audience. Some site categories of interest to youth librarians include: General Health, Parenting and Kids, Specific Health Problems, For Health Professionals, and Drug Information Resources. CAPHIS is the Consumer and Patient Health Information Section of the Medical Library Association (http://caphis.mlanet.org/consumer/index.html).

Child Advocate Home Page. Child Advocate and Child Mental Health. As stated by the publisher, "ChildAdvocate.net serves the needs of children, families and professionals while addressing mental health, medical, educational, legal and legislative issues." Provides references to health sources (http://www.childadvocate.net/).

Cool Nurse. Living Healthy Inc. Offers more topics than many other Web sites. Topics include prescription drug abuse, a condom tutorial, depression, diets, tattoos and body art, and anorexia and bulimia. It presents the tough topics on the homepage, addresses them head on. One section is for women and one for men. The site offers quizzes, a place to ask questions, and hotline numbers (http://www.coolnurse.com).

Consumer Health Complete. EBSCO. Provides "content covering all areas of health and wellness from mainstream medicine to the many perspectives of complementary, holistic, and integrated medicine." The publisher adds that this is "the single most comprehensive resource for consumer-oriented health content.... This full-text database covers topics such as aging, cancer, diabetes, drugs & alcohol, fitness, nutrition & dietetics, men's & women's health, and children's health" (http://www.ebsco.com/home/whatsnew/consumer_health.asp).

eLibrary Curriculum Edition. ProQuest. Contains reference materials, periodical, and digital items and includes health and medical information and a knowledge base of educational standards. A curriculum and reference resource for grades K–12 (http://www.proquestk12.com/productinfo/elibrary_ce.shtml).

Facts on File's Health Reference Center. Facts on File Inc. "[A] comprehensive encyclopedic database containing thousands of hyperlinked entries organized into four major categories: conditions and diseases, mental health, health and wellness, and body systems. It provides clear information on the causes, cures, key research, medical terms, symptoms, treatments and trends, and organizations in each field of study. Each content area is searchable by keyword and [an index]." List of links also allows the user to easily find more focused topics within each of the content areas (http://www.factsonfile.com).

GlobalHealthGuideInfo. Offers a user-friendly approach to a wide range of preselected consumer information topics (http://globalhealthguide.info).

GrolierOnline. Grolier. Constructed around the company's seven encyclopedia databases, this online system contains "age-appropriate" information and resources, including health information. For more information, visit http://auth.grolier.com/login/go_login.html.

Health and Wellness Center. Thomson Gale. "Provides reference material as well as full text periodicals and pamphlets from a wide variety of authoritative medical sources" (http://www.gale.com/HealthRC).

Health Information for Teens. United States Food and Drug Administration. Provides a serious approach to health issues of interest to adolescents. Information provided includes drug and alcohol use and abuse, birth control methods, and information on diseases that often affect teens such as mononucleosis (http://www.fda.gov/oc/opacom/kids/html/7teens.htm).

Health Library. EBSCO. "Offers a Web-based resource for their patrons to examine a comprehensive coverage of health, wellness, and other medical-related topics presented in an easy-to-understand manner" (http://www.epnet.com/thisTopic.php?topicID=81&marketID=6).

Health Source—Consumer Edition. EBSCO. "Provides access to the full-text of over 190 journals covering authoritative health information for consumers. Several health books and over 1000 health-related pamphlets are also available." Information about this source is available through the EBSCO Student Research Center (http://www.epnet.com/thisTopic.php?marketID=6&topicID=13).

Kid's Home Page. United States Food and Drug Administration. Especially designed for children, offers information on animals, news items, medical and drug vocabulary, fun quizzes, medicines in the home, wearing braces, links to other children's sites, feature item "Yorick, the Bionic Skelton," and a "parent corner" (http://www.fda.gov/oc/opacom/kids/default.htm).

Let's Face It. (Newsletter). University of Michigan School of Dentistry, Dentistry Library. Provides information and resources, including reviews of materials especially useful for dental and teeth care. Updated frequently (http://www.dent.umich.edu/faceit/organizations).

Medical Library Association. Concerned with making health care information accessible to medical professionals as well as to the general public for more than

100 years, the association's publication programs include a variety of pamphlet materials aimed at the health information consumer (http://www.mlanet.org).

National Library of Medicine Databases (NLM). Provides useful electronic databases offering extensive and freely accessible medical information from throughout the world. The services include MEDLINE, MedlinePlus, and PubMed. PubMed offers information in addition to that on MEDLINE (the primary citation database) including links to consumer health information. MedlinePlus is designed to be of use to the general public, and it has features that are user-friendly and that have subject approaches that have been preformulated with MEDLINE. All of these databases are described by NLM at http://www.nlm.nih.gov.

Native Health Databases. University of New Mexico Health Sciences Library and Information Center. "Contains bibliographic information and abstracts of health-related articles, reports, surveys, and other resource documents pertaining to the health and health care of American Indians, Alaska Natives, and Canadian First Nations" (http://hsc.unm.edu/library/nhd/index.cfm).

Natural & Alternative Treatments. EBSCO, NAT. Offers a complementary and alternative medicine database designed specifically for the consumer health researcher. Updated weekly (http://www.epnet.com/thisTopic.php?marketID=15&topicID=114).

NetWellness: Consumer Health Information. This is "a nonprofit site that offers high quality health information and educational services created and evaluated by the faculty of three major universities: University of Cincinnati, Case Western Reserve University, and The Ohio State University." The site gives comprehensive information on selected health topics. In addition, it offers information on health centers and provides access to an online reference collection. Experts are also available to answer questions from site users (http://www.netwellness.com/default.cfm).

NIH Curriculum Supplement Series. A series of interactive teaching units that combines cutting-edge science research discoveries from the National Institutes of Health.

Project Inform. A national, community-based organization that provides people living with HIV, their caregivers, and health care providers reliable and up-to-date information on treatments and HIV disease monitoring. In addition to providing information, it advocates for better services and encourages people to make informed health care decisions (http://www.projinf.org.html).

TeenGrowth. KG Investments. Provides real-world answers and options including birth control, pregnancy, and personal hygiene. Includes fun trivia and quizzes where teens can test their knowledge of pregnancy and sex (http://www.teengrowth.com).

Teen Health & Wellness: Real Life, Real Answers, Rosen Publishing Online. Based on the extensive line of health books for teens in the publisher's Coping series, this interactive database "provides students with comprehensive curricular support and self-help tools on topics including diseases, drugs, alcohol, nutrition, fitness, mental health, diversity, family life, and more." *Library Journal* said this about this one-stop self-help resource: "fully interactive online community center for teen health and wellness . . . authoritative." The site offers an interactive hotline service available only by subscription. (http://www.thwrlra.com/static/publicabout).

Teenage Health Freak. Teen Age Health Websites. Provides information written in diary and cartoon form which is a visually interesting approach to health information of interest to teens. Information is often given in diary or conversational form and includes information on sexually transmitted infections, smoking, weight and body images, moods, and cold sores (http://www.teenagehealthfreak.org/homepage/index.asp).

TeensHealth. Nemours Foundation. Provides subject categories such as body, sexual health, and drugs and alcohol with links to featured articles, hot topics, expert answers, journals, and so on. Offers clear and concise answers to health-related topics, in language the teens can understand. The Web site is also available in Spanish (http://www.kidshealth.org/teen).

United States Food and Drug Administration (FDA) Home Page. Offers links on the central homepage for the FDA to an abundance of information concerned with its governmental mission and mandates. Included here are a wide variety of health information, such as food safety and regulations, drugs, medical devices, biologics, cosmetics, and radiation safety and issues (http://www.fda.gov/default.htm).

University of Texas Health Science Center at San Antonio. *Multidiscipline Health Science Curriculum.* Contains a extensive amount of teaching materials of interest to teachers and youth . Available at: http://teachhealthk-12.uthscsa.edu/curriculum.htm

Part C. Other Important Considerations

Health Books and Films in Series

A great many books on health are published in series by various publishers. A direct approach to finding such series is through any of the book acquisition services. For example, using the keywords "health series" in *Books in Print* electronic database within its "Children's Room" section and limiting the search by the various options will most likely produce a number of hits, with many of these including reviews as well as annotations. Publishers indexed here include Franklin Watts' Human Health and Disease series (Scholastic), Curriculum Concepts (New Zealand), Image Paths Inc., Heinemann Library, Scholastic, Marshall Cavendish, and Kids for Health. Kids for Health also has a series of heath-related videos.

Sources of Pamphlets and Brochures

As mentioned earlier, many associations such as the Medical Library Association have pamphlets and brochures that relate specifically to health issues. The *Vertical File Index,* published by H. W. Wilson, is another source for finding such materials, as is ETR Associates, a nonprofit organization founded in 1981 with the mission of improving the health of families and individuals. Its publication program includes more than 1,000 pamphlets, books, posters, flip charts, displays, curricula, and videos (http://www.etr.org).

Materials in Other Languages and Cultural Contexts

Although dated now, *Informacion de Salud para los Consumidores,* edited by Alan Rees and published by Oryx Press of Phoenix in 1998, provides a good example of a type of guide that is always needed. This publication describes various consumer health brochures and pamphlets in Spanish issued by several U.S. federal and nonprofit agencies, including the National Cancer Institute, the Food and Drug Administration, and the Leukemia Society of America. The Internet now meets some of the information needs provided by this type of publication. Most if not all of these types of agencies and organizations include foreign language materials in their Web site postings. In addition to Spanish, Web sites often include materials in other languages, particularly Asian languages. The National Library of Medicine, the Department of Health and Human Resources, and other U.S. government agencies list their non-English publication through their many Web sites.

French Language Resources include:

In France:

- The French Ministry of Health provides information on research and health services at its official Web site http://www.sante.gouv.fr/drees/index.html. The ministry also addresses the needs of families, including health needs of children at this site (http://www.famille.gouv.fr).

- Health resources in France include government ministries and organizations that advocate for good health. Among these is Fondation Hôpitaux de Paris-Hôpitaux de France. This foundation is concerned with various aspects of health and in this role undertakes projects for children and adolescents who are ill and need health care (http://www.fondation-wyeth.org/rss_view.aspx?id=74).

In Canada:

- "CUSMeF-Patienets santé de l'enfant et de l'adolescent," operated by CHU Hôpitaux de Roaen, publishes the "Catalogue et Index des Sites Médicaux Francophones," which lists many French-language health resources throughout the world (http://www.cismef.org).

- French Language Health Services of the Ontario Ministry of Health and Long-Term Care also provides access to French-language materials (http://www.health.gov. on.ca/english/public/program/flhs/flhs_mn.html).

- The Société Canadienne de Pédiatrie is a professional association of pedestrians organized in 1922 to address the health needs of children. Its publication program provides useful information for persons who need help in meeting the medical needs of children http://www.cps.ca/Francais/defensedinterets/autochtones.htm).

The Weill Cornell Medical Library (Cornell University) published an extensive list of foreign-language consumer health materials available throughout the world in 2001. One feature of this listing is its introduction, which gives details on how to locate and evaluate foreign language materials (http://library.med.cornell.edu/Library/PDF/forlangcons.pdf).

The Medical Health Library at George Washington University maintains *Publicaciones en Español de la Administración de Drogas y Alimentos de los Estados Unidos* that list a great many American government publications in Spanish (http://www.fda.gov/oc/spanish).

Cultural and religious considerations are also important. In addition to language, some health care materials recognize the importance of culture and religion as well. For a listing of such materials consult *Health Materials in Languages Other than English* by Jacquelyn Coughlan (2006) available through the Web site of the State University of New York Institute of Technology (http://culturedmed.sunyit.edu/foreign/index.html).

Resources for Special Needs Children and Their Parents

Many advocacy and care groups exist for the support of children, parents, and caregivers of youth with special needs. A comprehensive and peer-reviewed list of support materials entitled *Knowledge Path: Children and Adolescents with Special Health Care Needs,* developed by Susan B. Lorenzo, is available through the Medical Health Center at George Washington University. This document includes references and descriptions of health hotlines, Web sites, electronic publications, print materials, databases, electronic newsletters and discussion groups. Search protocols are also included for locating specific subjects within various sites (http://www.mchlibrary.info/KnowledgePaths/kp_CSHCN.html).

Exceptional Parent Annual Resource Guide (published annually in January by Psy-Ed Corp, Oradell, NJ) provides guidance on specific disabilities, parent support, and assistive technology. It is also available through the Emergency Medical Services for Children (EMSC) at http://www.eplibrary.com/directories. EMSC offers other materials of interest to families with special needs children and youth.

Conclusion

As stated in the introduction to this chapter, health information is so abundant that its identification and selection can be an overwhelming task. Nevertheless, youth librarians have the expertise to engage successfully in this selection and acquisition process. Because of their unique perspective, they can also influence what is produced and published in health care information that will be of special use to youth. New technology also allows them to be involved in health care information dissemination through the design and promotion of health care information and current awareness services. Web sites and other electronic devices available to or managed by youth librarians in public and school libraries offer useful ways to promote health care information. Along with others who work with youth, librarians can make a difference in the health and welfare of youth throughout the world.

Chapter 12

Censorship, the Law, and Access to Health Information

Introduction

In previous chapters, we have discussed the need for health information for youth, the kinds of health information available, and the ways to bring care health information to youth. In this chapter, we consider some of the legal challenges that public and school librarians face in providing care health information as well as the obligations they face in seeing that appropriate health information is available to youth and their families. These obligations include understanding legal and court rulings concerning how and by whom health information may be provided. Although the legal examples are American, their underlying principles can apply to many other countries facing similar problems of providing access to health care information.

As we know, many of the types of health information needed by youth are controversial. These controversies are not only about birth control and family planning issues; even topics such as human anatomy can be attacked. An example of this is the concern voiced by some American school librarians regarding the 2007 Newbery winner, *The Higher Power of Lucky* by Susan Patron, illustrated by Matt Phelan (Atheneum/ Richard Jackson Books, 2006). The controversy is based on the book's mention of "scrotum" in reference to a dog's genitals. Teacher-librarian Dana Nilsson of Durango, Colorado, explained her objection to the book in this way:

> Part of my job is to introduce students to quality, age-appropriate literature. I would not be doing my job if I booktalked or recommended this book to young audiences. This book has some great qualities—it shows a girl in an insecure situation wanting stability in her life. The inclusion of genitalia does not add to the story one bit and that is my objection.[1]

Some argue that "scrotum" is a scientifically appropriate word, and, on the basis of sound sex education principles, using the word in the context of a story seems an appropriate way to introduce acceptable scientific vocabulary to children.

Anatomy has always been problematic for adults when faced with presenting anatomical facts to children and youth. This reluctance is longstanding and is probably based on religious considerations coming from Christian and Jewish traditions where nakedness was often associated with shame and rejection.

Early sex education materials encouraged this view. Figure 12.1 is an illustration from a book by Lyman Beecher Sperry titled *Confidential Talks to Young Men*, and it clearly shows the reluctance of the author to deal realistically with male genitalia.

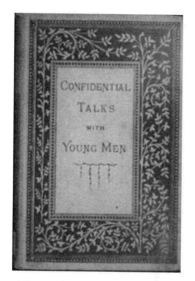
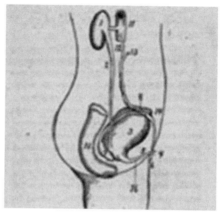

Figure 12.1. Male genitalia illustration from *Confidential Talks with Young Men*, published by F. H. Revell Co., 1893.

Censorship issues such as that presented in the Patron book will always arise, and procedures and policies must be developed to deal with censorship and the restriction of access to materials and information in accordance with laws and sound educational principles. As with any selection and acquisition issue, health information materials must be selected according to clear guidelines and policies. This includes not only books and reference materials, but also Web sites and their links. Customarily censorship issues are also more directed at school library materials and use in public schools than in public libraries.

English Law and the U.S. Legal Understanding of Obscenity

The basic reason for complaints and attempts to censor school library materials stems from conflicts in values and the fear that values differing from those of the immediate family, community, and perceived national values will cause harm to individuals, as well as to society and culture in general. U.S. law and court interpretations have some ambiguity concerning the rights of minors to receive information in comparison with rights of parents to control and direct the kinds of information minors may or may not receive in a public forum such as a school environment underscores legal ambiguity. This is particularly true regarding the rights of mature minors to receive information on such health-related topics as abortion, contraception, and sexual health.[2]

Laws regarding obscenity attempt to be clear, and adjudicated obscenity has no protection under the U.S. constitutional law. Challenges to health materials for youth are seldom based on charges of obscenity. Rather the concern centers on age appropriateness that can be used to justify the censorship and exclusion of certain health materials.

The United States and Canada, as well as other English-speaking countries, have been greatly influenced by English Common Law. Many of these countries' early censorship laws were directly influenced by both the common law and by English legislation and court rulings. Legal experts contend that modern English censorship laws began with the British Obscene Publication Act (Lord Campbell's Act) of 1857 and was further codified in *The Queen v. Hicklin* (L.R. 3Q.B.360) of 1869 in which the English high court ruled that the test of literary morality was "whether the tendency of the matter charged as obscenity is to deprave and corrupt." In this ruling, the test of obscenity as applied by the court was whether a father could read a work aloud in his own home. On the basis of this ruling, many literary works were seized, their authors and publishers prosecuted and books destroyed. In 1913, in *United States v. Kennerly* (209 F. 119), although sympathetic to the free expression of ideas, a court ruled against the defendant because the publication under review fell within the limits of the *Hicklin* test.

Even in its time the *Hicklin* legal test for obscenity was criticized for reducing literary standards to what was morally proper for the young and for forcing authors to avoid or distort social reality. This test of obscenity remained in British law for a century and in U.S. law until the 1930s.[3] In 1954, an English legal interpretation set aside the *Hicklin* test and established a distinction between "filth for filth's sake and literature." An English court judge ruled that literature should not be condemned because it deals with the realities of "life, love, and sex" and instructed the jury that sex is not dirty or a sin and that the literary-moral-legal test ought not to be what is suitable for a fourteen-year-old schoolgirl to read.[4,5]

In the 1973 landmark case of *Miller v. California* (413 U.S. 15), the U.S. Supreme Court decided what was meant to be a clear and unambiguous test of obscenity. *Miller* remains the fundamental legal guide and test for obscenity in the United States today. The basic guidelines which came out of this ruling involved whether

- the average person, applying contemporary community standards, would find that the work, taken as a whole, appeals to the prurient interest;

- the work depicts or describes in a patently offensive way sexual conduct specifically defined by the applicable state law; and

- the work taken as a whole lacks serious literary, artistic, political or scientific value.[6]

In this ruling, Justice Warren E. Burger reinstated the principle that community standards as applied in the *Miller* standards meant statewide standards, not just the standards prevailing in the local trial community.[7]

Although many First Amendment scholars consider the current American approach to regulating indecency as flawed and inconsistent, U.S. federal law and state laws today require that for items to be adjudicated "obscene" under law, they must be judged on the above tier of facts.

The U.S. Constitution is a rigid document. That is, it cannot be changed though normal legislative actions or mandates. The right of the American judiciary to interpret the meaning of the U.S. Constitution was established by the Supreme Court in 1803 in *Marbury v. Madison* (*Marbury v. Madison*, 1 Cranch 137, 5 U.S. 137 [1803]). This ruling meant that all laws, regulations, ordinances, and orders passed by governments and boards, including public library and school boards, that act under the authority of governments must conform to the principles of the Constitution.

Overview of Court Rulings Affecting School Library Collections

Important American court rulings that affect school library collections include *Tinker v. Des Moines Independent School District* (393 U.S. 503) in which the Supreme Court recognized in 1969 that students hold First Amendment rights, but a school board can place limits on those rights for good cause based on conduct that is disruptive to work and discipline of the school. In June 2007, the Supreme Court ruled in favor of Morse, thereby placing some limits on students' free speech within school environments (*Morse, Deborah, et al. v. Frederick,* Joseph MORSE v. FREDERICK [No. 06-278] 439 F. 3d 1114, reversed and remanded).[8] In 1972, in *President's Council, District 25 v. Community School Board No. 25* (457 F 2d 289), a U.S. court of appeals upheld the rights of a school board to remove *Down These Mean Streets* by Piri Thomas from libraries in the district. This court saw no infringements on First Amendment rights of students and considered that the board had acted in its role as guardian of public education. This ruling was important because it gave much power to local school authorities to control the contents of library collections.

Later a different court took another line of reasoning when it stated in *Minarcini v. Stongsville City School District* (541 F 2d 577) that the school board had overstepped its authority when it ordered the removal of Joseph Heller's *Catch-22* and Kurt Vonnegut's *Cat's Cradle* from its school libraries. This court saw the school library as a storehouse of knowledge and a privilege that had been created for students by the state and that such a right could not be taken away from them through the removal of books based on the board's displeasure with them.

Shortly thereafter in *Right to Read Defense Committee v. School Committee of the City of Chelsea* (454 F Supp. 703), a federal court ruled that the board had no right to remove *Male and Female under Eighteen: Frank Comments from Young People about Their Sex Roles*, edited by Nancy Larrick and Eve Merriam (1973), from the school library. In this ruling, the court stated that the school board did not have an absolute right to remove books from the library, that there were good public policy reasons for the school board not to have unquestioned power to censor, and that students have a right to read and to be exposed to controversial thoughts and language. This court held that such rights were subject to First Amendment protection.

In 1982, the U.S. Supreme Court handed down an important ruling concerning the removal of books from school libraries. *Board of Education, Island Trees, New York v. Pico* (457 U.S. 853, 867 [1982]), is considered one of the most important cases directly involving school libraries to reach the U.S. Supreme Court. The argument brought to the court on March 2, 1982, involved a situation in which the Board of Education of the Island Trees School District in the Long Island area of New York had removed several books from a high school library in the district without consideration of existing school policy. The central question presented to the court was this: Can a school board remove books from a school library in promoting moral, social, and political values and be consistent with the First Amendment?

Issues raised by this question centered on the motivation of the school board and the students' rights to receive information. In a five-to-four decision (a plurality), the court ruled in favor of the plaintiffs by declaring that a board of education cannot simply remove books because of the ideas, values, and opinions expressed in them.

In this ruling, the court defined the right of students to receive ideas and the right to learn as an "inherent corollary of rights of free speech and press," and it affirmed the right to receive information in a number of contexts. Through this ruling, students became beneficiaries of First Amendment rights ensuring access to information in school libraries. *Pico* gives further support to students' right to learn from materials already available, and it lends approval to such educational goals as encouraging individual autonomy and the appreciation of diverse points of view. As such, the ruling protects against the removal of books based on ideological content.[9]

Nonetheless, the court did allow books to be removed by boards of education for sound educational reasons and for legitimate purposes of limiting students' exposure to vulgarity. Nevertheless, the board's reasons for removal of books from libraries must be based on educational grounds that, if challenged, must stand up under court review.

Writing in the *Texas Law Review* in 1983, Tyll Van Geel outlined some of the issues and judicial conflicts and interpretations that faced the court in deciding this case. For example, the justices at both the Supreme Court and in lower courts had to face the three basic points: 1) the students' rights regarding freedom of belief, 2) the rationale for the government's desire to indoctrinate students, and 3) the role of the judiciary in protecting First Amendment rights within the context of public education. In an earlier ruling, the Supreme Court had recognized and protected students' rights to free speech and had insisted that schools remain a marketplace of ideas rather than as an institution to foster a homogenous nation. The court also insisted that public school officials cannot impose a "pall of orthodoxy" on the classroom.[10]

On the other hand, the Supreme Court and lower court rulings had likewise recognized the legitimate function of public schools to properly inculcate students. Such indications from the courts continue to give support to those who wish to have the rights of school authorities enforced and protected in overseeing policies and procedures such as the selection of materials for classrooms and libraries.[11]

First Amendment rights and challenges to government officials' decisions to remove materials from a school library could not be easily approached by the court in *Pico* using the traditional means of resolving First Amendment conflicts. The central test presented to the court was whether an order by a governing board to remove books is based on reasonableness and legitimate pedagogical concerns. The *Pico* decision also underscored the court's view that students not only have a right to receive information but also to learn and to be taught.

Although the court was clear to say that this ruling concerned only the removal of books from a school library by a board, it did present other constitutional issues. The role of government in restraining free speech of individuals is not clear or obvious when a government refuses to purchase a book for a library. As mentioned earlier, with *Pico* and other rulings, the court indicated that governmental boards may not prescribe orthodoxies to be adhered to within a school by the withdrawal of unacceptable books from a school library. The removal of books from libraries may be challenged on this as well on grounds that such removal is a violation of the right to receive information.

The selection and acquisition of materials might also be challenged if it is clear that the refusal to purchase certain items is a clear and persistent practice that in effect prevents certain ideas from being made available to students. Courts have recognized that a school librarian cannot buy all books or materials relating to a topic or idea and that officials must make decisions about what will be acquired, but *Pico* implied that constitutional rights have been violated if it can be shown that a persistent pattern of refusal to purchase certain types of materials is present. Records of selection decisions and official selection policies can possibly be used by courts in deciding whether unconstitutional practices have been systematically practiced.[12]

In line with rulings in *Pico*, Van Geel argued that to test whether government has impinged on First Amendment rights of free speech, courts must consider the motives of boards when they refuse to allow the purchase of materials and whether those motives present governmental restraint on the right of free speech for private individuals.[13] Courts have also implied that if a book has been removed from a library and if as a result of this removal students cannot gain access to the book through other means, then in effect they have been denied access to this material, and their constitutional rights may have been violated.[14]

Pico is now a legal standard set by the Supreme Court that lower courts follow in their determination of whether the First Amendment rights of students regarding library collections have been violated. For some years after the ruling, however, some observers felt that the educational justification for removal of books from libraries was so broad or "camouflaged" that the ruling would be of little help in the fight against school library censorship.[15] Nevertheless, the influence of *Pico* has slowly begun to appear in court rulings and legal reviews relating to both school libraries and other information-access issues.

In 1995, a federal district court found that the school board of the Unified School District no. 233 in Kansas had violated the First Amendment rights of its students by ordering the removal of *Annie on My Mind* by Nancy Garden from a school library in the district (*Case v. Unified School District No. 233*, (908 F Supp. 864, 1995). The court ruled, based on *Pico*, that books may be removed if they are "pervasively vulgar" or lacking in "educational suitability," but it is unconstitutional to do so if such removal will deny students access to ideas with which school officials disagree. In this case, school board members claimed that the book was removed by board vote because it was "educationally unsound," but testimony in the four-day trail convinced the court that the board had violated First Amendment rights because the court found considerable evidence of "viewpoint discrimination" on the part of the board. The court reasoned that the board had interpreted "educational unsoundness" to mean anything "other than their own disagreement with the ideas expressed in the book." The book in question had received numerous literary recognitions, including being selected by the American Library Association as one of the "Best of the Best" books for young adults. This judgment against the school district cost them more than $85,000 in court costs and fees.[16,17]

Censorship, the Internet, and the Impact of *Pico*

In recent rulings, the U.S. Supreme Court has extended to the Internet the highest level of First Amendment protection, and in doing so, the court has recognized the Internet's enormous reach and public forum appeal. In ruling that much of the Communication Decency Act of 1996 was unconstitutional, the high court recognized that Internet speech is to be afforded "strict scrutiny standards" for free speech (47 U.S.C. 230, 560-61) (declared unconstitutional in *Reno v. ACLU*, (521 U.S. 844 [1997]).

Strict scrutiny standards are the highest levels of constitutional tests that courts can consider in determining constitutional issues. The court in its ruling recognized that the government did have a legitimate interest in protecting children from harmful content found on the Internet, but it felt that some sections of the law as written were too broad to achieve that goal and that these sections would suppress a far greater spectrum of speech than was constitutionally permissible.[18] Regarding Internet access, it must not be forgotten that in *Pico,* the Supreme Court also established a broad rationale that students using school libraries have a "right to receive" information.

In early 2001, the Children's Internet Protection Act (CIPA) became law. The law specifies that schools and libraries that receive specific federal aid must protect children against receiving objectionable content via Internet transmissions. The law required schools to adopt Internet safety policies, to hold at least one public meeting to address the proposed policy, and to provide technology protection measures (i.e., filtering devices). According to statements made by those responsible for the law, safeguards were taken to ensure that the law was constitutionally sound based on prior court rulings regarding access to the Internet.

The American Library Association (ALA) believed strongly that CIPA was unconstitutional in the context of both the school and the public library. Nevertheless, ALA held that it lacked the legal standing to bring a lawsuit on behalf of schools that are fund recipients under the statute. Although not of direct benefit to school librarians, sections of CIPA were declared unconstitutional by a three-judge panel in the Eastern District of Pennsylvania in the spring of 2002. This ruling supported ALA's argument that the law violates constitutional principles. The judicial panel representing the court was not asked to address the school library section of the law and that part of the law remained in effect. In June 2002 the federal government announced that it would appeal this panel's interpretation to the Supreme Court. The U.S. Supreme Court in *United States v. American Library Association, Inc.* (02-361) (201 F Supp. 2d. 401, reversed) ruled in June 2003 that the law was constitutional, thus requiring public and school libraries to filter if they receive any federal funds. Nevertheless, the school library portion of the law has not been challenged and in theory remains untested in terms of its constitutionality.

The Commission on Online Child Protection, established in 1988, concluded that the most effective means for controlling children's access to objectionable online content was best set at the local level rather than through legislative mandates. Rather than relying on broad blocking technologies, which can negatively affect the instructional value of the Internet, the American Civil Liberties Union (ACLU) recommended that libraries identify and publicize links to age-appropriate content and that in public library situations privacy areas for viewing be maintained. In school situations, the ACLU and others recognized that teachers have a responsibility to guide and teach students the proper use of information found on the Internet.[19] The ruling of the Supreme Court in the CIPA case now makes these recommendations moot in cases in which libraries rely on federal support for these aspects of information technology.

To complicate further the issues involved in how governments can protect children from pornography and obscene materials on the Internet, in March 2007, in *ACLU v. Gonzales,* a lower court rejected the 1998 Child Online Protection Act (COPA) as unconstitutional because of its broadness and its effects on limiting free speech.[20]

Legal Considerations and the Rights of Youth

Legal theories are important in the study of censorship relating to information found in libraries because they can inform courts of developing issues, problems, and consensus within the legal community regarding questions of constitutional law. These legal theories and some court decisions in recent decades have added to the complexity of school library collection development and the responsibilities of librarians by widening the concept of the Free Speech Clause of the U.S. Constitution. This complexity is exacerbated through the introduction of a number of legal issues regarding youth and their rights. These concepts include the "right to receive information," "the right to receive information by mature minors independent of parents," "viewpoint discrimination," "content bias" "content neutral decisions," "content-based regulations," "the library as a government created 'public forum,' " forbidding schools to "impose orthodoxy in matters of opinions" while still allowing the "inculcating [of] values," "government speech, "government as educator," "educational speech," and "strict scrutiny [constitutional review] standards."[21-23] All of these legal concepts influence the development of school library collections for health information and offer direction for the roles and behaviors of school librarians, administrators, and school governing boards.

To reintroduce the concept of information needs for mature adolescents, Catherine J. Ross, in her article "An Emerging Right for Mature Minors to Receive Information" published in the *University of Pennsylvania Journal of Constitutional Law* (December 1999), considered the question of whether mature adolescents have constitutional rights to information that might be denied to them by parents and other authorities. She was particularly concerned about birth control and abortion information. As *Pico* indicates, the removal of books from libraries may be challenged on grounds that removal of books from a school library may be a violation of the right of students to receive information.

What Do School Librarians Know about Law and First Amendment Rights?

A 2002 study of school librarians in Texas indicated that school librarians may know little about court rulings concerning censorship and the free speech rights of students.[24] This study used a 71percent stratified random sample of school librarians from 207 schools in a region served by an education service center located in central Texas. The service area is comprised of 16 counties and represents small and large schools, as well as rural and metropolitan population areas. A 51 percent ($N = 105$) return of usable questionnaires was obtained. The sample and responses appeared to reflect the study population.

Frequency and percentage data suggest that school librarians in this survey were not well informed regarding federal court rulings regarding school library censorship. This may imply that they may not completely understand students' First Amendment rights of free speech and their rights to receive information. This showed a lack of knowledge of *Pico*.

When given the opportunity to consider the basic reasoning of the court regarding *Pico,* librarians generally agreed with the court. Findings in this study suggested that higher levels of education and librarian certification, higher levels of money spent on collection development, perception of a more liberal community, and higher levels of awareness regarding court rulings pertaining to school library censorship promoted a more proactive attitude to resist censorship. Based on principles of moral reasoning, Frances McDonald found that higher levels of education, service in larger size schools, service in higher grade levels, and membership in national and state associations suggested more acceptance of intellectual freedom principles and more positive attitudes in terms of resisting censorship. However, McDonald noted that there was more acceptance of intellectual freedom principles than with actual application.[25]

School librarians in the study generally believed that they would not feel threatened in having to explain *Pico* and its implications to their administrators. They also believed that their administrators would offer support to them in a censorship complaint. Terri Vrabel also found in a study of Texas school librarians that administrators supported librarians involved in censorship challenges.[26]

On the basis of a series of hypothetical questions presented to those in the survey, a large majority stated that they would accept with reluctance an order from their school boards to remove items from their collections. Sixteen percent indicated that they would challenge such orders and present evidence of legal problems that could arise from a removal order. Only a small minority indicated that they would remove an item without question.

When asked hypothetically if they did not agree with a removal order and wanted to resist it, to which outside sources of help might they turn? Librarians saw parents as being of little help and would not turn to them for help. This may not be surprising, as Katherine Chandler[27] and Vrabel discovered that parents instigated the majority of external censorship complaints. Chandler also found that librarians accounted for most of the internal school censorship challenges to materials. Participants viewed the Texas Library Association (TLA) and the American Library Association (ALA) as primary sources of help when faced with censorship attempts. This is somewhat surprising because rarely do these associations offer help directly to individual librarians involved in censorship challenges. Nevertheless, as we know, these associations do offer guidance through their philosophical stance and publication programs. On the other hand, librarians in the survey would not turn to the ACLU for help, an organization that has a history of direct involvement at the local level in First Amendment disputes. By only a slight majority, participants would turn to private legal counsel. Vrabel also found that few librarians sought help from community or professional organizations when faced with censorship attempts.

Overall in this study, higher levels of education, and higher types of certification, higher levels of monetary support for collection development, librarians' perceptions about the progressive nature of local communities, and individual judicial awareness of court rulings were significant predictors of librarians' strong reactions against attempts at official censorship of school library materials.

The Role of Library and Information Studies Education in Fostering Better Legal Awareness

From this study, what appears to be lacking among these school librarians is a deep, fundamental knowledge of or awareness of court interpretations of constitutional law and how these rulings affect school library collections and issues surrounding freedom of speech rights and the legal rights of students to receive information. Perhaps a new curriculum and new instructional approaches are needed to correct some of the inadequacies of the legal knowledge of school librarians in education programs. More professional development sessions at conferences and in workshops could also increase their awareness of their professional and constitutional responsibilities to protect students' First Amendment rights.

Teaching rules and application of law and school librarians' constitutional and professional responsibilities will need to be based on a fundamental understanding of community sociology and the political elements in community structures that determine the role of schools and the flow of information within school environments. The development of self-awareness and how it affects a professional's understanding of his or her responsibilities to protect students' First Amendment rights is absolutely necessary within the instructional process.

More research is needed to determine the types and level of instruction that youth librarians receive in their professional training regarding judicial and legal matters pertaining to censorship and First Amendment rights of youth. More research is also needed to help understand the levels of influence that such instruction might have on professional attitudes and behaviors regarding the obligations of school librarians to protect the First Amendment rights of students. Research is also needed to determine the types and effectiveness of instructional methodologies, curriculum, and instructional support materials needed to teach the legalities of constitutional rights and legal, professional, and ethical responsibilities of school librarians to defend freedom of access to information by youth. The "Library Bill of Rights" mandates this.

From recent court decisions and social and cultural pressures, it is clear that school librarians in the United States will be called on more and more to understand constitutional law and their obligations under the U.S. Constitution to defend freedom of speech issues within the school library environment. The importance of better legal training for school librarians is obvious, and implementation can begin by the emerging and broadening concept of the school and its library as a public forum.

Defined by the courts, a limited public forum is a traditional space such as a library or school, recognized by courts as appropriate for discussion, debate, and exchange of ideas, and the government cannot discriminate against viewpoints on subjects appropriate to the forum. However, the government (i.e., school boards) can exclude categories of speech that justifiably do not fall within the designed purpose of the forum.[28–30]

The instructional paradigm used to educate school librarians is somewhat standardized nationally and even internationally through the use of textbooks, state and national standards, and certification requirements. In the United States, and certainly elsewhere, a school librarian's education is based on national educational policies.[31] Theoretically, over the years such standardizations should have produced a rather uniform student product with a clear understanding of their obligations to protect the constitutional rights of students. The overall increase in censorship attacks on school library media collections, the emerging of laws such as the American Patriot Act of 2006, and the development of government-endorsed surveillance policies that have implications for limiting First Amendment rights strongly suggest that the prevailing methods of educating school librarians must be rethought. The right of youth to have appropriate health care information is one the core principles of freedom that must be protected.

Selection Policies and Censorship

As mentioned earlier in this chapter, all materials acquired by youth librarians must meet standards outlined in official selection procedures and policies. These procedures are an important part of the prevailing youth librarianship paradigm, and we need not go into them here because numerous books and articles discuss their purpose and how to formulate them. Links and Web sites must be considered in the selection process as carefully as other materials based on existing policies.

The Baltimore County Public Library and its "Connections: Children, Youth and Family Resources" is an example of this type of care and attention. Through its membership, "Connections" provides authoritative links to community services especially focused on facilitating direct connections with organizations that can provide services for youth and their families. "Connections" operates under the sponsorship of the Baltimore County Local Management Board whose members are appointed by the county executive officer. The board includes public agencies and private organizations that offer programs for children and their families. Agencies include the Baltimore County Public Library, the Baltimore County Public Schools, the Baltimore County Departments of Health, Recreation and Parks, Office of Community Conservation, the Office of Employment and Training and Social Services, the Police Department, and the Maryland Department of Juvenile Services

Web sites and links may be added to "Connections" by any organization, and in such cases the library advises that users must decide on the appropriateness of these Web sites and links based on their own needs.[32] Other public libraries may wish to establish a similar board for Web site and link recommendations. Schools always need to involve other school professionals in addition to the school librarian in making decisions about resources. Schools may also rely on recommendations by recognized authorities in the broad school community in selection decisions regarding Web sites and links.

Conclusion

Health information is too important to let challenges to it go unanswered. The United States and other countries have attempted to meet these needs in various ways while remaining sensitive to cultural and social expectations. Although the emphasis has been mostly on the school librarian's responsibilities in this discussion, public and school librarians must always be aware of their social and professional responsibilities to protect the right of youth to good, dependable, accurate, and age-appropriate health information. Using all the legal resources available, we must never forget the rights of youth to good health information.

Notes

1. Shannon Maughan, "Listservs Buzzing over Newbery Winner." *Publishers Weekly.Com*, February 19, 2007, and "Children's Bookshelf," February 15, 2007. Available at: http://www.publishersweekly.com/article/CA6416737. html?display=breaking, accessed February 19, 2007.

2. Catherine J. Ross, "An Emerging Right for Mature Minors to Receive Information." *University of Pennsylvania Journal of Constitutional Law* 2 (December 1999). Available from LEXIS/NEXIS Academic Universe, accessed February 19, 2007.

3. Kenneth L. Donelson and Alleen Pace Nilsen, *Literature for Today's Young Adults,* 6th ed. (New York: Longman, 1997), 413.

4. Martha Boaz, "Censorship." In *Encyclopedia of Library and Information Science,* 2nd ed., revised and expanded in 4 volumes (New York: Marcel Dekker; print published May 20, 2003; online published June 23, 2003), pp. 469–474.

5. Kenneth L. Donelson and Alleen Pace Nilsen, *Literature for Today's Young Adults,* 7th ed. (New York: Longman, 2005), pp. 376–377.

6. Donelson and Nilsen, 6th ed., pp. 414–415.

7. Donelson and Nilsen, 6th ed., pp. 415.

8. Linda Greenhouse, "Court Hears Whether a Drug Statement Is Protected Free Speech for Students." *The New York Times National*, Tuesday, March 20, 2007, A1.

9. Tyll Van Geel, "The Search for Constitutional Limits on Government Authority to Inculcate Youth." *Texas Law Review* 62 (October 1883): 197–297.

10. Van Geel.

11. Van Geel.

12. Van Geel.

13. Martin D. Munic, "Education or Indoctrination: Removal of Books from Public School Libraries." [*Board of Education, Island Trees Union Free School District no. 26 v. Pico*]. *Minnesota Law Review* 68 (October 1983): 213–253.

14. Van Geel.

15. Larry E. Dorrell and Anne Busch, "Censorship in Schools: The Impact of Christian Pressure Groups." *Knowledge Quest* 28 (January–February 2000): 24–26.

16. Munic.

17. "Recent Cases, Briefly Noted: Removal of Book from Library." *Entertainment Law Reporter* 18 (August 1996). Available from LEXIS-NEXIS Academic Universe, accessed February 19, 2007.

18. Joel Sanders, "The Regulation of Indecent Material Accessible to Children on the Internet: Is It Really Alright to Yell Fire in a Crowded Chat Room?" *The Catholic Lawyer* 39 (Summer–Fall 1999), 125. Available from LEXIS-LEXIS Universe, accessed Febuary 19, 2007.

19. Whitney A. Kaiser, "The Use of Internet Filters in Public Schools: Double Click on the Constitution." *Columbia Journal of Law and Social Problems* 34 (Fall 2000): 49–77. Available from LegalTrac, accessed Febuary 19, 2007.

20. People for the American Way, "Court Strikes Down Online Censorship Law as Unconstitutional." Available at: http://www.pfaw.org/pfaw/general/default. aspx?oid=23759, accessed March 24, 2007.

21. John S. Simmons and Eliza T. Dresang, *School Censorship in the 21st Century: A Guide for Teachers and School Library Media Specialists* (Newark, DE: International Reading Association, 2001).

22. Ross.

23. Randall P. Bezanson and William G. Buss, "The Many Faces of Government Speech." *Iowa Law Review* 86 (August 2001): 1377. Available at: LEXIX-NEXIS Academic Universe, accessed February 19, 2007.

24. W. Bernard Lukenbill, "Censorship and Students' Right to Information: Implications for a New Paradigm for Educating School Librarians." Unpublished paper, School of Information, University of Texas at Austin, 2006.

25. Frances B. McDonald, "Intellectual Freedom and Censorship Attitudes of Secondary School Librarians and Principled Moral Reasoning." Ph.D. dissertation, University of Minnesota, 1989, abstracted in *Dissertation Abstracts International* 50-A (1990): 3096.

26. Terri B.Vrabel, "Texas School Librarians' Perceptions on Censorship and Intellectual Freedom," Ph.D. dissertation, University of North Texas, 1997, abstracted in *Dissertation Abstracts International* 58-A (1998): 2521.

27. Katherine M. Chandler, "Intellectual Freedom and the Use of Trade Books in the Elementary School: Perceptions of Principles." Ph.D. dissertation, University of Minnesota, 1985, abstracted in *Dissertation Abstracts International* 46-A (1986): 833.

28. Mary Minow and Tomas A. Lipinski, *The Library's Legal Answer Book* (Chicago: American Library Association, 2003).

29. Michele Sipley, "Operation—Patriots Act—The Role of School Libraries in Promoting a Free and Informed Society." *Progressive Librarian* 22 (Summer 2003): 52–61.

30. Intellectual Freedom Committee, American Library Association, "Guidelines for the Development and Implementation of Policies, Regulations and Procedures Affecting Access to Library Materials, Services and Facilities." Adopted by the ALA Intellectual Committee, June 28, 1994. Available at: http://www. ala.org/Template.cfm?Section=Other_Policies_and_Guidelines&Template=/ ContentManagement/ContentDisplay.cfm&ContentID=13141, accessed October

23, 2003. Also available at: http://www.eff.org/Censorship/Academic_edu/CAF/library/access.policies.ala.

31. W. Berenard Lukenbill, "Learning Resources and Interactive Learning Principles." *Drexel Library Quarterly* 19 (Spring 1983): 91–116.

32. Baltimore County Public Library, "Connections: Children, Youth, & Family." Available at: http://www.bcpl.info/commpg/connections/connections.html, accessed February 17, 2007.

Chapter 13

Into the Future: Action Research for Health Care Information

Introduction

As we have suggested throughout this book, health information is dynamic and ever changing. If we are to provide good and reliable health information for youth, we must not only be aware of research conducted in areas ranging from medicine to sociology and social work, but we, as youth librarians, must take an active part in both conducting and presenting research. Research and good observational strategies can often provide ways to bring good health information services to the local library.

A "Starter List" for Action Research

In Chapter 8, we suggested that *How to Conduct Action Research* (2003) by Lesley Farmer[1] was a useful aid to action research. In her book, she discusses action research as a process, explaining how to collect and manage data, how to use statistics appropriately, and how to apply findings based on action research.

Following are some groups that have need for health information that action research can address:

- School-based health clinic personnel

- Librarians in institutional settings (e.g., hospitals)

- Parents (including all types of parent relationships—single parents, foster care; couples raising a minority child; and from all demographics—urban/suburban families, rural and small-town families, educational, economic, gender, race, and ageism)

- School librarians

- Public librarians

- Health professionals

- Youth

A Basic Action Research Question: Can Librarians Be Health Information Gatekeepers?

The role of the public and school librarian seems fundamental to health information dissemination in areas where information sources are scarce. Libraries are often the most visible places in rural and small-town communities where information is readily available without undue restrictions or requirements for use. Can youth librarians be forceful leaders in providing health information? Can they become health information gatekeepers? As you will recall, these questions were raised in Chapter 9 involving the discussion of the Lower Rio Grande Valley of Texas; we suggest that this is a viable research question to ask in any community.

Of course a researcher never knows the outcome of any research study. Should the result reveal confusion or even rejection of the gatekeeper role, there is no reason to abandon the idea. Negative responses to a good idea often reveal the need for educational strategies, public relations campaigns, and social marketing programs to educate and address some of these negative and often uninformed opinions. Chapter 7 discusses in more detail the practical and theoretical aspects of social marketing.

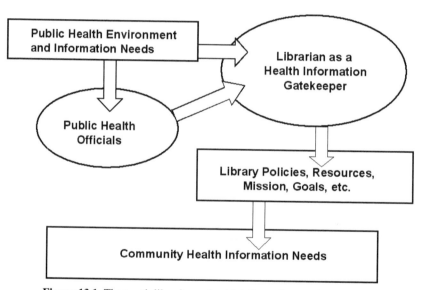

Figure 13.1. The youth librarian as health information gatekeeper.

Starter Questions for Action Research

The following are some "how-to" starter research questions that one might use to begin determining the needs for health information in the local library and community:

How can we better organize and disseminate health information?

How can we better promote health information?

How can we as librarians learn more about health information?

How can we teach health information literacy skills to our patrons?

How can we involve teachers and other professionals in learning about and using health information?

How can we better plan and promote health information programs and services?

How can we learn to design health information promotional materials and Web sites?

What are some good, workable collaboration strategies that we can use to involve community leaders in the library's role in health information?

How can we better manage health information programs?

How can we efficiently and economically train library staff to better disseminate health information?

How can we improve how we select health information materials of various types?

How can we encourage and influence the production and publishing of better and more appropriate health information for our communities?

The questions below can be directed at specific groups and/or services in most local communities and help to build profiles of users and their needs.

Questions for School-Based Health Clinic Administrators and Staff

1. Do school-based health clinics exist in this community? If so, what are some of the basic services offered?

2. How is the work of the clinic integrated into the curriculum and instruction in local schools?

3. Do health staff members work or collaborate with the youth in their communities in terms of building collections of health information? If not, what might be done to encourage this cooperation? What problems exist that might work against this collaboration?

4. In the opinion of health staff members, what do they see as their greatest successes?

5. What do they feel are their greatest obstacles to providing good services?

6. Do they see local librarians as health information gatekeepers?

Questions for Library-Based Institutional Services in Hospitals and Related Organizations

1. Do institutions in the community such as hospitals offer health care information services for youth?

2. Assuming that such programs exist, what types of programs and services, including outreach services, are currently offered by existing institutions? How do they augment services and cooperate with other health information providers?

3. What are some good examples of health information programs in small and rural communities that involve public and school libraries?

4. What are some characteristics that might account for successful programs?

5. What are some of the services and programs that can be easily adapted by other library programs?

6. What can librarians learn from these institutional programs? For example, what are some of the essential skills that youth librarians who want to become more involved in health information outreach and other services learn from these programs?

7. Based on the experiences from these programs, what are some of the basic health information services that youth librarians can offer without major adjustments to present operations?

Questions to Health Professionals in the Community

1. What are the major health issues that children and youth face in this community?

2. What kinds of services and information might help with these needs?

3. From the point of view of parents and other caregivers, what are the most pressing health information needs that now go unmet?

4. How might librarians in the community help meet some of these identified health information needs?

5. How often do health professionals communicate with youth librarians about community-based needs for health information?

6. Can and should librarians fulfill a gatekeeper role for health information?

Building Profiles of Users

Action research calls for procedures that will help build and develop profiles of users and potential users. Among these will be parents and youth. Following are some specific questions that might be asked either directly in conversation or through formal research approaches. Appendix A offers research strategies as well as a scenario of a small action research project.

Talking with Parents

These questions may be adapted to include a variety of parenting situations, including but not limited to, those listed earlier (including all types of parent relationships and from all demographics).

1. Within the last six months, have you had any medical situation that required information that addressed your needs specifically?

2. How would you describe this medical situation (e.g., mild, expected with children and youth of these ages, moderate, serious)?

3. To whom did you for turn for information?

4. Other than your physician, where did you go—for example, the Internet, the school nurse, the school library, the public library?

5. Have you ever gone to the local public library for health information? If not, what has prevented you from going there?

6. If you have children or youth in school, have you ever, or would you ever, go to the school library for health information?

7. Do you find the availability of health information in this area accessible?

8. Other than from physicians, do you find health information generally adequate (e.g., up-to-date, reliable, authoritative) in terms of meeting yours needs?

9. What do you suggest that professionals such as teachers, librarians, and counselors do to improve the availability of health information in this area?

10. Do you feel that librarians can fulfill a "gatekeeper" role in providing health information for this community and for your family?

11. Please make suggestions to make health information more available to parents in your situation.

Talking with Youth[2]

As with parents, these questions can be asked either formally in a structured research approach or as conversation. Health questions can be sensitive for children and youth to answer and for researchers and librarians to ask (based on laws, policies, and regulations). For these reasons, a list of possible health topics are provided here that can be adapted for use according to the needs of individual librarians and action researchers. In developing user profiles, it is also good to know demographic characteristics such as gender, age, race, and primary languages spoken in the home.

1. In the last six months, how many times have you visited a medical doctor?

2. Do you ever go to the public or school library for health information?

3. When you need health information, what do you like best—for example, a pamphlet, book, or magazine?

4. Have you ever asked an adult other than your parent(s) for health information?

5. Other than a medical doctor, who of the following are you most likely to ask or health information (responses can be ranked in order of your preference from most likely to least likely to ask):

   Family member (parent)

   Family member (brother or sister)

   Family member (uncle, aunt, cousin, grandparent, etc.)

   Pharmacist

   Friend or buddy

   Teacher

    Priest or minister

    School counselor

    School nurse

    Coach or PE teacher

6. If you had a question about a health issue, which of the following would you be most comfortable in approaching and asking for health information? These too can be ranked in order of preference.

    Doctor

    Nurse

    Family member

    Friends

    Neighbor

    Teachers

    Books

    Magazines

    Internet

7. Of the following sources, which do you generally prefer for your health information? As previously, preference ranking can be used for these.

    Newspapers

    Television

    Radio

    Public library

    School library

    City or county health departments

    Health organizations (e.g., American Heart Association)

    Hotline or crisis centers

    Internet

    Product labels or information

Research shows that the following are specific health topics of interest to youth. Depending on circumstances and situations, we can expect some of these to appear in conversations and interviews with youth.

    Human sexual reproduction

    Sexual behaviors

    Sexual problems

    Smoking and tobacco use

Anger management

Violence

Safety issues

Care and personal grooming

Hygiene

Disease management

Sports medicine

Exercise

Nutrition

An Action Research Design and Scenario

Recording and Reporting of Action Research

The following are elements that are generally expected in reporting an action research project. When these elements are present in your report, it reflects a project designed to ascertain useful health information resources for youth.

1. Introduction with statement of purpose

2. A brief overview of the important literature on health information for youth in recent years

3. Methods:

    Methods used for contacting youth

    Statement describing interviews and how responses were recorded

    Justification as to how responses were used to find resources that would satisfy needs and/or requests as stated by youth

    Description of evaluation criteria established for selecting sources

    Statement of how selected resources were verified as useful by interviewed youth

4. Findings and suggestions for resources (What kinds of resources are available and what recommendations were made, including how to improve available of resources?)

5. Cited references

Scenario of an Action Research Project in Progress

Purpose of the Study: To identify Internet sources used and appreciated by youth.

Setting: A community library serving a suburban area attached to a large city.

Investigator: A master's-level public librarian in charge of youth services.

Procedure: Selection of youth for interviews.

Informal conversations were held with youth as they came into the library. The library has two sections for youth under eighteen. The first section is for elementary and younger children, and this section is behind glass at the back of the library. The "Junior High" section is for ages twelve and older, including high school ages. This section is located in front of the children's department. It is not glassed in and is sectioned off with shelving so that it appears to be "separate" from the library. About seven to nine youth of high school age come into the library regularly and are known by the investigator both by appearance and by name.

Procedure: Interviews (as Described by Investigator)

I sat down with these youth for about five to ten minutes and asked them the following questions:

1. Do you ever look up health information like on sexually transmitted diseases, weight loss, or drug information, for either a school report or personal use?

2. Would you feel more comfortable asking a parent or teacher or looking it up yourself on a reputable site?

3. If you used an online resource, would you ask a librarian or teacher for a site, ask a friend, or would you search using a site like Google? Do you know of a Web site already?

4. If you have gone to any online Web sites, can you show me which ones? If you liked them, please tell me why or why not.

I also talked to a group of youth that I deal with on a monthly basis for topic lectures about various reading genres. I asked them similar questions and also told them to ask around and to look to see what they preferred and let me know. I got about five responses the following month, and they all came up with the same Web site: coolnurse.com. I don't know if they all just pitched in on one kid's response, or if that was the general consensus.

I also had about nine or ten kids tell me that they haven't had occasion to discuss anything or look anything up and that they basically [used what they heard, [about or found on] the Internet during surfing, and [learned about in] health and science classes.

I didn't exactly verify with them what I wrote; I just told them this was for some research … [and thanked them for their help].

Sources Suggested by Youth

Popular resources suggested by youth in interviews include coolnurse.com, Teen Age Health Freak, and Teen Growth. These are described in Chapter 11.

Summary

Because this project is currently in development, the final report will reflect characteristics as described in "Recording and Reporting of Action Research," previously discussed. Of course, styles of presentation vary with needs and circumstances for reporting.

Conclusion

Knowledge is power, and health knowledge and information are essential for good, sustainable living. Research, no matter how small, is a huge part of building knowledge about health and how health information and services are developed and promoted in libraries. Most youth librarians have opportunities to contribute to research in many ways. These opportunities are surprisingly abundant. Action research might involve observing and recording how patrons ask for and use information in the local situation, thus leading to modifications or improvement in how health information programs are developed and managed locally. Research can also be more broadly based, involving larger user groups, with rigorous scientific research methods applied.

Whatever the situation and approach, good methods of operations and management must be based on defensible research that offers effective and accountable program results. The future of health care and health information services depends on good research at all levels, coupled with a desire to promote the health and well-being of youth well into the twentieth-first century.

Notes

1. Lesley S. J. Farmer, *How to Conduct Action Research* (Chicago: American Association of School Librarians, 2003).

2. Questions based on Gilda Baeza Oretgo's "Health Information Seeking Behavior of Rural Consumers in the Big Bend Region of West Texas." Ph.D. dissertation, School of Library and Information Studies, Texas Woman's University, 2001).

Appendix

Action Research for Health Information

As we have noted throughout this book, research in all areas of health information is fundamental to providing good, reliable, and justifiable health information services and programs. The following questions offer some preliminary action research ideas for helping to advance our understanding of health information and how to make it more accessible to youth and their caregivers.

Some General Questions and Concerns

How to organize and disseminate health information

How to promote health information more effectively

How to learn about health information more effectively

How to teach health information literacy more effectively

How to involve teachers and other professionals in health information

How to plan and promote health information programs and services

How to design health information promotional materials and Web sites

What are good, workable collaboration strategies?

How to manage health information programs

How to train staff in health information dissemination

How to select health information materials of various types

How to encourage the production and publishing of better and more appropriate health information

How can librarians and school library media specialists better respond to the needs of parents and other caregivers?

Questions for Specific Providers and Consumers of Health Care Information

A. School-Based Health Clinic Questionnaire

1. Briefly describe your programs and its services.

2. Explain how the work of the clinic integrated into the curriculum and instruction.

3. Have you worked with the school librarians in your district to build collections of health information? Have you worked with public librarians in your district to build health information collections? If not, would you be willing to work with them? What potential problems do you envision with this?

4. What would you say are the greatest successes of your program?

5. What are the greatest limitations of your program?

6. Please provide any other insights you might have about your program.

7. Please feel free to provide any materials such as pamphlets or guidelines that you have developed relating to your program.

8. May we contact you for additional information?

B. Library-Based Institutional Services Questionnaire (e.g., hospitals)

1. What types of outreach programs are you currently offering or perhaps involved with or cooperating in with other health information providers?

2. What are some good examples of health information programs in small and rural communities that involve public or school libraries?

3. For those that have proved successful, what do you consider the major characteristics that account for these successes?

4. What are some of the services that these programs offer that you feel can be easily transferred to other library situations?

5. What are some of the essential skills that librarians who want to be more involved in health information outreach need to acquired or improve?

6. What are some of the basic health information services that school libraries and public libraries can now offer without major adjustments to present operations?

7. Other comments.

C. Health Professionals Questionnaire

1. In your professional judgment, what do you think are the major health issues that children and youth are now facing?

2. What kinds of services or information might help with these needs?

3. From the point of view of parents and other caregivers, what do you feel are their most pressing health information needs regarding the health of their children and youth?

4. How might the library or librarian in your school or area help meet some of these health information needs?

5. What are some of the major health information services that are needed in this community? Please consider their importance in regard to your professional situation and responsibilities.

6. In recent months, have you talked to a school or public librarian about the need for health information?

7. A gatekeeper is generally considered someone in a position of authority who controls access to or has some manner of influence on how resources and information are dispersed to others. Do you feel that the librarians in your school or community fulfill or should fulfill this gatekeeper role? Please explain your reasons.

8. Other comments.

D. Parenting Profile Interviews

These questions may be adapted to include a variety of parenting situations, including but not limited to single-parent families, foster care families, and others as defined in Chapter 11.

1. Within the last six months, have you had any medical situation requiring health information?

2. How would you describe this medical situation (e.g., mild and expected with children and youth of these ages, moderate, serious)?

3. To whom did you for turn for information?

4. Other than your physician, where did you go for information—for example, the Internet, the school nurse?

5. Have you ever gone to the local public library for health information? If not, what has prevented you from going there?

6. If you have children or youth in school, have you ever, or would you ever, go to the school library for health information?

7. Do you find the availability of health information in this area accessible?

8. Other than from physicians, do you find health information generally adequate (e.g., up-to-date, reliable, authoritative) in terms of meeting yours needs?

9. What do you suggest that professionals such as teachers, librarians, and counselors might do to improve the availability of health information in this area?

10. Please add any comments that you would like about making health information available to parents in your situation.

E. Youth Profile Information

Chapter 13 provides suggestions for youth research. Although not directed completely at youth, Gilda Baeza Ortego's "Health Information Seeking Behavior of Rural Consumers in the Big Bend Region of West Texas" (Ph.D., dissertation, School of Library and Information Studies, Texas Woman's University, 2001) will be useful for those working with youth because she provides insight into how to ask about health information needs.

Figure A.1 places many of the above questions into an organized conceptual framework. If need be, these categories can stand independently of each other.

Figure A.1. Research interview protocol for librarians as health information gatekeepers.

Interview Subjects in Selected Geographic Areas

• Recognized leaders in school librarianship

• Recognized leaders in public librarianship

• Selection of recognized health agency administrators

Objectives of the Interviews

To ascertain subjects' concept of the role of the library in health information

Public Librarians

Objective: To determine their views of the librarian as "gatekeeper" of health information.

Read a definition of gatekeeper: A gatekeeper is generally considered someone in a position of authority who controls access to or has some manner of influence on how resources and information are dispersed to others.

1. If someone told you that you were a community gatekeeper of information, would you feel comfortable with this designation? (Ask for reasons for these beliefs.)

2. What are the characteristics that would prevent this idea from developing in your community?

3. What characteristics would enhance the development of this concept in your community?

4. What services do you now offer that might be called "health information" and be a part of the gatekeeper role?

5. Of the following services, which would you be willing to offer? State "none" if you feel none of these are relevant.

    Provide:

    • Fiction and nonfiction books on health

    • Audiovisual materials on health

- Community information on health
- Programs on health issues
- Outreach activities to the community on health issues
- Professional and academic materials on health issues (selectively)

Work with:

- Other agencies and groups on health information and issues

Please rank these in terms of importance and adaptability.

- Do you currently have any contact with government health (not school-related) officers?
- Do you have any contact with school authorities related to health information?
- Within the context of this community, would it be easy for you to establish contact with government and school authorities?
- Other comments:

School Librarians

Objective: To determine their views of the librarian as "gatekeeper" of health information.

Read a definition of gatekeeper: A gatekeeper is generally considered someone in a position of authority who controls access to or has some manner of influence on how resources and information are dispersed to others.

1. If someone told you that you were a school gatekeeper of health information, would you feel comfortable with this designation? (Ask for reasons for these beliefs.)

2. What are the characteristics that would prevent this idea from developing in your school community?

3. What characteristics would enhance the development of this concept in your school community?

4. What services do you now offer that might be called "health information" and be a part of the gatekeeper role?

5. Of the following services, which would you be willing to offer? State "none" if you feel none of these are relevant.

   Provide:

   - Fiction and nonfiction books on health
   - Audiovisual materials on health
   - Community information on health
   - Programs on health issues

- Outreach activities to the community on health issues
- Professional and academic materials on health issues (selectively)

Work with:

- Other agencies and groups on health information and issues

Please rank the following in terms of importance and adaptability:

- Do you currently have any contact with government health (not school-related) officers?
- Do you have any contact with public librarians related to health information?
- Within the context of this school community, would it be easy for you to establish contact with government and other school authorities?
- Other comments:

Health Officers

Objective: To obtain information regarding their concept of librarians in a gatekeeper role of providing health information.

Read a definition of gatekeeper role: A gatekeeper is generally considered someone in a position of authority who controls access or has some manner of influence on how resources and information are dispersed to others.

1. If someone told you that public and school librarians were gatekeepers of health information, would you feel comfortable in their accepting this role or designation? (Ask for reasons for these beliefs.)

2. Have you ever considered the public library and the library director as important providers of health information?

3. Have you ever considered the school library and the school librarian as important providers of health information?

4. Have you ever considered librarians as "health information gatekeepers" in your community?

5. Do you have any contact with the librarians here in this community in your role as a government officer?

6. If you had the opportunity, what health information services might you request of the school and public librarians? State none if you feel none of these are relevant.

    Provide:

    - Fiction and nonfiction books on health
    - Audiovisual materials on health
    - Community information on health
    - Programs on health issues

- Outreach activities to the community on health issues
- Professional and academic materials on health issues (selectively)

Work with:

- Other agencies and groups on health information and issues

7. Do you have any contacts with other public agencies (e.g., school and public libraries) concerned with providing health information?

8. Within the context of your community, would it be easy for you to establish contact with other agencies such as schools and public libraries that have an interest in providing health information?

9. Other comments

Selected Bibliography

Entries marked with an asterisk (*) indicate that these are recommendations from "Young Adult Services Professional Resources: A Selected Five-Year Retrospective Bibliography with Some Class Exceptions," by Mary K. Chelton. Available at: http://yahelp.suffolk.lib.ny.us/YA_Bibliography7_04.pdf.

Health, Health Information, and Community

Abdelhak, Mervat. *Health Information: Management of a Strategic Resource*. 3rd ed. St. Louis, MO: Saunders/Elsevier, 2007.

"Abstinence-Only Education Policies and Programs: A Position Paper of the Society for Adolescent Medicine." *Journal of Adolescent Health* 38 (2006): 83–87. Available at: http://www.adolescenthealth.org/PositionPaper_Abstinence_only_edu_policies_and_programs.pdf.

American Association for the Advancement of Science. *The Challenge of Providing Consumer Health Information Services in Public Libraries*. Washington, DC: AAAS, n.d.

Andreasen, Alan E. *Social Marketing in the 21st Century*. Thousand Oaks, CA: Sage, 2006.

Anspaugh, David, and Gene Ezell. *Teaching Today's Health*. San Francisco: Pearson Benjamin Cummings, 2007.

Beckwith, Harry. *The Invisible Touch: The Four Keys to Modern Marketing*. New York: Warner Books, 2000.

_____. *What Clients Love: A Field Guide to Growing Your Business*. New York: Warner Books, 2003.

Berkowitz, Eric N. *Essentials of Health Care Marketing*. 2nd ed. Sudbury, MAMA: Jones and Bartlett, 2006.

Berns, Roberta M. *Child, Family, School, Community: Socialization and Support*. 7th ed. Belmont, CA: Thompson Higher Education, 2007.

Bishop, Kay. *Collection Program in Schools: Concepts, Practices, and Information Sources*. 4th ed. Westport, CT: Libraries Unlimited, 2007.

Bodenheiner, Thomas S., and Kevin Grumbak. *Understanding Health Policy: A Clinical Approach*. Norwalk, CT: Appleton & Lange, 1995. [Note: This is a continuing series.]

Bowden, Virginia M., et al. "Health Information—Hispanic Outreach in the Texas Lower Rio Grande Valley." *Journal of the Medical Library Association* 92 (April 2006): 180–189.

Burns, Barbara J., and Kimberly Hoagwood. *Community Treatment for Youth: Evidence-Based Interventions for Severe Emotional and Behavioral Disorders.* New York: Oxford University Press, 2002.

Children's Health, the Nation's Wealth: Assessing and Improving Child Health. Board on Children Youth and Family. Washington, DC: National Academies Press, 2004.

Davis, Hilton. *Counseling Parents of Children with Chronic Illness or Disability.* Leicester: British Psychological Society, 1993.

*"Developing Adolescents: A Reference for Professionals." American Psychological Association, 2002. Available at: www.apa.org/pi/pii/develop.pd.

*Di Prisco, Joseph, and Michael Riera. *Field Guide to the American Teenager: A Parent's Companion.* Cambridge, MA: Perseus Books, 2000.

DiClemente, Ralph J., et al., eds. *Handbook of Adolescent Health Risk Behavior.* New York: Putnam Press, 1996.

*Dorman, Gayle. *Planning Programs for Young Adolescents. Center for Early Adolescence.* Distributed by Search Institute Thresher Square West, Suite 210, 700 Third St., Minneapolis, MN 55415.

Farnham, Kevin M., and Dale G. Farnham. *MySpace Safety: 51 Tips for Teens and Parents.* Pomfret, CT: How-To Primers, 2006.

Fee, Elizabeth. "Public Health and the State: The United States." In *The History of Public Health and the Modern State.* Dorothy Porter, ed. Amsterdam: Editions Rodopi, 1994, pp. 233–235.

Fink, Arlene. *Evaluation Fundamentals: Insights into the Outcomes, Effectiveness, and Quality of Health Programs,* 2nd ed. Thousand Oaks, CA: Sage, 2005.

Gal, Iddo, and Ayelet Prigat. "Why Organizations Continue to Create Patient Information Leaflets with Readability and Usability Problems: An Exploratory Study." *Health Education Research* 20, no. 4 (2005): 485–493.

Gestwicki, Carol. *Home, School and Community Relations: A Guide to Working with Families.* 6th ed. Clifton Park, CA: Thomson Delmar Learning, 2006.

Hayman, Laura L., et al., eds. *Chronic Illness in Children: An Evidence-Based Approach.* New York: Springer, 2002.

_____. *Health and Behavior in Childhood and Adolescence.* New York: Springer, 2002.

Heineman, Toni Vaughn, and Diane Ehrensaft, eds. *Building a Home Within: Meeting the Emotional Needs of Children and Youth in Foster Care.* Baltimore: P.H. Brookes, 2006.

Hofrichter, Richard, ed. *Health and Social Justice: Politics, Ideology, and Inequity in the Distribution of Disease.* San Francisco: Jossey-Bass, 2003.

Hornik, Robert, ed. *Public Health Communication: Evidence for Behavior Change.* Mahwah, NJ: Lawrence Erlbaum Associates, 2002.

Huff, Robert M., and Michael V. Kline, eds. *Promoting Health in Multicultural Populations: A Handbook for Practitioners.* Thousand Oaks, CA: Sage, 1999.

Kawachi, Ichirô, and Lisa F. Berkman, eds. *Neighborhoods and Health.* New York: Oxford University Press, 2003.

Kawachi, Ichirô, and Sarah Wamala. *Globalization and Health.* New York: Oxford University Press, 2007.

*Kaye, Cathryn Berger. *Complete Guide to Service Learning: Proven, Practical Ways to Engage Students in Civic Responsibility, Academic Curriculum, and Social Action.* Minneapolis, MN: Free Spirit, 2004.

*Konopka, Gisela. "Requirements for Healthy Development of Adolescent Youth," *Adolescence* 8 (Fall 1973): 1–26. Available at: http://www.cyfernet.mes.umn.edu/youthdev/konopka.html.

Kotler, Philip, et al. *Social Marketing: Improving the Quality of Life.* 2nd ed. Thousand Oaks, CA: Sage, 2002.

LaVeist, Thomas. *Minority Populations and Health: An Introduction to Health Disparities in the United States.* San Francisco: Jossey-Bass, 2005.

_____. ed. Race, *Ethnicity, and Health: A Public Health Reader.* San Francisco: Jossey-Bass, 2002.

*Lesko, Wendy Schaetzel. *Maximum Youth Involvement: The Complete Gameplan for Community Action.* Rev. ed. Youth Activism Project, 2003 (PO Box E, Kensington, MD 20895).

Lyons, John S. *Redressing the Emperor: Improving Our Children's Public Mental Health System.* Westport, CT: Praeger, 2004.

Maibach, Edward W., and Roxanne Parrott, eds. *Designing Health Messages: Approaches from Communication Theory and Public Health Practice.* Sage, 1995.

Marmot, Michael, and Richard G. Wilkinson, eds. *Social Determinants of Health.* 2nd ed. New York: Oxford University Press, 2006.

*McClaughlin, Milbrey W., et al. *Urban Sanctuaries: Neighborhood Organizations in the Lives and Futures of Inner-city Youth.* San Francisco: Jossey-Bass, 2001.

*McIntyre, Alice. *Inner City Kids: Adolescents Confront Life and Violence in an Urban Community*. New York: New York University Press, 2000.

Minkler, Meredith, ed. *Community Organizing and Community Building for Health*. 2nd ed. Rutgers University Press, 2004.

Mondimore, Francis Mark. *Adolescent Depression: A Guide for Parents*. Baltimore: Johns Hopkins University Press, 2002.

Nielsen-Bohlman, Lynn et al., eds. *Health Literacy: A Prescription to End Confusion*. Washington, DC: National Academies Press, 2004.

*Nikkah, John. *Our Boys Speak: Adolescent Boys Write about Their Inner Lives*. New York: St. Martin's, 2000.

Ortego, Gilda Baeza. "Health Information Seeking Behavior of Rural Consumers in the Big Bend Region of West Texas." Ph.D. dissertation, Texas Woman's University, 2001. *Dissertations Abstracts International*, 62-A (October 2001): 1258.

Patel, Kant, and Mark E. Rushefsky. *Politics of Public Health in the United States*. Armoonk, NY: M. E. Sharpe, 2005.

*Perlstein, Linda. *Not Much Chillin': The Hidden Lives of Middle Schoolers*. New York: Farrar, Straus and Giroux, 2003.

Pipher. Mary. *Reviving Ophelia: Saving the Selves of Adolescent Girls*. New York: Putnam,1994.

Pollack, William. *Real Boys: Rescuing our Sons from the Myths of Boyhood*. New York: Henry Holt, 1999.

Pollack, William S., with Todd Schuster. *Real Boys' Voices*. New York: Random House, 2000.

Ponton, Lynn E. *Sex Lives of Teenagers: Revealing the Secret World of Adolescent Boys and Girls*. New York: Dutton, 2000.

Porter, Dorothy, ed. *The History of Public Health and the Modern State*. Amsterdam: Editions Rodopi, 1994.

Porter, Michael E., and Elizabeth Olmsted Teisberg. *Redefining Health Care: Creating Value-Based Competition on Results*. Boston: Harvard Business School Press, 2006.

Power, Thomas J., et al. *Promoting Children's Health: Integrating School, Family, and Community*. New York: Guilford Press, 2003.

Prothrow-Stith, Deborah, with Michaele Weissman. *Deadly Consequences*. New York: HarperCollins, 1991.

Quart, Alissa. *Branded: The Buying and Selling of Teenagers*. New York: Perseus, 2002.

*Ravitch, Diane. *Language Police: How Pressure Groups Restrict What Students Learn*. New York: Knopf, 2003.

Reagan, Patricia A., and Jodi Brookins-Fishere. *Community Health in the 21st Century*. 2nd ed. San Francisco: Benjamin Cummings, 2002.

*"Reflection: The Key to Service Learning." 2nd ed. National Helpers Network, 245 Fifth Ave., Suite 1705, New York, NY 10016-8728.

*Scales, Peter, and Nancy Leffert. *Developmental Assets: A Synthesis of the Scientific Research on Adolescent Development*. Minneapolis, MN: Search Institute, 1999.

Siegel, Michael M. D., and Lynne Doner. *Marketing Public Health: Strategies to Promote Social Change*. Sudbury, MA: Jones and Bartlett, 2004.

Slack, Warner V., et al., eds. *Consumer Health Informatics: Informing Consumers and Improving Health Care*. New York: Springer, 2005.

*Slaytorn, Elaine Doremus. *Empowering Teens: A Guide to Developing a Community Based Youth Organization, 2000*. Available from CROYA, 400 Hastings Road, Lake Forest, IL 60045.

Steele, Ric G., and Michael C. Roberts, eds. *Handbook of Mental Health Services for Children, Adolescents, and Families*. New York: Springer, 2006.

Strauch, Barbara. *Primal Teen: What the New Discoveries about the Teenage Brain Tell Us about Our Kids*. New York: Doubleday, 2003.

*Strauss, Susan, with Pamela Espeland. *Sexual Harassment and Teens: A Program for Positive Change: Case Studies, Activities, Questionnaires, Laws, Guidelines, Policies, Procedures, Resources, and More*. Minneapolis, MN: Free Spirit, 1992.

Sutherland, Anne, and Beth Thompson. *Kidfluence: The Marketer's Guide to Understanding and Reaching Generation Y Kids, Tweens, and Teens*. New York: McGraw-Hill, 2003.

Taffel, Ron, with Melinda Blau. *Second Family: How Adolescent Power Is Challenging the American Family*. New York: St. Martin's, 2001.

Taublieb, Amy Beth. *A—Z Handbook of Child and Adolescent Issues*. Boston: Allyn and Bacon, 2000.

*Treadwell, Henrie M. *Safe Passages through Adolescence: Communities Protecting the Health and Hopes of Youth*. Battle Creek, MI: W. K. Kellogg Foundation, 1998.

United States Institute of Medicine. *Unequal Treatment: Confronting Racial & Ethnic Disparities in Health*. Edited by Brian D. Smedley et al. Book and CD-ROM ed. Washington, DC: National Academies Press, 2002.

United Way of America. *Measuring Program Outcomes: A Practical Approach*. Alexandria, VA: United Way of America, 1996.

*Van Hoorn, Judith Lieberman, et al. *Adolescent Development and Rapid Social Change: Perspectives from Eastern Europe.* Albany, NY: State University of York Press, 2000.

Warner, Debra G., et al. "High School Peer Tutors Teach MedlinePlus: A Model for Hispanic Outreach." *Journal of the Medical Library Association* 93 (April 2005): 243–252.

Weinreich, Nedra Kline. *Hands-On Social Marketing: A Step-by-Step Guide.* Sage, 1999.

Weinstein, Estelle, and Efrem Rosen. *Teaching Children about Health: A Multidisciplinary Approach.* 2nd ed. Belmont, CA: Wadsworth/Thomson Learning, 2003.

Willard, Nancy E. *Cyber-Safe Kids, Cyber-Savvy Teens: Helping Young People Learn to Use the Internet Safely and Responsibly.* San Francisco: Jossey-Bass, 2007.

Wiseman, Rosalind. *Queens Bees and Wannbes: Helping Your Daughter Survive Cliques, Gossip, Boyfriends and Other Realities of Adolescence.* New York: Crown, 2002.

Witte, Kim, et al. *Effective Health Risk Messages: A Step-by-Step Guide.* Thousand Oaks, CA: Sage, 2006.

World Health Organization. "Youth and Health Issues." Chapter 4 in *World Youth Report 2003.* Available at: www.un.org/esa/socdev/unyin/documents/ch04.pdf.

Wright, Bradford W. *Comic Book Nation: The Transformation of Youth Culture in America.* Baltimore: Johns Hopkins University Press, 2001.

Wurzbach, Mary Ellen, ed. *Community Health Education and Promotion: A Guide to Program Design and Evaluation.* 2nd ed. Gaithersburg, MD: Aspen, 2002.

*"Youth on Board: Why and How to Involve Young People in Organizational Decision-Making." Washington, D.C. National Center for Nonprofit Boards, 2000 (Suite 900, 1828 L St., NW, Washington, DC 20036-5104).

Zeyenhuizen, Joanne Marily. "Information Needs of Parents of Hospitalized Chronically Ill Children." Master's thesis, Dalhousie University. *Master's Thesis Abstract International* 34 (February 1996), p. 286.

*Zollo, Peter. *Getting Wiser to Teens: More Insights into Marketing to Teenagers.* 3rd ed. Ithaca: NY: New Strategist, 2004.

School Library Media Centers and Public Libraries: Management, Services, and Collection Development

Baker, Lynda, and Viginia Manbeck. *Consumer Health Information for Public Librarians.* Lanham, MD: Scarecrow Press, 2002.

Barclay, Donald A., and Deborah D. Halsted. *Medical Library Association Consumer Health Reference Service Handbook.* New York: Neal-Schuman, 2001.

Buddy, Juanita. "Keeping Current Library Media Specialists: Addressing the Student Health Epidemic." *School Library Activities Monthly* 22 (Octber 2005): 56–58.

Casini, Barbara, and Andrea Kenton. *The Public Librarian's Guide to Providing Consumer Health Information.* Chicago: Public Library Association, 2006.

*Chelton, Mary K., and Colleen, Cool, eds. *Youth Information Seeking Behavior: Theories, Models, and Issues.* Lanham, MD: Scarecrow, 2004.

"Coping With...." series. Publishers within the Greenwood Publishing Group offer a number of titles that deal with various health issues. Some of these include:

Using Literature to Help Troubled Teenagers Cope with End-of-Life Issues. Janet Allen, ed. 2002.

Using Literature to Help Troubled Teenagers Cope with Family Issues. Joan F. Kaywell, ed. 1999.

Using Literature to Help Troubled Teenagers Cope with Health Issues. Cynthia Ann Bowman, ed. 2000.

Using Literature to Help Troubled Teenagers Cope with Identity Issues. Jeffrey S. Kaplan, ed. 1999.

Using Literature to Help Troubled Teenagers Cope with Societal Issues. Pamela S. Carroll, ed. 1999.

*Doll, Carol A., and Pamela Petrick Barron. *Managing and Analyzing Your Collection: A Practical Guide for Small Libraries and School Library Media Centers.* Chicago: American Library Association, 2002.

Dresand, Eliza T., et al. *Dynamic Youth Services through Outcome-Based Planning and Evaluation.* Chicago: American Library Association, 2006.

DuMont, Rosemary. *Reform and Reaction: The Big City Public Library in American Life.* Westport, CT: Greenwood Press, 1977.

Durrance, Joan C., et al. *How Libraries and Librarians Help: A Guide to Identifying User-Centered Outcomes.* Chicago: American Library Association, 2005.

Eisenberg, Michael B., et al. *Information Literacy: Essential Skills for the Information Age.* 2nd ed. Westport, CT: Libraries Unlimited, 2004.

*Immroth, Barbara, and Kathleen de la Pena McCook. *Library Services to Youth of Hispanic Heritage.* Jefferson, NC: McFarland, 2000.

*Jones, Patrick, and Patricia Taylor. *Creating a Core Collection for Young Adults.* New York: Neal-Schuman, 2003.

*Junon-Metz, Gail. *Coaching Kids for the Internet: A Guide for Librarians, Teachers, and Parents.* El Dorado Hills, CA: Library Solutions Press, 2000. Also available as ERIC Reproduction document no. ED 438 788.

Kellerman, Frank. *Introduction to Health Sciences Librarianship: A Management Handbook.* Westport, CT: Greenwood Press, 1997.

Kids Still Welcome Here! An Update of Public Library Policies That Promote Use by Young People. Albany, NY: New York Library Association, Youth Service Section, 2004. Available at: http://www.nyla.org/content/user_12/ysskids.pdf.

Kids Welcome Here!: Writing Public Library Policies That Promote Use by Young People. Albany, NY: New York Library Association, Youth Services Section, 1998.

*Kuhlthau, Carol Collier. *Seeking Meaning: A Process Approach to Library and Information Services.* 2nd ed. Westport, CT: Libraries Unlimited, 2004.

*Kuntz, Jerry. *KidsClick! Web Searching Skills Guide with CD-Rom.* New York: Neal-Schuman, 2001.

*Lane, Nancy, et al. *Techniques for Student Research: A Comprehensive Guide to Using the Library.* New York: Neal-Schuman, 2000.

LaTour, Kathleen M., and Shirley Eichenwald-Maki, eds. *Health Information Management: Concepts, Principles, and Practice.* 2nd ed. Chicago: American Health Information Management Association, 2006.

Lerch, Maureen T., and Janet Welch. *Serving Homeschooled Teens and Their Parents.* Westport, CT: Libraries Unlimited, 2004.

Lukenbill, W. Bernard. *Collection Development for a New Century in the School Library Media Center.* Westport, CT: Greenwood Press, 2002.

_____. *Community Resources in the School Library Media Center: Concepts and Methods.* Westport CT: Libraries Unlimited, 2004.

*Marlow, Ann. *Learning to Learn: A Guide to Becoming Information Literate.* New York: Neal-Schuman, 2002.

Medical Library Association. *Communicating Health Information Literacy.* Chicago: Medical Library Association, 2005.

Merida, John L. *Health Information Management Technology: An Applied Approach.* 2nd ed. Chicago: American Health Information Management Association, 2006.

Nelson, Rosemary, and Marion J. Ball, eds. *Consumer Informatics: Applications and Strategies in Cyber Health Care.* New York: Springer, 2004.

Nichols, C. Allen, ed. *Thinking Outside the Book: Alternatives for Today's Teen Library Collections.* Westport, CT: Libraries Unlimited, 2004.

Nichols, Mary Anne. *Merchandising Library Materials to Young Adults.* Westport, CT: Libraries Unlimited, 2002.

Rees, Alan, ed. *Consumer Health Information Source Book,* 7th ed. Westport, CT: Greenwood Press, 2003.

Smith, Mark, ed. *Managing the Internet Controversy.* New York: Neal-Schuman, 2001.

Van Orden, Phyllis. *Selecting Books for the Elementary School Library Media Center.* New York: Neal-Schuman, 2000.

*Weisner, Stan. *Information Is Empowering: Developing Public Library Services for Youth at Risk.* Katie Scarborough, ed. 2nd ed. Oakland, CA: Bay Area Library and Information System, 1992.

Research Methods and Theory

Bandura, Albert. *Social Learning Theory.* Englewood Cliffs, NJ: Prentice Hall, 1977.

Chibucos, Thomas R., et al., eds. *Readings in Family Theory.* Thousand Oaks, CA: Sage, 2005.

DiClemente, Ralph J., et al. *Emerging Theories in Health Promotion Practice and Research: Strategies for Improving Public Health.* San Francisco: Jossey-Bass, 2002.

Dillman, Don A. *Mail and Internet Surveys: The Tailored Design Method.* 2nd ed. New York: Wiley, 2000.

Farmer, Lesley S. J. *How to Conduct Action Research.* Chicago: American Association of School Librarians, 2003.

Glanz, Karen, et al., eds. *Health Behavior and Health Education: Theory, Research, and Practice.* 3rd ed. San Francisco: Jossey-Bass, 2002.

Gostin, Lawrence O. "Public Health Theory and Practice in the Constitutional Design." Available at: http://law.case.edu/student_life/journals/health_matrix/11-2/59102.pdf.

Israel, Barbara A., et al. *Methods in Community-Based Participatory Research for Health.* San Francisco: Jossey-Bass, 2005.

Krueger, Richard A, and Mary Anne Casey. *Focus Groups: A Practical Guide for Applied Research.* 3rd ed. Thousand Oaks, CA: Sage, 2000.

Nutbeam, Don, and Elizabeth Harris. *Theory in a Nutshell: A Practical Guide to Health Promotion Theories.* 2nd ed. Sydney; New York: McGraw-Hill Book Company, 2004.

Rogers, Everett M. *Diffusion of Innovation.* Glencoe, IL: The Free Press, 1962.

Scot, Beverly. *Consulting on the Inside: An Internal Consultant's Guide to Living and Working Inside.* Alexandria, VA: American Society for Training & Development, 2000.

"Social Cognitive Theory." University of South Florida, Community and Family Health. Available at: http://hsc.usf.edu/~kmbrown/Social_Cognitive_Theory_Overview.htm.

Wagstaff, A. "The Demand for Health: Theory and Applications." *Journal of Epidemiology and Community Health* 40 (March 1986): 1–11.

Index

AAAS. *See* American Association for the Advancement of Science

Abstinence sex education programs. *See* Sex education, information programs, and curriculum

ACLU. *See* American Civil Liberties Union

ACLU v. Gonzales, 170

Acoma Clan and Pueblo (New Mexico), 55

Action research. *See* Research

Adolescents. *See* Youth

Adopters, early. *See* Diffusion and innovation theory and approaches

Advisory boards, 91

AIDS/HIV health and knowledge, 67, 89–96

AIDS Risk Reduction Model in critical care (ARRM), 67

American Association for the Advancement of Science (AAAS), 47–48, 112; Library Initiative program and, 47–48

American Civil Liberties Union, 168–69, 171

American Library Association (ALA), 168–69

American Medical Association (AMA), 1, 28, 156

American Red Cross, 120

American Society for Training and Development (ASTD), 118

Annie on My Mind (Garden, Nancy), censorship of, 168

Anomalous state of knowledge theory. *See* Information seeking behavior

Arkansas Children's Hospital Library, 88

ARRM. *See* AIDS Rick Reduction Model in critical care (ARRM)

Assessment. *See* Evaluation

ASTD. *See* American Society for Training and Development (ASTD)

Atlantic Canada Educational Foundation, 81

Attachment family theory, 56

Aurora, Illinois, region, health information, 5; Teen Advisory Group (TAG) and, 5, 91; Teen Health Information Network (THINK), and 5, 91

Aurora Public Library, 90–91; health information for youth and, 90–91; Teen Health Information Network (THINK) and, 5, 91

Austin, Texas, 42–43, 97–98

Australia: Children's hospitals and, 32; Health care and, 132; Institute of Health and Welfare, 132

Avoidance of conflicting information theory. *See* Information seeking behavior

Avoidance of information theory. *See* Information seeking theory

Baker, Lynda, 116

Baker and Taylor (company), 148

Baltimore County Pubic Library, "Connections" and, 173

Bandura, Albert, 109

Barclay, Donald A., 148

Barriers to health information, 77; Rio Grande Valley of Texas and, 126–28. *See also* Culture and society; Families, theories of; Information seeking behavior; Language

Barton, Clara, 119–20

Bates, Marcia, 85

Baylor University Medical Center, 130

Behaviorism in family concepts, 60

Benne, K. D., 107

"Berrypicking" theory, 85

Best Books for Young Adults (ALA), 168–69

205

About the Authors

W. BERNARD LUKENBILL, Professor, The Information School, University of Texas at Austin, holds a BS degree from University of North Texas, an MLS from the University of Oklahoma, and a PhD from Indiana University. He has been a high school librarian and has authored other books for Libraries Unlimited.

BARBARA FROLING IMMROTH holds an AB from Brown, an MA in libraianship from the University of Denver, and a PhD from the University of Pittsburgh. She has both public library and school library experience. She is a past president of the Association for Library Service to Children, the Texas Library Association, and Beta Phi Mu International Library and Information Science Honor Society.